Birds o

DESTINY

CW01338036

MADHAVA KUMAR TURUMELLA

BlueRose ONE.com
Stories Matter

BLUEROSE PUBLISHERS UK Ltd.
London
Copyright © 2025 Madhava Kumar Turumella
All rights reserved.
No part of this book may be copied, reproduced, stored, or transmitted in any form or by any means—electronic, mechanical, photocopying, recording, or otherwise—without prior written permission from the author or publisher.

The author retains the moral rights to be identified as the creator of this work.

This book is primarily published and distributed in Great Britain and is also available in other global marketplaces.

ISBN: 978-93-7018-376-6

Designed and distributed by **BlueRoseONE.com** with global reach. Printing and fulfilment are managed through international distribution networks, ensuring availability based on order locations.

For publishing inquiries, visit **www.BlueRoseONE.com**

BlueRose Publishers UK Ltd,
Unit 3, 6-7 St Mary at Hill, London

+44 7386286323

First Edition: May 2025

Birds Of Destiny

Disclaimer:

This book is a work of fiction. Names, characters, places, and incidents are products of the author 'Madhava Kumar Turumella's imagination or used fictitiously. Any resemblance to actual persons, living or dead, events, or locales is purely coincidental. The content within these pages includes mature themes, explicitly detailing sexual content, suicide, injury, and horror elements. It is intended strictly for adult audiences. Reader discretion is strongly advised, and the book is unsuitable for individuals under 18. The views and opinions expressed in this book are solely those of the author and do not reflect any official policy or position. Any assumptions made by the readers are not the author's responsibility. All rights are reserved by 'Madhava Kumar Turumella.' No part of this publication may be reproduced or used in any manner whatsoever without the express written permission of the author, except in the case of brief quotations embodied in critical articles and reviews. This book is for entertainment purposes only, and the author assumes no responsibility for any actions taken by the reader.

"When Sulabha, the yogini, used her yogic powers to enter King Janaka's mind and gain control over it, the king found himself powerless. Though fully aware, he was unable to direct his own thoughts or actions. Thus, the mighty King Janaka, a renowned emperor, was reduced to being a mere puppet, as Sulabha completely dominated and governed his inner world."

– (Based on the Mahabharata, Shanti Parva: Janaka-Sulabha dialogue)

"How should ye not fight for the cause of Allah and of the feeble among men and of the women and the children who are crying: Our Lord! Bring us forth from out this town of which the people are oppressors! Oh, give us from thy presence some protecting friend! Oh, give us from Thy presence some defender!" - Verse (4:75) The Holy Quran

Satyam eva jayate nānṛtaṁ Satyena panthā vitato devayānaḥ

Yenākramantyṛṣayo hyāptakāmāḥ Yatra tat satyasya paramaṁ nidhānam

Mundaka Upanishad, Chapter 3, Section 1, Verse 6

Truth alone triumphs, not falsehood. Through truth, the path is laid out for the gods and by that path the sages whose desires have been completely fulfilled, reach the highest abode of truth.

ARS BONI ET AEQUI
THE ART OF INTEGRITY AND EQUITY

Author's Note

Dear Reader,

This book is not confined to a single genre–because neither is the human experience.

I began writing this story not with the intention of creating a political thriller, a love story, a science fiction tale, or a spiritual parable–but simply to follow the emotional and philosophical processes unfolding within me. What emerged was a layered narrative, shaped by memory, longing, faith, heartbreak, divine mystery, and speculative wonder.

You will encounter characters who move across borders–geographical, emotional, and metaphysical. You will meet Sarma, a man driven as much by love as by destiny; Kamala, whose presence lingers even in absence, like incense after a ritual; and a world where the ancient and the futuristic coexist, often in quiet conflict. You will see the sacred and the scientific collide–not to confuse you, but to reflect the complexity of our modern spiritual crisis.

Some scenes may read like fragments from a personal memoir. Others may pulse with the urgency of a thriller. And some may evoke the cadence of Vedic scriptures or resemble breaking news headlines. This is intentional–or rather, instinctual. I followed the flow as it came. Especially in Chapter 5, you will notice I wrote an elaborate explanation on a very new concept called Conscious Intergalactic Entities. It may appear lengthy and momentarily take you away from the pace at which the novel is progressing. But know that this detour is deliberate. Unless you absorb the perspective offered in Chapter 5, you may not be able to grasp what I, as the author, perceive as truly happening in the world around us. The knowledge explored there helped me navigate life. It continues to help me heal. And I believe it might do the same for you.

I did not write this book to follow a formula. I wrote to explore what it means to live and love in a fragmented, hyper-connected world. It is not a puzzle to be solved, but a mirror held up to the soul—a reflection of our collective inner turbulence and our search for transcendence.

If you find the structure unusual, I encourage you to read with the patience and openness of a traveller—one who does not rush to reach a destination but embraces each shift in landscape as part of the journey.

Thank you for choosing to walk this path with me.

Warm regards,
Madhava

Previously in The Riddles of Destiny

In The Riddles of Destiny, we followed Siddhanta Sarma–a powerful Brahmin priest deeply versed in occult rituals–whose life near the baryte mines of Kodur, Andhra Pradesh, took a dark turn with the mysterious suicide of his gifted student, Manasi. Sarma's relentless quest for truth plunged him into a chilling confrontation with the ghostly entity Śākini, unveiling an unknown, malevolent force that defied even death's understanding.

Simultaneously, India's covert intelligence operations grappled with the bizarre death of General Bakshi, head of military intelligence. It was originally reported as a family suicide. Dr Sood, the sceptical head of India's Research and Analysis Wing (R&AW) partnered with Dr Rao, a retired scholar and expert in the occult, to investigate these unsettling incidents. Their journey exposed a network of sinister sorcery orchestrated by Bikku Tāntrik, whose manipulation of dark forces caused devastating psychological harm even to seasoned military figures.

Complicating matters further was the enigmatic Lucian Wrathborne, leader of an influential organization wielding the Brain Activity Transformer (BAT)–a potent device capable of remotely controlling human minds and inciting chaos. The clandestine use of BAT hinted at an ominous blend of advanced technology, psychological warfare, and dark mysticism.

The novel culminated in Sarma's perilous confrontation with these dark forces, yet significant questions about his destiny and the larger threats remained unanswered. Now, in Birds of

Destiny, the narrative shifts from abstract riddles to stark realities. Sarma, emotionally vulnerable and spiritually shaken, faces deeper intricacies of love, betrayal, reincarnation, and heightened interfaith tensions. The riddles have become realities—and destiny demands a heavier price.

CONTENTS

1. LET US FLY 1

2. DIVINE INTERVENTIONS 21

3. THE INSIDERS 51

4. NOW YOU SEE IT, NOW YOU DON'T 84

5. CONSCIOUS INTERGALACTIC ENTITIES (KIEs) 122

6. FLIP THE TABLES 161

7. ṬUYŪRUN WAḤSHIYYA – SAVAGE BIRDS 179

8. ATTATAYIS 193

9. SHIKHANDI 211

10. PROOF OF CONCEPT 234

11. KAALA SARPA 258

12. KALKI 293

13. HORNET'S NEST 333

1. LET US FLY

Birds, birds, scores of dead birds raining down from the sky... In less than ten seconds, the lifeless bodies carpeted the ground.

Year: September 11, 1992

Place: Kharan, Balochistan, Pakistan.

Imran Khan looked at the sky. It seemed eerily normal. "What could have caused these birds to fall dead from the sky?" he wondered. "Ya Allah... Reham..." Imran lifted his palms, outstretched, praying for Allah's mercy on the birds.

He was conveying his Intention (Niyyah) to perform Umrah. As he prepared to say his prayers, "Labbaik Allahumma Umrah," Imran was interrupted by Noor's terrified cry. "Baba..."

Noor is a teenager. Rest of the children were hiding behind Noor. All their faces carried fear.

"Do not look at them. Go inside," Imran instructed. The children, including Noor, hurried indoors. Imran knelt beside a bird. Its feathers still soft but lifeless.

"This is a bad omen. Something grave is going to befall our Ummah," said Sheik Adil, his white beard swaying in the desert wind.

Sheik Adil was Imran's uncle, an authority on Islamic scriptures, having performed Hajj many times. "Allah is cautioning us to be mindful. We are peace-loving people, minding our own business. But events around the world are not showing good signs," he said.

"Are we peace-loving?" Adam, Imran's elder son, challenged. "What about the bloodshed we caused? The wars we waged? I'm not sure we are truly peace-loving,"

"Astaghfirullah," Adil exclaimed, his eyes flashing with anger. He scrutinized Adam as if seeing him for the first time.

Adam shrunk under Adil's gaze, realizing his mistake. Speaking disrespectfully was unacceptable in their family. He lowered his eyes.

"May Allah have Reham on all of us," said Hamid, another uncle.

Adil turned to Imran, his anger palpable. "This is why I told you to send your boy to a regular Madrasaa. Instead, you sent him to England. Look what those devils taught him."

"It is okay," Imran said calmly. "Adam is only questioning our history. You are our elder, the best among us. If you think Adam has overstepped, guide him. Who else will teach our children if not the learned like you?"

Adil's anger abated slightly, but his displeasure remained. "I shall teach this boy a lesson," he thought.

The congregation prepared for the Niyyah in silence, Adam's question hanging heavily in the air.

"What time is your flight?" asked Fatima, Imran's wife breaking the tension.

"It departs at 7 pm. Have you packed everything?" Imran asked.

"Yes."

"Adam, go inside and see if Noor has prepared her prayer paper. She said she would give me a list of her wishes to carry to the holy land," Imran directed, wanting to diffuse the situation further.

Adam went inside, grateful for the reprieve.

There are other pilgrims who have assembled there to travel with Imran to perform Ummah. They were all carrying suitcases. All suitcases were stacked-up there. One of the suitcases was a perfectly concealed suitcase looking like COMxBAT. The suitcase is carried there by Sajjad, Adil's assistant.

Adil is not happy with what had transpired with Adam. COMxBAT was fully tuned into Adil and registered the bio-electrical brainwaves that recognize the pattern at which the emotion of Anger in Adil is triggered. Each human maintains a unique point in his brainwave at which they trigger the emotion of anger. All humans think. These thoughts generate emotions. Emotions are triggered by thoughts. Some people are easily prone to anger, some it takes a bit effort to get angry, some other it takes a lot of thoughts before it triggers anger. One of the functions of COMxBAT is to recognize the pattern at which the emotion of anger is triggered. Each being on this planet, not just humans carry a unique physical signature. COMxBAT is tuned into these signatures. It is capable of noting down the emotional patterns of 50 people who are in its blast zone. There are a total forty people assembled there to make the journey of ummah.

Hamid was lost in thoughts. Imran noticed Hamid's absentmindedness. "What happened?" He asked.

"My sister Ruksana, I was expecting her to come. But she did not come. I don't know what happened." said Hamid.

"Why don't you ask Sheik Adil? With the power of his prayers, he can make Ruksana appear" suggested someone. They have a point. Lately, Adil had noticed something strange–his prayers, even the smallest ones, seemed to be answered almost instantly. Was this a test from Allah? A divine blessing? He didn't know, but he dared not question it. Instead, he chose to immerse himself further in his religious duties, afraid that even the slightest disobedience might cause this mysterious connection to disappear.

Hamid looked at Adil and asked "Sheik, please pray for me I want to see Ruksana before I embark on this journey." Adil is pleased with the special recognition he got.

"Ruksana will come in fifteen minutes," Adil said. The green colour COMxBAT came alive and silently sent a signal to satellite SANI which relayed the signal to another COMxBAT located quite close by. A back-up COMxBAT stored at Sajjad's place. Ruksana is Sajjad's wife.

Ruksana was doing something. Her mind fully occupied with thoughts. Even Though she was supposed to go to Imran's place she got busy and temporarily forgot. COMxBAT has suppressed that part of thought where she was supposed to go to Imran's place. But the moment Adil said "Ruksana will arrive in 15 minutes" the back-up COMxBAT released the chokehold it had on Ruksana's memory to attend Imran's home. Ruksana was in the middle of something–what was it? She couldn't remember. Something felt... off.

Then, like a door unlocking in her brain, a thought rushed in. Imran. Hamid. The send-off. **How could she have forgotten something so important?** She gasped, a cold shiver running down her spine. It was as if the memory had been locked away, only to be released at the exact moment she needed it.

Shaking off the uneasy feeling, she grabbed her things and hurried out. She had to reach Imran's place in time.

As Adil said exactly in 15 minutes, Ruksana appeared. Everyone was pleased to see that.

"Yeah Sheik Adil, it looks like Allah has given you a special power. What you say seems to be happening," said someone. Adil was very pleased with that outcome. He noticed that off late Allah is granting any reasonable wish that he conveys. He is able to pray for lost donkeys when owners of the donkeys come to him in distress. He can also pray and get the humans that he wants to speak to. It is as if he is blessed with the power of telepathy. Since the time Adil started noticing that Allah is granting his wishes, he became much more religious. He became too strict in his religious observations. He does not want to disobey any command of Allah. Everyone around noticed the radical transformation in Adil. But all are happy because Adil is pleasing Allah and in return Allah is blessing Adil. All started having respectful reverence towards Adil. And no wonder then that Adil got extremely upset when Adam challenged him.

A mini bus has arrived to carry them to the airport. All suitcases were loaded onto the top of the minibus. A helper was loading the suitcases onto the top of the bus.

He reached for the green suitcase which is a COMxBAT, but Sajjad's hand shot out, gripping his wrist.

'Not this one,' he said firmly.

The man hesitated, surprised by the sharpness in Sajjad's tone.

'It's for Adil bhai–his medicine. I'll carry it myself.'

The helper nodded, stepping back. But as Sajjad lifted the suitcase, he felt the weight of its secrets pressing down on him.

Everyone got into the bus. Imran was the last to board, as he was waiting for a small piece of paper. Noor wanted to express her prayers to Allah in her own creative way. She decided to write down her heartfelt supplications–a personal letter to **Al-Rahim, the Most Merciful**. Though it is customary to pray directly, she wished for her father to carry her words in his heart while circumambulating the **Kaaba, the holiest site in Islam, located in Mecca, Saudi Arabia**.

The bus driver sounded horn showing his impatience. Noor came running out and handed over the paper to her father. Imran boarded the bus as soon as Noor handed him her paper.

Inside the bus, hushed voices murmured **duas**, the rhythmic clicking of prayer beads filling the space between conversations. Imran, one of the last to board, paused at the door, adjusting his bag. He glanced back toward the town as if committing it to memory before stepping inside.

The driver, a man with salt-and-pepper hair and a calm demeanour, called out in a steady voice, "**Sab tayyar hain? (Is everyone ready?)**"

A few nods, a quiet chorus of "**Insha'Allah**", and with that, the bus rumbled forward, rolling onto the long, dusty road leading out of Kharan.

The journey was long but peaceful, stretching through arid landscapes where the wind carried the scent of dry earth. Occasionally, a lone herder tending to his camels or goats appeared in the distance, a reminder of the simplicity of life in these lands. Inside, some pilgrims closed their eyes in silent reflection, while others recited **Talbiyah**, the pilgrimage prayer:

"Labbayka Allahumma labbayk... Here I am, O Allah, here I am."

Hours passed, the bus steadily moving toward the nearest airport. As they approached the outskirts of Karachi, the surroundings changed–wider roads, scattered buildings, the signs of a bustling city waking up.

“Stop the bus” ordered Sajjad just after they reached the outskirts of Karachi. The bus came to a screeching halt.

Sajjad got down the bus and said to Adil "I will take your leave. May your pilgrimage be successful"

"Is he not flying with us?" asked someone. "No. He is Adil's assistant. He came to help. But he will not be flying with us." Sajjad went along with his big and a green suitcase.

The bus moved again and reached the airport. At the airport, the group was guided through a special processing area. Officials, well aware of the significance of their journey, handled their documents swiftly.

"May Allah accept your Umrah," one officer said with quiet reverence as he stamped their papers.

Beyond the glass windows, the charter plane stood waiting, its sleek body gleaming under the morning sun. The pilgrims moved forward, stepping onto the tarmac. Some looked up at the sky, whispering their final prayers before boarding.

Imran took a deep breath. This was it–the moment they had all been waiting for. He placed his right foot on the first step of the boarding stairs and whispered, **"Bismillah."**

With hearts full of devotion, the pilgrims ascended into the plane, ready to leave behind the world they knew for the holiest journey of their lives.

Ruksana went to the nearest shop which had a telephone and dialled India. She is from Villupuram in Kerala district in India. She got married to Sajjad and migrated to Pakistan. Hamid is Ruksana's cousin brother.

Ruksana is from a rich family. Her parents have their own telephone at home. Ruksana conveyed the happy news that everyone has now left for Umrah.

"What about Sajjad? Is he not going?" asked her mother begum.

"No, he is not going. He said he would take me with him. Maybe we will go in another three months... I don't know" said Ruksana.

"Okay" said Begum. They had a few more minutes of conversation and Begum kept down the phone.

Her mind not at ease. "I don't trust that man," Begum muttered after putting down the phone. "He's too secretive. And ever since Ruksana married him, she speaks less as if she's hiding something too."

She was very reluctant to give Ruksana in wedding to Sajjad. But because Hamid and his family are there in Pakistan she got convinced. The reason for her reluctance is that Sajjad is not a strict believer. But she has ten daughters. And their wedding is an important aspect that she cannot ignore. Since Ruksana's father's untimely death Begum is handling all home affairs by herself. She got assurances from Hamid and did her enquiries before giving Ruksana away in wedding to Sajjad. Still her mind is weary....

She recollected how she met Sajjad. One and half years ago, in the year 1991 she travelled to Kadapah to offer prayers at the **Ameen Peer Dargah**, also known as **Pedda Dargah**, and she met her distant relative Hamid's family who came from Pakistan to offer prayers at the Dargah. Sajjad was working as an auto driver there. Hamid and Sajjad are known to each other. That is how Ruksana became Sajjad's wife. After his wedding immediately within a month, Sajjad permanently migrated back to Pakistan.

Imran sat on the airplane, with Wahid beside him. After everyone said a prayer, the flight took off. The passengers settled in, their minds at ease.

"What did Noor give you, brother?" Wahid asked.

Imran touched his coat pocket, feeling the neatly folded paper inside. He pulled it out. "A prayer paper," he said, unfolding it carefully.

The paper was a delicate shade of light rose, adorned with four roses printed at each corner. Noor had taken every care to show her reverence while preparing it. A faint scent of attar, sprinkled on the page, drifted into the air. Imran inhaled deeply, letting the fragrance fill his senses. Wahid glanced sideways at the paper in Imran's hand, noticing the beautifully written Urdu script. At the top, Noor had titled it: "My Application to Al-Rahim."

"Masha Allah! Allah has gifted you the most precious daughter," Wahid said. "Not only is she outwardly beautiful, but her heart is full of love for Allah. She's given you an application to carry to the Holy Land?"

"I had no idea she planned this," Imran admitted. "Noor thinks differently. When I told her I was going for Umrah, she decided to write this application. It's her wish that I read it while circumambulating the Holy Shrine."

They both leaned in, curiously reading her words.

Dear Allah,

If You will it, even the bitterest of enemies can become friends. I pray that my father and my brother Nayeem reconcile.

May there be peace across the world.

May You grant a good education and wisdom to all my siblings.

May I always hold unwavering devotion to You in my heart.

May You protect all of us.

May Your kind gaze never leave us.

"Such beautiful wishes," Wahid murmured. "She wants you to read them at the Holy Shrine?"

"Yes," Imran replied. "And she's been very clever about it. If I read these wishes before Parvardigar (the Sustainer), and I don't reconcile with Nayeem, then it would mean Allah has not granted her request."

Wahid smiled. "She's put you in a tight spot. Noor knows how to bend people to her will. The ball is in your court now—you can't delay making peace with Nayeem."

Imran sighed, both amused and touched by his daughter's wisdom. Noor and Nayeem were his children from his first wife. He and his family had lived in Bangladesh with Noor's maternal grandparents, but during the Bangladesh Liberation War, Noor's mother had died. At the time, Imran was a senior civil servant in the Pakistani government, so they had migrated. Both Noor and Nayeem had returned with him to Pakistan, but

Noor's maternal grandparents left property in both her and Nayeem's names.

Nayeem, however, had grown increasingly radical, something Imran could never condone. He had tried to steer his son away from extremism, but Nayeem refused to listen. After several arguments, he left for Bangladesh, choosing to live at his grandparents. Though he rarely called, he still spoke with Noor and Fatima.

Fatima had raised both Noor and Nayeem as if they were her own, and for that, Nayeem held her in the highest regard.

"He is my son. Allah knows how much I love him," Imran said, his voice heavy with emotion. "But he is walking a dangerous path. You know how much I despise violence. We must strive for peace, not war."

"InshaAllah... he is still young. He will find his way back," Wahid reassured him. "Let us pray that Allah softens his heart."

"Young?" Imran scoffed. "He's twenty-five years old! Look at Noor—she's six years younger, yet at nineteen, she prays for peace while he spends his time plotting revenge. That fool doesn't even understand who his real enemies are."

His face flushed with frustration and eyes heavy with sorrow for the son who refused to listen.

After a brief silence, Wahid changed the subject. "And how is Mustafa's education going? You sent him to India to study—how is he adjusting?"

Mustafa and Adam were twins, yet their interests and temperaments couldn't be more different.

"Alhamdulillah, he is studying well," Imran replied. "But he's struggling with homesickness–especially missing home-cooked food."

"Where is he studying?"

"He joined B.Tech at Osmania University in Hyderabad. He's living in the Old City."

Wahid nodded thoughtfully. "Ah, the Old City... full of our Muslim faith followers. Good people. Mustafa will be fine there, InshaAllah."

"That is the hope," Imran said.

Wahid's curiosity deepened. "And what about Adam? He wasn't interested in studying in India?"

Imran smiled. "Though they are twins, they are nothing alike. Mustafa is drawn to technology–he loves anything technical. That's why he's studying Electrical Engineering at Osmania. The University College of Engineering (UCE), Osmania University, is one of India's oldest and most respected engineering colleges, founded in 1929. By the 1990s, it had well-established programs in various branches, including Electrical and Electronics Engineering (EEE)."

He paused before continuing.

"But Adam... he's different. He has no interest in machines or circuits. His passion is nature. He wants to study the wonders of Allah's creation. So, we sent him to England to pursue Zoology."

Wahid smiled. "That is fascinating. I'm sure Adam will find what he's seeking in life, InshaAllah." Then, as if remembering something, he asked, "Fatima has relatives in Hyderabad, doesn't she?"

"Yes, distant relatives," Imran confirmed. "Fatima's grandparents were from Hyderabad. Her grandfather was related to the Nizam."

The Nizam of Hyderabad—a title that once belonged to one of the wealthiest men in the world during the early 20th century—held a significant place in history.

"We are thinking of sending Noor there as well," Imran added. "She would be a great help to Mustafa—he would finally get home-cooked meals. And Noor herself wants to pursue further studies in India."

"That's a good idea," Wahid agreed. "She would be a great support for her brother."

After a moment, he asked, "Is Nayeem coming to Jeddah Airport?"

"Fatima mentioned he has some work in Jeddah," Imran said. "He also wants to send gifts for his mother and sister, so yes, he might meet us while we're on our way back."

As the plane began its descent, the King Abdulaziz International Airport came into view—its vast structure gleaming under the sun. It was one of the largest airports in the world, designed to accommodate millions of pilgrims arriving for their sacred journey.

Riyadh, Saudi Arabia. A discrete building hosts the MENA (Middle East and North Africa) joint intelligence sharing headquarters.

It was 4 PM local time. Prince Taif had just completed his Asr prayers, his mind momentarily at peace before duty called once more. A man of formidable intelligence, he had been personally appointed by the King to lead the nation's intelligence division. Fluent in multiple languages, an elite fighter pilot, and a master strategist, he had honed his skills at Britain's prestigious Sandhurst Military Academy. Yet, what truly set him apart was his profound knowledge of Islamic studies, a depth of understanding that shaped both his leadership and his vision for the future.

A soft knock at the door interrupted his thoughts.

"Chief, may I come in?" Binasad's voice carried through. He was the second in command, trusted and efficient.

"Please, come in, brother," Prince Taif replied, his tone warm, exuding both kindness and authority.

Binasad stepped into the room. Prince Taif studied him for a moment, his eyebrows slightly raised.

"What is it?"

"The charter flight from Pakistan has landed," Binasad reported.

Prince Taif let out a thoughtful hum, turning to gaze out of the window. Outside, a few desert birds soared in formation, their movements precise, disciplined. A fitting metaphor, he mused.

"Tap Sheik Adil," he finally said, his voice measured. "The man who claims to have a direct connection to Allah."

Binasad frowned slightly. "Any particular reason?"

Prince Taif exhaled slowly. "The Pakistani government is concerned. 'Special powers from Allah'—claims like that can spark unrest, even rebellion. Our ummah suffers from many such figures." His voice was even, though tinged with scepticism. "We must separate the wheat from the chaff. If Sheik Adil possesses true divine gifts, he deserves our honour and respect. But if not..."

He turned to Binasad, holding his gaze for a long moment before finishing his sentence.

"You know what to do."

A knowing silence passed between them.

"Understood." With a slight nod, Binasad turned and left the room.

For the last one month, Prince Taif felt a stirring in his soul—a quiet, persistent unease that deepened with every prayer. Each time he completed his daily salah, a whisper seemed to echo in his mind, an urgent call from Allah—

"My son, watch out..."

It was subtle, yet powerful. As the head of intelligence, vigilance was his duty. Watching out was second nature. But this... this felt different.

'What am I meant to watch out for?'

The question gnawed at him. A divine warning gripped his soul, yet its meaning remained elusive.

Saudi Arabia, the guardian of the Two Holy Mosques, bore the sacred responsibility of leading the Islamic world. Whenever Muslims faced turmoil, it was their duty–no, their divine calling–to steer the ummah out of danger. Prince Taif knew this well. His role was more than that of an intelligence chief; he was a servant of Allah, entrusted with safeguarding not just the Kingdom, but the entire Muslim world.

And yet, this cautionary voice that accompanied his prayers unsettled him.

'What is this warning I keep receiving from Allah?'

The unease remained, an unanswered question hanging over his faith and duty.

Noor's voice carried through the room, weaving its way into the hearts of those who heard it. She was singing her favourite song, "Hum Dekhenge", a powerful poem by the renowned Faiz Ahmed Faiz. His words, rich with longing for divine justice, echoed like a prophecy, stirring something deep within her.

Hum dekhenge,

laazim hai ke hum bhi dekhenge,

hum dekhenge...

We shall witness,

It is certain that we too, shall witness,

The day that has been promised,

Of which has been written on the slate of eternity...

Lost in the melody and meaning, Noor sang with devotion, her voice carrying the weight of hope and conviction.

With most of the men from the tribe having travelled to the holy land for pilgrimage, the women of the community had begun to gather more freely, their bonds strengthening in their absence. That afternoon, Ruksana arrived, carrying a steaming casserole of halim, a dish she had specially prepared. As she stepped into the hall, Noor's melodious voice caught her attention, and she stood still, captivated.

"Jab zulm-o-sitam ke koh-e-giraan

roo_ii kii tarah ud jaayenge,

hum mahkoomon ke paaon tale

yeh dharti dhaR dhaR dhaRkegii,

aur ahl-e-hakam ke sar uupar

jab bijlii kaR kaR karkegii...

hum dekhenge."

When the mountains of tyranny will be blown away like cotton,

Under our feet—the feet of the oppressed—

The earth will shake with a deafening tremor,

And above the heads of our rulers,

Lightning will strike.

The song had a way of stirring the soul, awakening something primal and profound. Noor let the final note linger, the depth of the lyrics still reverberating through her.

"Masha Allah... You sing so beautifully," Ruksana finally said, breaking the silence.

Startled, Noor turned around. She had been so immersed in her singing that she hadn't noticed Ruksana standing behind her.

"Thank you, Ruksana," she said, a hint of embarrassment in her voice. "When did you arrive? I didn't even notice."

"I came in when you started singing," Ruksana replied with a smile. "You were so lost, I didn't want to disturb you. But Noor, you must share your talent! Bollywood music directors would love to hear your voice. You could have an incredible career!"

Noor's cheeks flushed at the compliment. "Oh, my singing is nothing," she murmured, suddenly shy.

Just then, Fatima entered the hall.

"Ruksana, how are you?" she greeted warmly.

"Salaam, Aapa," Ruksana responded respectfully. "I made some halim and thought of sharing it with you." She handed the casserole bowl to Fatima.

"That is so kind of you," Fatima said, motioning for Ruksana to sit. As they settled in, Ruksana turned to Fatima.

"Noor has real potential," she said enthusiastically. "She could become a great singer. I was just telling her she should consider Bollywood."

Fatima smiled gently. "Insha Allah... Allah has blessed my beti with many talents. He will guide her to where he wishes to use them."

A thoughtful look crossed Ruksana's face. "Sajjad told me you're thinking of sending Noor to India to be with Mustafa?"

Fatima nodded. "Yes, Mustafa has been struggling with food. He misses home-cooked meals. You know how it is–he prefers Noor's cooking over mine. So, we're planning to send her to India." She chuckled lightly.

Ruksana grinned. "For Mustafa, you and Noor are both like mothers. But it's not just him–everyone loves Noor's cooking. If she doesn't become a famous singer, she could easily be an incredible chef."

Noor laughed softly. "I don't know about that, but I do love cooking," she admitted.

"What will she do in Hyderabad while she is there looking after her brother? I am sure Noor would not want to stay idle." asked Ruksana.

"I want to learn how to mix Music using computers. So, I am planning to join a computers course which can teach me that." replied Noor.

"Oh! that is nice to hear. Please also consider traveling to Kerala. You know my family is there. If you need any help, let my mother know," said Ruksana. She turned towards Fatima and asked "When will she leave?".

"Insha Allah, after her father returns from the pilgrimage," Fatima replied.

The conversation flowed effortlessly, drifting from Noor's future to stories of family and shared memories. An hour passed before Ruksana finally took her leave, leaving behind the warmth of companionship and the lingering echo of Noor's song.

2. DIVINE INTERVENTIONS

Date 22 May 1991. Place: Mokkavari Palle, between Kadapah and Kodur, Andhra Pradesh, India...

Early in the morning, Sarma woke up from a disturbed sleep. After completing his morning rituals, he pulled out a bicycle and rode towards a nearby village situated an hour's cycle away. While he used the charity school-issued motorcycle for important work, he preferred a cycle for anything leisurely. That day, he wanted to meet a potter near Mukkavaripalle. Sarma was trained in low-cost housing and civil engineering.

Many people in Indian villages could not afford a house to live in. A sustainable architect had created a design that allowed one to build a large enough permanent structure for two people to live in, costing less than 200 dollars. The design could last for 25 years. Sarma had gone to Sevagram, one of Mahatma

Gandhi's Ashrams in Wardha, to train as an architect for building such low-cost housing. The particular design required special tiles made by a potter. That morning, Sarma was on his way, slowly pedalling his cycle. As he crossed Mokkavaripalle village, the ring finger of his left hand began giving very mild pain signals. It meant Sarma had entered a space where danger might be lurking.

All animals in nature are designed to sense danger instinctively. Humans also have this ability, known as biomimicry design. One can train one's body to receive such signals. Sarma had trained his left-hand little finger to signal when he entered any space where danger was present. He had also trained his body to signal when he was in the presence of someone harbouring ill intentions towards him.

Sarma's ring finger continued to give him signals. He stopped his cycle, got down, and looked around. He was riding through a hamlet. There were houses on both sides of the road. It was 7 am. Everything seemed normal, yet the signals suggested danger. As he was contemplating, he saw Ranganna standing in front of a house with folded hands.

"Sarma ji, I made a big mistake. Please save me!" he yelled.

Sarma was bewildered. He was not expecting to see Ranganna there that morning.

"Ranganna, what are you doing here?" he asked, walking his cycle towards Ranganna. A crow sitting on a nearby tree made a loud noise and flew away hurriedly into the sky. Ranganna did not reply. Instead, he roared like a caged animal–a sound only the dead make.

Sarma stopped in his tracks. "Has Ranganna died? Is it his ghost calling out for help?" he thought.

"Ranganna, what happened? When did you pass away into the realm of the dead? Oh, Ranga... It was only the day before we enjoyed drinking tea together. I told you to stay away from helping Kaamini. Did she push you into the realm of the dead?"

There was no reply. His head awkwardly tilted, and he was looking towards the road. A truck was coming from somewhere, heading towards Tirupati on that highway...

"Sarma ji, please save me... Śākini is haunting me. She is trying to capture and enslave me. Oh... Oh..." Ranganna wailed and ran into the house.

"So, Śākini is after Ranganna. If I find her, I can reason with her," Sarma thought, looking around for any signs of Śākini. She was nowhere to be seen...

Meanwhile, the truck sound grew louder. Sarma stepped a few feet away from the road to let the truck pass. But the driver was in a trance. He abruptly swerved off the road, driving straight toward Sarma.

Suddenly, a small boy emerged from the house–the same house Ranganna's ghost had entered. The boy ran onto the road into the merciless path of the monster truck. Ranganna's ghost was right behind him, chasing him. "Don't be afraid; I am a friendly ghost. Don't run," he tried to assure the frightened boy. Both ran straight in front of the truck. A loud thud followed. The force of the speeding truck threw the boy's body six feet into the sky. Ranganna yelled, but he was already dead–nothing could kill what was already killed.

The truck did not stop after hitting the boy, instantly killing him. The driver drove straight towards Sarma. Sarma dropped his cycle and jumped into the bushes to save himself. The front wheel of the truck crushed Sarma's cycle, but the truck did not stop. It sped away towards Tirupati.

Sarma, an accomplished athlete trained in martial arts, had no trouble jumping away from the truck's path. The bushes cushioned his fall. He got up unscathed, bewildered, dusting off the dirt from his body. The villagers came running, gathering around the child's lifeless body, wailing loudly. A few of them angrily dug a trench on the road to prevent speeding vehicles. The atmosphere was filled with agony and sorrow. Sarma felt sorry for them, but there was nothing more he could do. Ranganna's ghost vanished the moment the truck hit the boy.

Sarma picked up his damaged cycle. An auto heading towards Kodur was passing by. Sarma loaded his cycle into the auto.

The auto driver, while driving, remarked, "It looks like the gates of hell have opened... Death is everywhere."

"What do you mean? Has anyone else died on this road?" Sarma asked, thinking the monster truck may have killed others.

"No, sir, haven't you heard the news? They assassinated Rajiv Gandhi in Perumbudur, just a few hours from here," replied the auto driver.

Rajiv Gandhi was the leader of the Congress Party and a former Prime Minister of India. He was a visionary for India's development. Sarma admired Rajiv Gandhi. His mother and Rajiv Gandhi shared the same birthday. Many of Sarma's relatives were Congress supporters. The news of Rajiv's death came as a shock.

Before he could ask for further details, the auto reached the next village, where a cycle repair shop was located. Not sure if the repair could be done there, Sarma requested the auto driver to wait.

"Please wait for a few minutes. If the repair shop can't manage to fix my cycle, I will have to find another shop," Sarma said.

"Sure, I will wait," the auto driver replied.

"What's your name?" Sarma asked, as was customary.

"Sajjad," replied the auto driver.

Luckily, the cycle repair shop could fix the damage. "Thank you for waiting, Sajjad. You can go now," Sarma said, paying him.

Sarma handed his cycle to the shop for repair. With nothing else to do, he started walking back towards the charity school where he taught. As he walked along the side of the road, he heard the roar of the monster truck again. He turned around. It was the same truck.

To his horror, the truck drove straight towards him again. Sarma thought he was going to die that day. He could see the truck approaching fast. But then, a miracle happened... A Hanuman temple stood on the side of the road. Devotees had dug a large pit for construction work. The truck's left tire fell into the ditch, breaking the axle with a loud snap. The engine roared violently before falling silent. The truck could no longer move. It was as if Lord Hanuman himself had broken its legs for killing innocent children and causing harm.

Had that ditch not been there, Sarma would have been crushed. Unknown divine forces foresaw future events and intervened. Some things cannot be explained rationally. On that day, when the gates of hell seemed open, the divine intervened to save Sarma.

The driver of the truck got down and ran away from the scene before anyone could capture him.

Sarma reached the school. A police jeep was waiting for him at the school gates. The driver greeted Sarma and said, "Sir, I am waiting here to pick you up. Chandra sir sent me."

Sarma knew Chandra well, so he climbed into the jeep. The two-way radio crackled. It was Chandra. He asked the police driver to give the receiver to Sarma.

"Sarma, yesterday I came to see you, but you were not there. Today, I wanted to come, but we are all waking up to the horrible news of Rajiv Gandhi's assassination. Everyone is busy with this unexpected event. But I was hoping you could travel to Karjat. We will find a job for you there," said Chandra.

Sarma hesitated for a few seconds before replying, "But sir, I can't travel..."

"Why? Do you need a few more days?" Chandra asked.

"No, Sir, sorry, I will not leave this charity school," Sarma replied, still unsure how to explain.

"Why?" Chandra asked, completely surprised by the answer that came next.

"I just got married," Sarma said.

"What! Married? When? With whom?" Chandra's tone rose in astonishment.

"She is my colleague, my fellow school teacher. We fell in love, and we got married. But I can't explain it like this. Can we meet?" Sarma asked.

"Sure... But not now. As I said, we are dealing with a major terror crisis. Can you come over to Tirupati? My driver will bring you."

"I don't need your jeep. I will travel by bus. I will come to meet you by evening," Sarma said before stepping out of the police jeep.

But little did he realize that major trouble was waiting for him, as the school administration was livid that he had married a teacher without their permission.

Sarma reached the school gates.

"Teacher... Teacher..." He heard a voice calling him in a hushed tone.

He looked around and saw Cinnu, a student, hiding behind a bush.

"Hey, Cinnu... What is it? Why are you hiding?" Sarma asked.

"Teacher... Kamala Teacher is calling you. She asked me to tell you not to go towards the Charity Admin Office. She asked me to bring you to her room as soon as I found you. I have been waiting here for the last two hours," Cinnu said. "Please follow me, I will take you to Kamala teacher."

Sarma followed Cinnu. All women teachers who worked for the charity school lived in the quarters allocated to them within the school premises. It was a strictly no-go zone for men unless accompanied by a student or administration staff.

Cinnu led him to Kamala's dwelling, a small independent house.

"Teacher, I will wait for you outside," Cinnu said as he sat on the ground.

Sarma walked up to the door and knocked. It was unlocked.

Kamala had been waiting for him. The moment she saw him at the door, she pulled him inside and hugged him, sobbing bitterly.

Sarma was caught off guard. "What happened? Why are you crying?" he asked, concern filling his voice.

"They are furious that I married you. They called and questioned me about our marriage. I told them it was none of their business–that I am madly in love with you and that's all that matters," Kamala lifted her head, looking into his eyes. Tears rolled down her cheeks, her thick black hair falling over her shoulders. Her beautiful face, contorted with emotion, bore the weight of the storm within her.

"Hey... we are only married. It's not a crime. I love you, and I'll explain it to them," Sarma reassured her, gently trying to loosen her grip so he could return to the Charity Administration office.

"No, please don't go. I am terrified. I feel they will kill both of us." She tightened her embrace, refusing to let go. Sarma could sense it now–she had been threatened with dire consequences.

"Don't worry. They can do no such thing. I will talk to them. Let me go," he said firmly.

"No..." Kamala clung to him. "They said they would kill you. Please, let's run away. Right now–before anything happens to us," she pleaded, her voice steady but desperate.

"Look... do not worry. You are new to India and its environment. Let me handle this." Sarma pressed a kiss to her forehead, inhaling deeply as if drawing out all her worries.

He never told Kamala this, but he feared losing her in this reincarnation. When he breathed her in, he recognized a scent beyond the physical–a unique, signature fragrance that only the soul of one's beloved emits. It was a scent he had known across lifetimes, the signature that bound their souls together. Otherwise, how else could one explain the unbreakable pull between two beings? Why did two souls in love fall into an undeniable gravitational force?

Sarma held her forehead in his hands and kissed it again. He wanted to inhale her fears and exhale his strength into her. He knew they had rushed into marriage, and she is younger than him. Kamala did not fully understand the pull he had over her, the magic that had compelled her to say 'yes' the moment he asked her. It was beyond reason. It was fate.

"Hopefully, I will get a chance to explain this to her," Sarma thought. "Nothing will happen. Let me go and sort this out for us."

Kamala reluctantly loosened her grip. But her pounding heart sensed an unknown danger.

Sarma walked out of the room and headed toward the Charity Administration office.

It was 10 a.m. The children were already in their respective classes.

"Hey, Sarma..." someone called.

Sarma turned in the direction of the voice. It was Bala Krishna Reddy, the charity administration office manager. But he was not in the office. He was standing near the small gate at the rear of the school. The small gate led into the forest. Sarma approached Bala.

"We must talk," Bala Reddy said, his voice laced with contempt. He was a heavily built, six-foot-tall man. People feared him.

"Talk about what?" Sarma asked, though he already knew the answer.

"About the affair between you and Kamala teacher," Bala said bluntly.

Sarma frowned. He did not like the way the word *affair* was uttered, but he did not retaliate. Words are harsh. Words are weapons. Words, when used with intention, can invoke a thought in another person. Thought results in emotion, and every emotion eventually leads to action. This is why wise men say that a word unspoken remains a slave to you, but a word that escapes your lips makes you its slave.

Sarma understood Bala's intent–to provoke him. But he refused to let rage take hold. "We are both adults. What happens between me, and Kamala is between us," he replied, ignoring the insult.

Bala looked uneasily around as if he did not want anyone else to overhear their conversation. "Can we go for a walk into the forest? Let's not discuss this here. Follow me." He walked ahead. Sarma followed.

For five minutes, they walked in silence. The towering trees and thick bushes surrounded them, devoid of any other human presence. Suddenly, Bala stopped and turned to face Sarma. A bald eagle circling above let out a cry–a warning. The forest animals shared this sacred bond, forewarning one another of unseen dangers.

Sarma understood the cue and silently thanked the eagle for its caution.

Bala abruptly lunged, pulling a hidden stick from the bushes and swinging it furiously at Sarma's head. Sarma ducked swiftly, heart pounding, then seized Bala's arm. Twisting sharply, he leveraged Bala's own momentum against him, flipping him effortlessly over his shoulder. Bala slammed into a tree trunk with a grunt, crumpling to the ground, dazed and groaning.

"Never try that again," Sarma warned coldly, stepping back.

Bala had not known that Sarma was trained in Martial Arts. He was merely a ruffian who used brute force to intimidate others. But Sarma's counterattack, steeped in self-confidence, had completely overpowered him.

Sarma stepped forward. "You called me to talk, but instead, you tried to attack me. If you touch me again, you will find yourself in a hospital." With that, Sarma turned and walked back toward the school. He had a class of children to teach.

"We aren't done yet. I'm going to tell Mannemma," Bala shouted after him.

Mannemma–a trustee of the charity, a powerful woman. Once the wife of an influential man, she had taken his place after his death.

"So, it was Mannemma who sent Bala Reddy to attack me..." Sarma thought. But he brushed aside the speculation and immersed himself in teaching his students.

Sarma got busy teaching for the next hour.

After teaching the class he went straight to Mannemma's quarter.

He knocked and entered her place. Mannemma seated on a chair. She was an old lady. Wearing a white saree and white jacket. Her grey hair is unkempt. There was no electricity so one of her assistants was fanning her using a handmade palm leaves fan.

Mannemma gave an extremely stern look at Sarma. She did not talk. But her expression is like "You made a mistake so it is your duty to give me an explanation kind of look".

"Bala Reddy attacked me. Why did you ask him to do that! It was uncalled for," said Sarma.

Mannemma's expression quickly changed. "I told that hot headed idiot to do no such thing" She said, "Are you hurt?"

while saying that Mannemma looked at the assistant who was fanning her "Go and fetch Bala Reddy tell him drop everything he is doing and come to me at once". Assistant left the room allowing only Sarma in front of her in the room.

"I did not ask Bala to attack you. But I think you deserve such a punishment, though... If I decided to attack you then you must know that you will not be standing there in front of me" She has a point. Mannemma commands great respect. If she decides to attack there would have been a mob of twenty or thirty people to carry out her order. Sarma felt sorry for quickly jumping into a conclusion without knowing the facts.

Sarma did not reply.

"Everyone in the school is telling me you married Kamala?" Mannemma came straight to the point.

"Yes"

"But she came to teach at our school only two months ago. We gave many assurances to her parents from America that we will provide safe living conditions. This is totally unexpected." she said.

Sarma remained silent.

"A marriage means there have to be people, priests and wedding invitations. Both sides agree all this is necessary. Since you and Kamala are both from the same Caste your parents may have agreed. But why rush?!" Mannemma asked.

Sarma knew she was right. He could have asked permission from everyone and do a proper marriage. But how could I tell her the longing he felt when they went onto the mountain for a date... He felt if he did not make her his wife at that moment then the universe will not give him that chance for a very long time and that he felt Kamala was his wife in his many past incarnations but they got separated by people surrounding them... He felt the separation anxiety from Kamala. But Sarma did not reply... Giving any such explanation will only infuriates Mannemma and worsens the situation.

"What kind of marriage is that? I know you are a priest, I guess you do not need another priest..." she asked

"It was a Gandharva style marriage" Sarma replied. Hinduism has eight types of weddings. One of them is Gandharva.

When a man and a woman fall in love, they can marry by mutually exchanging wedding vows. The trees, the animals, the air, the sky, the earth and the gentle drizzle falling from the sky are the witnesses to the wedding of the couple. The presence of no other humans is necessary for Gandhrva style weddings. There is a very famous folk story called "King Dushyanth and Shakuntala" in which they fall in love in the forest and get married in Gandharva style.

"But a wedding is incomplete without fire" said Mannemma.

"True"

"Where did you find fire on the mountain?" asked Mannemma.

"Fire is always present. It is there in the Sun, In our body as jatharagni. It is the fire that keeps our body warm. Fire is one of the five elements the universe is made of. If I die the fire inside me leaves me, if you or her or anyone dies the fire in then leaves them. That is why they say fire has to be there for wedding. Two healthy humans who are not sick maintain healthy human body temperature. They are eligible for wedding. The sacred fire that we light is symbolic in other weddings." said Sarma.

The erudite reply from Sarma proving how fire is present but becomes internal in the romantic Gandharva style wedding only further infuriated Mannemma. But before Mannemma replied Bala Reddy came into the room. Without looking at Sarma he asked Mannemma "Did you call for me?"

"Yes... Did you attack Sarma?!" Mannemma demanded to know. "I told you to do no such thing. What happened to you? Apologise at once to Sarma," she commanded. Bala Reddy looked at Sarma and said sorry.

"Your apologies are accepted, but never do that again" replied Sarma.

Mannemma looked at Sarma and said "Okay. I understand you both are adults and your marriage is legitimate. But that does not pacify our concerns. Our charity administration owes an explanation to her parents. I am still horrified imagining the scene of meeting her parents. We called her parents. I think her father is on his way from New York. It will take a few days for him to arrive. They requested us to keep you both separate." Mannemma said...

"Okay. I don't mind but I need to discuss this with Kamala" replied Sarma.

"No. I already spoke to her. I do not know what kind of magic you used but that poor girl went into your total submission. She thinks only of you. I never witnessed any such thing before in my eighty-five years of life. I guess because Kamala is brought up in America they think differently there. I failed to convince her to stay away from you, therefore I am asking you. Respect our wishes and stay away from her. Though you both think you are wife and husband we need her parents to come down." Said Mannemma.

"What do you want me to do?"

"Stay away from Kamala. If she insists on staying together with you, I expect you to convince her."

"But we are married." Sarma protested

"Show me some respect, Sarma. As your elder, I'm asking for your word–you will keep your distance from Kamala until her parents arrive." Mannemma looked at Sarma.

Sarma understood. "Okay. I will stay away till her parents come down"

"Good, I am glad you agreed to respect me." Mannemma got up indicating that the conversation was over.

Sarma walked out of the room. He went straight to Kamala. He told her what had transpired. "I am going to Tirupati for urgent work. But all is sorted. Nothing to worry about. We will talk more after I am back".

Kamala gripped Sarma's arm tightly, her voice shaking. "I'm scared. Everything feels wrong since we married–as if some shadow's waiting to tear us apart." She hesitated, eyes glistening with tears. "Please don't leave me alone."

"Don't be afraid. I will be back from Tirupati by late evening." Sarma assured.

After that, Sarma went to the bus stand and boarded a bus to Tirupati. Little did he realize that by the time he returned Kamala would be gone.

In the bustling temple town of Tirupati, IBSB maintains a significant operational presence, having commandeered the entire fourth floor of the building also serving as the regional police headquarters. Upon arrival, Sarma navigated his way directly to the fourth floor and immediately reported his presence to a detective, one of Chandra's trusted officers.

Chandra was deeply engaged in a meeting when Sarma arrived. After a brief wait, the doors to the meeting room swung open and Chandra emerged, his demeanour commanding yet accessible. He was closely followed by six of his subordinates, each holding the rank of Superintendent of Police. Chandra's presence was both imposing and reassuring, reminiscent of a majestic lion leading a strategic hunt alongside his trusted companions. Among this group was the superintendent in charge of the highly respected and feared special police unit known as the Greyhounds. Sarma was filled with a sense of warmth and respect; Chandra not only noticed him but also showered him with attention and affection, treating him much like an elder brother would, affirming his importance and belonging in that moment.

The air was thick with tension, a reflection of the nation's mood following the shocking assassination of one of India's most prominent leaders. This event sent shockwaves through the corridors of power and law enforcement communities alike.

As Chandra approached, his sharp eyes locked onto Sarma, who stood in anticipation and respect. "Hello brother Sarma, glad to see you. Follow me," Chandra said with a nod, leading the way to his office. Sarma followed closely behind, his steps quick with a mix of nervousness and eagerness.

Once settled in the privacy of his office, Chandra wasted no time delving into the heart of the matter. "Only a few days ago in Karjat I was embroiled in a deep discussion about you with some people whom I highly admire and respect. We all concurred that you have a penchant for unpredictability in your life's journey. I'm well aware of the chaotic entanglements your girlfriends often bring...But boy..." Chandra paused, his gaze piercing as he scrutinized Sarma, "the news of your marriage was a bolt from the blue, completely beyond my wildest imaginations."

Chandra's police eyes pierced into Sarma trying to assess the depth of Sarma's soul. Sarma became a bit unsettled under that raw gaze of Chandra. He moved uneasily in his seat.

"Tell me everything about this woman you've married and the circumstances that led to your union," he demanded with a mix of curiosity and concern.

Sarma recounted the series of events that culminated in his marriage to Kamala.

Chandra patiently listened to every word Sarma narrated without interrupting. This is something which Sarma highly appreciated. Sarma only knew people who either do not bother to ask him about his version of the story or disrespectfully interrupt him in the middle. And the worst kind are the ones who trouble Sarma based on hearsay. To be able to ask the other human about their version and permit oneself to listen patiently without any mental chatter is a great quality that leads to unbiased discernment. It cuts through the hard rock of hidden human emotional iceberg like a diamond.

"So, your wife Kamala came from America to teach at the local charity school?", Chandra asked.

"Yes," Sarma confirmed, his voice a mixture of fondness and worry.

Chandra leaned back in his chair, his gaze searching Sarma's face. "Do you know anything about her background for you to quickly jump to such a monumental decision? Marriage means being able to support your wife. have you thought about how you'll manage financially? She's American–her expectations might be different. Even simple things, like a trip home, can cost a fortune. Are you prepared for that?" Chandra probed, his tone serious yet empathetic..

Sarma hesitated, looking away briefly. "Honestly, I hadn't thought that far ahead."

Chandra nodded slowly. "That's something you'll need to consider, friend. Love is wonderful–but the practicalities can't be ignored."

Sarma's heart sank. Sarma felt someone had shown him a mirror of reality. A pang of realization hit Sarma; he could barely sustain himself, let alone fund international travels: "No sir, you know my financial situation is quite constrained. I cannot afford such expenses," Sarma replied. Suddenly he felt thirsty. Chandra seems to have expected that reaction. "Are you thirsty? Here, take a sip of water." He slid a glass of water across the table for Sarma to drink.

Then, leaning forward, he posed a poignant question, "All human relationships are economic relationships. You know who articulated this concept?" Chandra inquired.

"Yes sir, it's rooted in dialectical materialism. Karl Marx discussed these ideas," Sarma responded, eager to demonstrate his grasp of such philosophical underpinnings.

A flicker of approval crossed Chandra's features. "Indeed, you possess a deep reservoir of knowledge and the capacity for unconventional thinking. You are a person of considerable potential. Remember, Kamala might view you through the lens of love—a partner who would stand by her side irrespective of the circumstances. I believe that is what happened in your case. But just because she stands by you does not mean the people surrounding her stand by you. They will put you to the test. They will check your finances. But I am sure you will figure out a way to support Kamala." said Chandra.

"Thank you, sir," Sarma responded, a slight relief softening his tense demeanour.

"Now, about traveling to Karjat—can you make the journey?" Chandra inquired.

"No, sir. As I mentioned, I'm not in a position to undertake any travel currently."

"Understood. There's no rush. Take your time to discuss your future plans with your wife and keep me updated," Chandra advised with a supportive nod.

Sarma took leave. He went to the bus stand and returned to his home.

It was late in the evening he reached home. Someone was waiting for him at the door. It was the Charity school human resources officer Shankar. He was holding an envelope in his hand. He handed over the envelope as soon as Sarma approached and said "Sarma, you are fired"... That was totally unexpected. Sarma took the envelope and opened the letter inside. It said that the Charity has terminated his teaching services with immediate notice due to gross misconduct.

"You are asked to vacate the charity premises immediately. We are sent here to see you off from here," Sarma carefully looked. There is a mob of twenty plus people with bow sticks waiting a little bit away. Shanker came prepared with his mob to evict Sarma using force if necessary.

"Give me a few minutes. I will have to pick up my stuff." Saying that Sarma went into his room. He packed his bags and started walking towards the school ladies quarters. He will have to pick up Kamala.

"Bus stand is not towards that side," Shanker said.

"I am going to fetch Kamala." Sarma replied.

"Kamala is not there. They sent her away at noon after you went to Tirupati," Shanker replied.

This revelation staggered Sarma. His heart raced as panic gripped him. "What?... Is this Mannemma who is doing this?"

"I don't know. I only follow orders. You will not find Kamala there. I suggest you leave this place immediately. Otherwise, you know your life is going to be in danger."

Sarma got the point. He felt highly disappointed. His anxiety levels shot up. His mind went numb. "Is Kamala safe?" he asked, his voice strained with concern.

"Of course, she's safe," Shankar replied, though his tone offered little comfort.

Sarma carried his bags and walked towards the bus stand. In twelve hours his world turned upside down. He needed help. He recollected Chandra. He boarded a bus to Tirupati. By the time he reached police headquarters it was 10 in the night. He started feeling tired. The 4th floor is nearly empty.

"Where could I find Chandra sir?" He asked a police constable.

"They all went to Sri Perumbudur. They won't be back until tomorrow noon" replied the constable.

Sarma has not had any food the whole day. Hunger is evading him. He certainly did not expect to lose Kamala so abruptly. He recollected her sobbing. Standing in front of him and wiping her tears. He acted like a hero. Told her everything is going to be alright. But now the harsh reality that he lost her has hit him in the face like a brick.

"How did I let this happen? Where did I make a mistake..." The intrusive thoughts started haunting him. He desperately wanted Kamala by his side. She held his hand, her eyes giving that loving comfort was all he needed for his wayward soul to anchor himself back to reality.

He opened his bag. There is a book called "mantra pushpam" printed by Ramakrishna Mission. In that book he has hidden a scented red rose flower. It is a special flower. On the day they decided to go on a date and got married, Kamala tucked that red rose on the right side of her hair. God, she appeared the prettiest woman on this whole planet. She appeared like a special gift God sent on to earth exclusively for him.

As a child Sarma was attacked many times by those who considered his feeble little vulnerable existence on this earth would somehow threaten the existence of their countries. There is no dearth to the diabolical thinking of some humans. Sarma developed empathy and an understanding to see the soul rather than the human body and judge by what sort of activities that body was compelled to participate in participating. Sarma did not judge Nalini for being a prostitute due to that discernment. He was happy to be her friend, visit her home and accept her hospitality. His love was unadulterated. It was not lustful.

Kamala shared with him the troubles she had while growing up as a child of immigrants in an alien culture. She carries her shadow. But Sarma did not bother. He saw Kamala as a soul mate who stood by him incarnation after incarnation. She is a friend, a companion and a rock to lean on for support in every incarnation.

Kamala standing in front of him wearing that scented red rose flower in the red colour dress kick started in him an anxiety. An unbearable separation anxiety that haunted him every incarnation. So, he asked her "Kamala, let us marry". She giggled.

"Sure... right now?"

"Yes! right now"

"Okay. I am ready. Let's do it. Let us become wife and husband."

There was drizzle from the sky. The atmosphere turned festive. They exchanged wedding vows "Till death do us apart" ...

But now they are separated. She cried. She warned him. She looked for him to come up with a plan. But he totally fumbled it like a fool. The thought he fumbled flicked a switch in his mind. Depression engulfed Sarma like a dark blanket. A very familiar devil called anxiety sneaked into his soul and tried to take control over him.

Kamala did not know Sarma carefully collected the scented red rose and kept it in his prayer book. He took the rose out. It has already turned dark and withered. But he inhaled the scent. He was thinking Kamala's scent had touched that flower. He was not wrong. That flower acted like an anchor and brought him back to his senses.

The jeep screeched to a halt in front of a dimly lit roadside restaurant. Chandra stepped out, his boots crunching on the gravel as he made his way to a public telephone booth next to the restaurant. He dialled his office back in Tirupati, his fingers drumming impatiently on the worn metal.

The phone rang twice before a police attendant picked up, his voice sleepy and disinterested until he recognised Chandra's voice. "Get police detective Shree over the phone,". The attendant's tone snapped to attention. "One moment, sir," he said, quickly handing over the phone to Detective Shree, who was buried under a mountain of paperwork.

"Jai hind Sir," Shree greeted, his voice crisp over the phone.

"Shree, what have you found out about Kamala who is teaching at Kodur mining school?" Chandra's voice was tight, urgent.

Shree hesitated, flipping through his notes. "Yes, sir, we've received the initial findings. Because that girl arrived from America we already have some information. I've dug deeper since."

"And?" Chandra's voice bore into him.

"It's complicated, sir, and I'm afraid the details are unsettling," Shree began cautiously, detailing the findings. As the words spilled out, Chandra leaned against the booth, his face shadowed, the muscles around his jaw tightening.

"Who else is privy to this new found information?" Chandra cut sharply.

"Just me, sir. I took the initiative to visit her village alone, considering the sensitivity," Shree responded, his voice low.

"Okay. Just drop this finding. Destroy anything you have. This conversation didn't happen. And Shree, keep it away from Sarma at all costs."

"Understood, sir, since this is anyway a very private matter which you wanted me to dig up, I did not compile any official report." Shree assured him, his voice equally grave.

"Okay good. Sarma would be heartbroken if he ever comes to know this news. He repeatedly proves that he is naive through his actions." Chandra said. His tone is not hiding the irritation after listening to Shree about Kamala.

As they spoke, a new urgency crept into Shree's tone. "Sarma is here at the station."

Chandra paused, taken aback. "Who... Sarma?"

"Yes sir"

"What is he doing at our police station at this late hour?"

"Don't know sir. I see him slumped at the reception bench, He looks beat," Shree observed Sarma over side glance.

"Put him on," Chandra ordered, a sigh escaping him as he braced for more complications.

Sarma's voice came through, weary but hopeful. "Hello Chandra sir"

"Hey Sarma what are you doing there at this odd hour?. I thought you were back to Kodur"

Sarma explained everything that transpired.

"Okay. That reaction from the school administration is unexpected but not out of line. Obviously they would not tolerate indiscipline. What is your plan? Your next move?" asked Chandra.

"I have to find Kamala. I am planning to go to her relatives place." said Sarma.

"No. Do not do any such thing."

"Why sir?" asked Sarma.

"I can't explain over the phone. But forget Kamala for now," Chandra's voice was firm, his usual warmth absent.

Sarma would hear this "Forget Kamala" advice from many people for a long time to come.

"Why sir?" Sarma asked again. The confusion in his voice is palpable.

"Focus on yourself for now. She would be okay. She has your address?" Asked Chandra.

"Yes sir" replied Sarma

"Good. She would reach out if necessary. Sarma, don't go chasing shadows, not without talking to me first."

Sarma noticed a visible change in Chandra's voice when he was speaking of Kamala. He was not showing the same affection towards Kamala like he did earlier when Sarma explained about their magical marriage over the mountaintop.

"Okay sir," Sarma's voice was tinged with defeat.

"So what do you want to do?" Chandra asked.

"Sir...." Sarma hesitated for a few seconds, "Now that I lost the job at the school I need another employment. You asked me to travel to Karjat. Is that option still open for me?" Sarma asked

.

"Of course. I am glad you decided to go to Karjat. When can you travel?" Chandra said.

"Today sir, the train to Bombay is in another few hours" Sarma said.

"Okay good. Give the phone to Shree".

Sarma handed the phone receiver to Shree.

"Shree.."

"Yes, sir"

"Goto the train station with Sarma. Buy him a ticket to Karjat. Also, give Sarma some cash. Sarma is highly shy. He would not accept or ask for cash help from anyone. He thinks he has to earn money and should not accept any handouts. So use your detective brain. Tease out of him how much cash he has in reserve with him. And give him enough to survive him for a month in Karjat" said Chandra.

"Yes, sir" saying that Shree handed the receiver back to Sarma.

"Sarma, here is what you do. Shree will drop you at the train station. He will also give you some cash. Stay at Hotel Savera in Karjat. There is already a room reserved in our department's name. Tell them you are working for us on a temporary assignment. Stay in Karjat. I will come over there in a few days." Chandra gave the marching orders to Sarma. His words were clipped, each syllable a direct command.

"yes, sir" Sarma replied, a new resolve settling in his voice.

Sarma headed towards the train station, his shoulders heavy but his steps determined, embarking on the late train to Karjat. As the countryside blurred past, Sarma reclined in his seat, the exhaustion of the day pulling him into a restless sleep.

A phone rang in a bungalow In Mayur Vihar, New Delhi. Vinay, who runs an international mining and minerals company, was on the other end.

"Hello Sulfikar here," said the caller. "Sarma's been kicked out just like we thought."

"Great. Now complete your job."

"On the contrary our job got complicated," replied Sulfikar.

"What happened?"

"Sarma went to IBSB. He asked for Chandra."

There was silence for a few seconds from the otherside. "Does he know Chandra?!" The voice was anxious, like someone who walked into a cave and poked a sleeping bear. The outcome would be deadly.

"Looks like it. We have been on his tail since this morning after our initial failed attempt using a truck. We were looking for an opportunity to complete our job. But he went and met Chandra in Tirupati. We did our enquiries. It seems Chandra treats Sarma as his younger brother. He is highly affectionate and very protective of Sarma."

"You found a stupid driver. We should now be discussing the money and financial opportunities that the 3rd party promised for finishing off Sarma. Instead your Incompetence is putting us in danger. Every step we make leads us more into our exposure. Now you tell me Chandra knows Sarma. You know how complicated this makes our job!?" Vinay asked. "Where is Sarma now?"

"He is at the train station. Bought a ticket to Karjat."

"Follow him... But abandon the idea of killing him. Just watch and report." Vinay said. "Did you manage and close down the truck accident situation as something completely unrelated?"

"Yeah. There is nothing to worry about."

"Good. Travel to Karjat. But do not make any more moves towards eliminating Sarma until I do my enquiries. It looks like Sarma is not going to be an easy target. Do not make any more moves. Just follow him and report to me on his moves."

"Got it." Sulfikar hung up in Tirupati, walked to the train ticket counter. He bought a ticket to Karjat and boarded it.

Vinay sat back for a few minutes to contemplate his next move. He called a number in Indore. The person in Indore who received the call called a number in Bali Island and said "Target is moved but not eliminated. We came to know that the target is of higher value than we initially estimated. Vinay wants to renegotiate the price based on the efforts involved."

After that there was a long silence between parties involved in Delhi, Indore and Bali. Thus, unbeknownst to Sarma a divine intervention gave a breather to him for a few months. Someone most high up in the heavenly realms moved Sarma out of danger.

3. THE INSIDERS

Year 1991, Place: Hotel Savera, Karjat, INDIA

Sarma slumped onto the edge of the hotel bed, a temporary refuge while he waited for Chandra's arrival in Karjat. He ran his fingers through his hair, his thoughts spiralling back to Kamala. He is desperately missing Kamala. He does not even know where she is. He has no idea which condition she is in. She was sobbing when he left her. That face of her is vividly imprinted in his soul. Her tear-stained face lingered in his mind, a haunting echo from both this life and a past one. A past life incarnation memory came haunting him. He did it again. He had left her crying before, a century ago, the reincarnation memory gnawing at him.

"How could a man leave his beloved when she is in such a vulnerable condition?" he pondered. 'Oh, but he can...' he recollected the haunting words of Kamini, "your priest is ruthless".

"Am I that ruthless?... Why do I have to act so stubborn? Just because Chandra asked him not to make contact with Kamala does not mean he has to obey him. Let me contact Kamala...," he thought. The isolation is unbearable. 'Or perhaps there is a letter from her to my home,' thinking that Kamala may have sent a letter to his home gave Sarma hope. He called his home in Guntur. The wealthy next door neighbours have a phone. Sarma's sister came to answer the phone.

"Is there any mail for me?" Sarma asked, his voice tinged with urgency.

"Yes," came the reply, simple yet carrying the weight of relief.

"Can you read it to me?" His heart raced as he listened.

Kamala's words flowed through the receiver. Kamala is safe. But she was missing Sarma terribly. She does not know where she is in India because her father is moving her to various places. In a gist, Kamala asked Sarma to temporarily find a job because working in Charity school is not an option anymore. But find a job that can bring Sarma to the USA. Kamala is going away to the USA. Her parents are taking her back.

"But we are married," Sarma whispered to the empty room, the walls echoing his frustration. He slammed the receiver down, a mix of anger and helplessness washing over him.

With a heavy heart, he picked up the phone again and dialled Chandra's office number in Tirupati. Despite the busy tone of the office, Chandra answered.

"Sarma?" his voice came through, strained yet attentive.

"Sir, I received a letter to my home from Kamala," Sarma managed, his voice thick with emotion.

"Good. What did she write?"

Before he could respond, a choked sob escaped Sarma's lips, travelling through the phone line to Chandra's ears.

"Hey, Sarma... Are you crying?" Chandra's tone softened.

"Sir, I am missing her terribly. I don't know what came over me but I can't stay away. Please permit me to search for Kamala." Sarma's plea was heartfelt, his voice breaking.

A brief silence fell, heavy and thoughtful.

"Sarma, listen. You control yourself. I'm nearly done here in Tirupati. It is now time to concentrate on the special assignment for which we wanted your assistance in Karjat. I will board the train to Karjat in three days. Let's meet then and talk about everything. Just control yourself for a few more days," Chandra advised calmly.

Reluctantly, Sarma agreed and hung up the phone, his mind racing. He must go to the USA. He knows if he asks, Chandra can find him a job in the police. But Sarma's priority is to find a job that can give him an opportunity to goto the USA. Resolute, he picked up a local newspaper and flipped through to the job listings. There an advertisement caught his eye:

"WANTED - Systems Analyst: Seeking a skilled individual proficient in statistics and C++ for our Sleep Research Lab. Help pioneer groundbreaking studies. Walk-in Interviews available."

A walk-in-interview means that candidates can directly approach the reception, where interviews are organized depending on availability. Sarma decided to try his luck and attended the interview three days later. But what has transpired there was something else altogether. Sarma saw Bhetala trying to attack the head of the Sleep research Lab Dr Avasthi. After rescuing Dr Avasthi, he spoke to Priya and returned to his hotel, his thoughts overwhelmingly occupied with Kamala and the imminent arrival of Chandra. The train from Tirupati was scheduled to arrive in Karjat by midday. Although Priya had wanted Sarma to stay, he did not because his mind was totally occupied with the thoughts of Kamala. He wants to meet Kamala before she leaves India. Needing Chandra's help for this, Sarma left the lab and headed back to the hotel.

"Has Mr Chandra arrived?" Sarma asked the receptionist, his voice tense with anticipation.

"Yes," the receptionist replied, "He checked in an hour ago but left immediately. He left a message for you--he will meet you tomorrow morning at breakfast"

Sarma's heart sank as he realized he had to wait yet another day. His anxiety was escalating, and impatience clawed at him. Anyone who sees him in that state would not believe that he is one of the most powerful spiritual warriors who can fearlessly enter the realms of the dead to seek answers. Since losing Kamala he has become somebody else. He seemed to have transformed into someone unrecognizable, a change that Sarma himself disliked but felt powerless to resist. The only person Chandra who could offer tangible help is busy with his police investigative duties. Love is not just a priority, there are many other priorities in this world. Saving the community and society at large from danger takes higher priority. Such high priorities seek sacrifice. So Sarma would have to wait, to sacrifice his immediate desires for a greater cause.

As discussed over the phone they met at the hotel for breakfast. Chandra came straight to the point. "Yours sounds more like puppy love," said Chandra.

"What is puppy love, sir?" asked Sarma.

"Dogs are of pure love, so the puppies blindly follow any human that pets them," said Chandra.

"I was trying to understand the love you had towards Kamala. How many girlfriends did you have before Kamala that expressed love like Kamala?"

"None sir. Kamala is the only one"

"You see that is where your problem lies. You grew up in abandonment. Your family always made you a ready-made scapegoat for every problem they committed." said Chandra.

Sarma shrunk under the analysis. He felt sorry for himself.

"Do not feel it is your mistake. You are a very loving and caring person. Nobody can take away that nature from you. You are like a healer. Only sick people go to the doctor to get healed. After they are healed some people might abandon the doctor because they do not want to pay the healer's fees," said Chandra.

"I don't know who I am... Sometimes the delusion of a reincarnation takes over me. I also think I time jump between dimensions. I can not rationally explain my passion towards saving the vulnerable or my unconditional love towards some people who enter my world, or my passion towards Kamala, except that I can only attribute it to the reincarnation. A forgotten memory, a longing kicked in and I fell head over heels. If you call that a puppy love then so be it. But I do not expect anything from anyone when I decide to help. I sincerely believe GOD put me in those people's path for their healing and for my healing as well," replied Sarma.

"Yes, the other day we were discussing reincarnations as well..." Chandra paused before talking further "See... you do not expect. But this is a highly transactional world. They do not expect to come across a rare soul like you who does things out of love, without any expectation. They suspect your motives at any instance."

Sarma did not reply.

"Kamala expressed love for you in an American way. Teens who are brought up in that culture express love without any inhibitions. There Is nothing wrong with that. Whereas in our Indian culture we teach inhibition. However much your past girlfriends liked you they may have never uttered the word 'I love you'. Whereas Kamala may have said I love you too many times" said Chandra.

Sarma felt enlightened with that analysis.

"Yes, sir. Kamala is the only one who I thought could understand love. Is it because of the way she expressed her love?" asked Sarma. He wants to know more.

Chandra is happy. He wants Sarna to maintain distance from Kamala. His police enquiries are ringing all kinds of alarm bells regarding Kamala's surroundings. His priority Is to save Sarma. Kamala is an educated girl. She will make her choices. Time will tell of her character based on the choices she makes. "Exactly.. You are like a puppy. You will fall head over heels for anyone who shows love for you. Sorry to say Kamala bagged you." Chandra said bluntly.

"Sir, I sense that you don't like Kamala" Sarma felt hurt. He thought Chandra would support him.

"No, my boy. Don't be silly. I am with you. I want to support you. Anyways, what did she write in the letter?"

Sarma explained that Kamala wants him to find a job. A job that can bring him to the USA.

"We are thinking of recommending you to the police service," said Chandra. "I know you have fantastic analytical capabilities, you are good with statistics and computers. You will be an asset to our police work. Think how much you can save the world." Chandra looked at Sarma to see if his words managed to motivate Sarma. But Sarma is not at all absorbing. He appeared lost.

"What?" asked Chandra "are you listening to what I say?"

"Sorry sir, my priority now is to find a job that can take me to the USA," said Sarma. "It is as if my destiny is calling me there...I can't join Police now"

"I understand but you know it is difficult to travel to the USA without preparation. Why don't you join us, settle down in life here in India for a few years. Police will train you. You can pick up a lot of skills. Besides, who knows by that time your Kamala may return to be with you?"

Those words gave temporary solace to Sarma.

"No sir... If it were two weeks ago, I would have highly appreciated a chance to join the police. But now I want to find a job that can take me to the USA. But I do not mind helping you on an adhoc basis as a consultant. But I do not want any strings attached which will stop me from pursuing my goal to reach my wife" replied Sarma.

"Alright. So how do you want to do that... finding a job... where do you want to work? Let me know if I can recommend you for a few companies that can give you employment. Hopefully after they realize how good you are, they may give you a chance to travel to the USA on a project. In that way you can reach your wife" suggested Chandra.

"I applied for a job, sir. I attended the interview. There are a lot of scientists working there. I am selected." said Sarma.

"Oh congratulations. But know that doing that job will not take you away from you helping us with the police work." said Chandra.

"Sure sir. As I said I am always available to assist you" Sarma was about to explain further but there was someone who walked into the breakfast area looking for him.

"Chandra sir, what a pleasant surprise. Nice to see you here. I did not know you were staying at this hotel," said the person.

Chandra stopped speaking to Sarma and looked up. It is Circle Inspector John.

"Hey John, good morning. Nice to see you. Yes, I stay at this hotel. What brought you here this early morning?" asked Chandra.

“I am here to look for someone called Priest Siddhanta Sarma from Andhra Pradesh. Hotel receptionist told me he is here having his breakfast. So, I am looking for him.” John looked around the breakfast room. There are not many having breakfast.

“What a serendipity...” exclaimed Chandra with a surprise in his eyes. “Here is the priest Sarma you are looking for. He is right in front of me.” said Chandra introducing Sarma to John.

John did not expect Sarma to be with Chandra. But seeing Chandra and Sarma together made him feel happy. “Hello sir, I am Sarma. Why are you looking for me?” asked Sarma, extending his hand. John shook the hand of Sarma. He removed his police cap and sat at an empty chair at the table.

John looked at Chandra “It is divine guidance Sarma is already with you. How do you know Sarma?” he asked.

“He helps us sometimes in our Andhra Pradesh police work. Why are you looking for Sarma?”

Chandra asked.

“I will tell” saying this John looked at Sarma “Are you at the Sleep research lab yesterday?”

“Yes sir, I was there attending a job interview” replied Sarma.

“Okay but we found a burnt suitcase. I met Priya there.” said John.

“Yes sir, I told Priya about that suitcase. Priya mentioned your name. She said that I must meet you and explain what has happened.”

Till that time Chandra was curiously listening to the conversation and asked "What happened? What burnt out suitcase?"

Sarma turned to Chandra and replied "There is a suitcase sir. It is specially made. It is heavy. But I noticed that it has summoned Bhetala. It sang a song and Bhetala was attracted to that song. He attacked Prof Avasthi and tried to kill him," replied Sarma.

Chandra and John both looked at each other. Their police minds tried to comprehend the narration Sarma gave. It is irrational. But they can't refute the fact that there was someone hurt and there is a suitcase. "Where is this suitcase now?" asked Chandra looking at John.

"It is left at the Sleep research lab only. It is part of the construction equipment. We can't confiscate it as evidence. It is not directly linked to any crime scene. Except Sarma's priestly word we cannot even directly connect the suitcase to any crime!" said John.

"Impound the suitcase immediately" ordered Chandra. He stood up and looked at both of them and said "No... On second thought, let us go asap to the Sleep research lab and pick up that suitcase. We must see what it contains" saying that Chandra walked out of the hotel followed by John and Sarma. All three reached the Sleep research lab.

They went straight into the lift and reached the second floor and entered the room where the construction is taking place. There is a fresh suitcase similar looking. "Is this the suitcase?" asked Chandra.

Sarma went a little close to the suitcase. He touched it with his palm. He closed his eyes and contemplated for a second and replied "No sir… It is not the same. I saw the suitcase before it burnt down yesterday. It sings songs… It emits vibrations. But this suitcase is doing no such thing. I do not think it is the similar kind"

"Okay they must have switched the suitcase. If it is not the same then let us find the old suitcase which was burnt down yesterday," Chandra said. That they went back to the reception.

"Who is doing the construction on the second floor?" asked John.

"It is TOP NOTCH CONSTRUCTIONS sir," saying that the receptionist gave the name and number of the construction company. The office is not far from where they are. All three of them went to the construction company. Though they call it a company it is too small. It is a shop located in a row of shops. A very unassuming shop. On the top of the shop there is a red colour board "TOP NOTCH CONSTRUCTIONS". The shop owner was just opening the shutter when the police jeep stopped in front of the shop. John got down first and went straight to the person, who was standing there curiously looking at the jeep.

"Hi, who is in charge this construction company?" asked John.

"I am sir. My name is Ravindra," replied the person.

"Ravindra, Are you doing construction work at Sleep research lab?"

"Yes sir"

"Yesterday there was a fire at the sleep research lab. We are looking for a suitcase typed device which is broken down, where is it?"

Ravindra looked puzzled. He did not understand why senior level officers from the police came early in the morning looking for construction equipment.

"We are a small construction company sir. We started recently picking up business. We do not own all equipment which we use at our construction sites. The suitcase you are referring to helps us curate the concrete. We call it concrete Induction Heating." said Ravindra.

"Okay where is this Concrete Induction Heating, does it look like a suitcase?" asked John. Chandra and Sarma were listening to the conversation.

"It is not with us sir. As I said, we are a small business. These induction heating systems are made of electro magnetic circuits. They are very recent technology made in Italy, and highly expensive. But we are offered by a 3rd party contractor who is trying to market their products. We rent this electro magnetic induction heater for a lower rate. It helps us to significantly reduce the time of construction. So, we use them" replied Ravindra.

"Give me the address of the 3rd party," asked John.

"Oh, they are not local sir, they are from Hyderabad. They bring the induction heaters and replace them. That person came yesterday and replaced the damaged induction heater. He took the damaged induction heater with him," replied Ravindra. He gave the visiting card of the person who is supplying the induction heaters on rent. It says "Construction supplies leasing, Old City, Hyderabad. Owner: Nayeemuddin". The card has a phone number but no address.

"Why is there no address?" asked John.

"I don't know sir"

"What kind of business are you doing? Why do you engage 3rd parties who have no fixed address?" asked John. His raised voice expressing a command to know the truth mixed with an agony that he had left an extremely vital piece of evidence has hit him hard. The Top Notch Constructions owner Ravindra shrunk at that demanding question.

"I do not know sir. We are a small company growing locally. We do hire supplies. Because I know Nayeem I did not mind hiring his supplies. But it is not entirely true that there is no address. We know the address. He lives close to Charminar in Hyderabad. I usually meet him in an irani chai shop when I go to Hyderabad on work," replied Ravindra.

John looked at Chandra who was patiently listening to the conversation. "Where else did you do construction work during the last three months?" asked Chandra.

Ravindra invited them into the shop. He opened a desk and pulled out a ledger. There are a few entries. Chandra pulled the ledger towards him and glanced at it. The entries he saw there made the hairs on his neck stand up. Two names Valeria Heights apartment and Travellers Bungalow are noted in the ledger.

Chandra pushed the ledger towards John and pointed to the entries and asked "do you see any connection?" Chandra asked.

John has many years of police service behind his belt. He immediately connected the dots. "My GOD! General Bakshi's family perished in Valaria Heights, and Acharya's death happened in Traveller's bungalow", John's eyes became red. The anger in his face is palpable. He looked at Ravindra and said "You are under arrest".

Ravindra started sweating the moment he heard "You are under arrest".

"Sorry sir, we have no idea what you are implying. What did we do? Why are you arresting us" Ravindra was trying to say something else. But suddenly his face turned pale. He clutched his chest and fell on the ground. John tried to administer CPR but It was a massive heart attack. Ravindra's death was instant. They called for an ambulance. Lots of curious onlookers gathered around. John rushed back to the police jeep and summoned an ambulance. There is nothing else they could do. John suddenly recalled something.

He turned towards Sarma. "Sarma, you said that there was a suitcase connected that sent killer signals to cause a heart attack to Professor Avasthi?", saying that John looked around the place "But I do not see any construction activity ongoing here?"

"That is because Ravindra's heart attack is genuine, sir" replied Sarma "Not every event that we encounter is linked to the underworld demonic attacks. In this case, this person Ravindra may be genuinely sick. Your questioning may have caused him tension."

"Can your super powers detect if they are killed by poisons such as cyanide?"

"No, sir"

"Hmmm...We must get a toxicology report," John did not ask any further questions.

Ambulance arrived and the crew picked up the lifeless body of Ravindra. John also summoned the police forensics team. He called Sri Ram the head of Toxicology. "Sriram, your boys are bringing in samples from a deceased person named Ravindra. I want you to prioritise the report. Give us a full picture on what happened to him, what he ate, whatever you can find in his body, any minute detail, I want to know."

After giving out his instructions, John looked at Chandra and asked "What now?"

"At least we have a solid lead. Let us follow this up" suggested Chandra. "Let us go back to the police station".

They all got into the jeep. The driver drove them to the police station.

"Sir, do you need me?" asked Sarma, unsure of what he will do at the police station.

"No Sarma. Stay at the hotel. We will follow up with the leads. I will send someone to fetch you in case we need you". They dropped Sarma at the hotel and went to the Karjat police station.

Sulfikar was following up all the events from a distance. As soon as Sarma went into the hotel he hastened to the nearest public telephone booth and called Vinay in Delhi.

"Hi, Sulfikar here," he announced.

"Go ahead," Vinay responded from Delhi.

"I have something critical to report. It appears Sarma is acting as a Spiritual Consultant for the police."

"That doesn't surprise me," Vinay retorted. "Sarma has always been sought after by influential figures. We've been trying to dim his light since he was a child, yet he consistently outsmarts us."

"That is strange. I thought you hired me to deal with someone that you barely knew. Now you are saying that you've been after this priest since he was a child?" Sulfikar's voice tinged with disbelief.

"It's a long story. You are local to our operations at the Kodur mines, so I reached out to you. We've sent others before, but none succeeded," Vinay explained.

"Didn't you think that is an important detail you should have shared with me?" Sulfikar pressed.

"How does it matter? You still proved yourself to be a failure." Vinay snapped back. "Did you find out what kind of consultancy the police are seeking from Sarma?"

"They're investigating some murders in Karjat. Police suspect there is some witchcraft involved," Sulfikar replied.

"The murders of the military general and Acharya the spiritual leader?" Vinay questioned.

"Yes, those. The police believe there's an occult angle, and Sarma is aiding their investigations," Sulfikar confirmed.

"That's Interesting. It'd be interesting to see what Sarma uncovers," mused Vinay, pausing before adding, "Here's what you should do--befriend Sarma."

"Okay, but how should I approach him?" Sulfikar asked.

"Sarma is somewhat naive. He values friendships, which makes him vulnerable. My men have gotten close to him using that tactic. He's passionate about spirituality, helping the underprivileged, teaching kids, and advanced computing. He entertains mad ambitions. His devotion to GOD really irritates me. Conversations with him always lead to spirituality. That is quite irritating. Just make up a story around one of these interests and say that you need his guidance. He'll be eager to help."

"But would he not suspect? He seems to be having some spiritual powers otherwise why would police value his consultancy so highly? What if he figures it out?" Sulfikar's brow furrowed with concern as he paced in the telephone booth, sunlight creating his shadow dancing on the walls.

Vinay, relaxed against the back of his chair, waved a dismissive hand. "Oh, don't worry about that. We also used to worry about that angle in the past. But he follows a certain code of conduct. He does not consciously suspect people who approach him. He says it is his priest's duty to be available to everyone who approaches him seeking help. He thinks he can't be discriminative with people who seek his help." Vinay's voice carried a hint of mockery. "We used his naivety to our advantage before."

Frustration edged Sulfikar's voice as he pressed, "Then how come you failed to eliminate him? Why must I clean up your mess?" This time Sulfikar stressed the word 'failed' to push back the insult.

Vinay leaned forward, his expression serious. "Divine interventions. There seems to be a force that is shielding Sarma. Every time we try to harm him, he gets helped by something inexplicable. This is why I did not tell you that we failed in the past. But your failure also proved our suspicions. Sarma is untouchable. That surprises me. His circle is too small. Yet he manages to escape," replied Vinay.

"I've seen him," Sulfikar mused, a plan forming. "Desperately trying to reach Kamala. He has totally fallen for her, openly weeping for her. He is begging Chandra to help him to reach her. He is seeking to go to the USA. Maybe I can approach him as a job agent from the middle east offering him job offers? That is my immediate act because I always carry that prop with me"

Prop means the necessary visiting cards and other preparations which make the other person fall for their deception. Sulfikar carries visiting cards with him to back up his act as an employment agent.

Vinay's eyes lit up. "Perfect. Do that. Approach him as a job agent. Just keep him in your company. Move around him. Entice him with career opportunities. He would take the bait," said Vinay.

"Alright." Sulfikar had put down the phone and went back to the hotel. He found Sarma at a breakfast table, his coffee untouched, lost in a maze of worry. Looking lost in his thoughts.

Sulfikar approached, confidence cloaked around him like a second skin. "Hello, I am Sulfikar," he extended his hand with a practiced ease. "How are you?"

Sarma, startled, returned the handshake "Do I know you?"

"Not likely, but I saw you at the Sleep research labs yesterday. You were there for an interview, right?"

"Yes, that was me," Sarma replied, his interest piqued. "You also attended the interview?"

"No... No... I run a boutique employment agency. We scout potential candidates for positions in the Middle East. I was there to see the candidates who do the walk-in interviews. I pick up the candidates and offer them a better salary. It is easy to find potential employees at that place." Sulfikar replied.

"Oh. Glad to know you." Sarma said.

"How did it go? You got your employment?" Sulfikar asked.

"I think so. They are positive that they will offer me a job."

"Oh congratulations. That is wonderful news. If you ever need any employment in the Middle East do let me know. You know gulf states offer insane tax-free salaries for potentials like you." Sulfikar said.

"Definitely. Please let me know your contact details". Sulfikar gave him a card. It read "Lucky employment agency, Lower Parel, Bombay. Branch Office: White Field, Bangalore"

Sarma took the card and said thanks to Sulfikar. Heartened by the conversation, Sarma retreated to his room to rest, the weight of his uncertainties momentarily lifted.

Next day he received a call from the Sleep Research Lab confirming his employment. Sarma is elated. A job in hand would temporarily put a halt to his impending poverty. He could use that money in case Kamala comes to join him they have financial security. Overjoyed, he immediately informs Chandra, who is swamped with following up with the leads generated through Top Notch Constructions.

"I am glad you found employment. Please be available. We are actively pursuing to recover the suitcases which you said are linked to these horrible crimes. Continue concentrating on your job. Good luck" Chandra said.

Sarma went to the Lab to join. He approached the receptionist and informed her that he is there to join the job as Systems Analyst. Receptionist asked him to wait. After ten minutes of waiting Dr Rashmi approached Sarma. She is the one who interviewed him for the job as a Statistical Systems Analyst.

"Hi Sarma, congratulations" Dr Rashmi greeted.

"Thank you Ma'am..." Sarma replied. He is grateful that Rashmi thought he was capable of doing the job. It would be a huge gamble upon her part. "For believing in my abilities. I will not let you down." Sarma promised without even knowing what he was about to get into...

"You are welcome. Please come let me explain the job." Sarma followed Rashmi. After introducing Sarma to everyone Rashmi had shown Sarma his work desk. They spent an hour in front of the computer where Rashmi took him through the necessary details of the job.

"We have a research conference happening in Bangalore. I am going to attend. I want you to join me. There will be various international delegates at the conference. I need data from some of the research papers going to be presented there. So, I expect you to compile data from those papers." Dr Rashmi said.

"Sure Ma'am. When do you plan to travel?" Sarma asked.

"In ten days" said Dr Rashmi "And one more thing. Do not Ma'am me. Call me Rashmi"

The telephone at John's desk rang. It was the head of toxicology.

"Jai Hind, sir" Sriram greeted.

"Hi Sriram, Jai Hind. What news? Did you find anything?"

"Ravindra died of cyanide poisoning." Sriram replied.

'I knew it...' thought John. He thanked Sriram and put down the phone.

Chandra was sitting in the cabin and reading through a file. John went to Chandra and said "Chandra, we got confirmation. Ravindra was murdered. They found cyanide in his system".

Chandra was not surprised. He got up from his chair and said "This is the most tangible proof we have in our hands now. Till now we only have suspicions based on Sarma's report that there is a suitcase device involved in making humans act like killer robots. This is the proof. Why would they go to eliminate the supplier if there is no truth behind our suspicions?!"

"You are right. So, what now?" asked John.

"I need to call Delhi. I will let you know, but let us continue the rest of the evidence gathering exercise" said Chandra.

After John left the cabin, Chandra called Dr Sood at Delhi.

"Jai Hind, sir" greeted Chandra.

"Jai Hind, Chandra" replied Dr Sood. His heart is heavy and mixed with grief. All government security agencies are busy with the aftermath of Rajiv Gandhi's assassination. "How is it going?"

"Aghora is gone to North India to complete the rituals related to his disciple"

"Hmm..." said Dr Sood "it is certainly a tragedy that we tried our best to evade. Has Sarma reached Karjat?"

"Yes sir, in fact that is the reason I called you. I have something extremely important to report" said Chandra.

"Tell me..."

"There seems to be a device involved which can control human minds" Chandra came straight to the point.

"What?... A mind controlling device? Who said this?" Dr Sood asked.

"Sarma...We are looking for his help to understand the mindset of Bikku Tantrik and how they are connected to General Bakshi's death."

"Correct"

Chandra's voice crackled through the phone line, heavy with urgency. "Well... Now the problem is larger than we anticipated," he began, the seriousness of his tone clear even through the static. "Sarma encountered something alarming. He says that there is a suitcase-type device involved in summoning Bhetala."

"How did Sarma come across this information?" Dr Sood asked, his voice tinged with disbelief.

Chandra paused briefly, allowing the gravity of his report to resonate. "He went to apply for a job at the sleep research lab. There he seems to have tried to stop Bhetala. And Bhetala led Sarma towards this device," Chandra explained. "And there is more to this story. We traced the presence of similar type of devices at the apartment where General Bakshi's family perished and also at traveller's bungalow where Acharya committed murder suicide."

Dr Sood rose from his chair, his movements slow, deliberate. He peered out of the window where dark clouds loomed ominous on the horizon, the still air heavy with the threat of a storm.

"Chandra. This is an extremely important detail. Where is this device now? Have we secured it?" Dr Sood pressed, turning back from the window, his expression grave.

"We haven't yet, sir. We identified the supplier of these devices and are planning a trip to Hyderabad for further inquiries," Chandra replied.

"Do this—send Vyas for the inquiry. You, however, need to come down to Delhi immediately. I'll arrange for a meeting with some key personnel who need to be briefed about this matter," Dr Sood instructed. Vyas is a senior level police officer who is responsible for anti-terror operations within the Hyderabad region.

"Understood, sir. Jai Hind," Chandra responded, then hung up and dialled Vyas immediately.

"Vyas, track down a construction equipment supplier named Nayeem for us," Chandra instructed, providing the necessary details.

By evening flight, Chandra was en route to Delhi, the urgency of the situation propelling his actions.

At 7 pm, Chandra proceeded directly from the airport to the secretive corridors of the Ministry of Defence. The receptionist recognized him immediately, nodding respectfully before guiding him to a secluded meeting room. Dr Rao and Dr Sood awaited, alongside a third figure. After greeting each other Dr Sood introduced the new comer "Chandra, this is Brigadier Bipin. He is joining us as a part of this special task force from the Ministry of Defence."

Chandra then launched into a comprehensive briefing on the unsettling developments. The room absorbed every word in somber silence, understanding the gravity of the information shared.

"That is both dangerous and deeply troubling," Dr Rao commented once Chandra finished. "We know certain ancient mantras had mind-controlling capabilities. Our scripture Mahabharata has a story regarding mind controlling, but such esoteric knowledge has long since vanished. What you are describing surpasses simple hypnotism; this is complete subjugation of the will, transforming people into mere automatons."

Brigadier Bipin, visibly shaken, added his concerns. "So, this device compelled General Bakshi and his family into suicide?!" His voice trembled with a mix of anger and sorrow. "Where is this device now?"

"We are still trying to locate it," Chandra replied calmly.

"How many people are aware of this situation?" Dr Sood interjected, his strategic mind racing ahead.

"Including those of us here, the count is eight: Professor Avasthi, Dr Priya, Priest Sarma and Circle Inspector John," Chandra listed.

Dr Sood nodded slowly. "We must entertain the possibility that there is a device that can truly control minds. It can make healthy individuals to either commit suicide or commit horrific acts. We do not yet grasp the full extent of this threat," said Dr Sood. "Do you know why they targeted Professor Avasthi at the sleep research lab?"

"Interestingly, this came to light purely by chance when Priest Sarma applied for a position at the sleep research lab run by Professor Avasthi. And what is more interesting is that Professor Avasthi is a very close friend of the late Dr Kotwal." replied Chandra.

"Dr Kotwal the head of our nuclear research? The one who died a few years ago in a car accident?" Brigadier Bipin clarified, connecting dots.

"Exactly," Chandra confirmed.

Silence enveloped the room for a few heartbeats.

"So, our Defence, our Nuclear research, and our spiritual leaders are targeted." Dr Sood stated gravely. "How come nobody was able to see this till today?"

Dr Rao's eyes met Dr Sood's briefly, a flicker of understanding in his gaze. "It happens. Sometimes the brightest of minds can fail to see the patterns. Just take it easy," he said, his voice steady, infusing a calm into the charged atmosphere of the room.

"We need to ring-fence this information. No one should have a clue about it until we understand the breadth of this issue. This is highly confidential information till the day we know how widespread this problem is within our systems. Assume everyone is an outsider until our investigation is complete. We must use what we know to protect our nation."

"Understood, sir." Chandra responded, nodding solemnly.

Bipin shifted in his seat, breaking the heavy silence. "What do we call this mission?"

"The Insiders," Dr Sood declared, his eyes narrowing slightly as gears turned in his head, piecing together a strategy robust enough to safeguard India's critical interests and advance the goals of India as a nation.

In the year of 1991, an elite group of fewer than ten individuals was quietly assembled for a mission shrouded in utmost secrecy--The Insiders. Their singular focus: national security, with an aim to defend India against the mind controlling tactics of the sinister forces. Their aim was to make India a nuclear power, and to make India economically prosperous. Every other personal interest of "The Insiders" is offered as a sacrifice at the altar of national duty.

After the meeting they all came out of the room. It is 10 pm. They filtered out of the room, exchanging brief nods and murmurs of farewell. All departed except Chandra, who lingered behind. The old Ministry of Defence building loomed around him, its corridors dimly lit, barely touched by the weak glow of aging bulbs. Outside, occasional headlights of the cars passing by the building cut through the darkness, casting long, eerie shadows across the walls that danced like Specters.

"Dr Sood, could I have a moment, sir?" Chandra's voice broke through the quiet.

As Dr Rao and Brigadier Bipin disappeared into the night, Dr Sood turned towards Chandra, his silhouette framed by the ghostly light. "What is it?" he inquired, his tone a mixture of curiosity and wariness.

"It is about Sarma," Chandra began, his voice low and uneasy.

Dr Sood leaned in, his brow furrowing. "What about him?"

"He's not been himself lately. He's completely lost his focus."

"Why? What happened?" Dr Sood's concern was palpable.

Chandra hesitated, then dropped the bombshell. "He got married."

"What?!" Dr Sood's voice echoed slightly in the corridor. "When did this happen? Does Dr Rao know?"

Chandra shook his head, recounting the recent events. "I haven't told Dr Rao yet."

Dr Sood nodded "Hmm.. He needs to know." He paused before switching topics. "So, Sarma is working at the Sleep Research Lab now?"

"Yes, he landed the job there."

"That's fortuitous. Given that the Sleep Research Lab ties into our investigations, he's exactly where we need him to be."

Chandra shifted, bringing up another concern. "What about Gorak Aghora? Should we call him? He is in the Himalayas performing special rituals for his departed disciple."

"Is Gorak aware of Mission Insiders?" Dr Sood inquired sharply.

Chandra explained, "We initially wanted Gorak's insight to probe into Bikku Tantrik's mind. But Sarma's already uncovered a crucial clue, making Gorak's involvement unnecessary now."

"Still, Gorak might want to assist Priest Sarma. Remember, he was near Tirupati searching for him."

"Perhaps inform Gorak of Sarma's location. Let Sarma decide what help he wishes to accept," Dr Sood suggested, then added, "Anything else?"

"That is all, sir. Good night," Chandra replied, taking leave.

"Good night. Where are you headed?" Dr Sood called after him.

"To Hyderabad on a midnight flight, sir. I need to oversee the evidence collection personally," Chandra responded, with determination in his voice.

"Excellent. Carry on with it. Keep me posted on your findings," Dr. Sood said, then added thoughtfully, "You know, it feels like Confluence."

"A confluence?" Chandra echoed, puzzled.

"Yes, a serendipitous alignment. Perhaps, a divine intervention. What will we tell anyone why such a young person is involved or doing with the elite of the power circles?" asked Dr Sood.

"I see your point. We need to create a perfect cover for Sarma."

"Exactly. Sarma's deep involvement in our work, his sudden marriage--these could provide the perfect cover. Sarma madly falling in love and crying out for his beloved will give a perfect smoke screen for all of us. Everyone's focused on his personal drama. People will feel sympathetic to his story and try to help. We are also folks trying to help Sarma. We can do our work in the background. Sarma's love story would be a perfect cover for all of us to get involved" Dr Sood said.

"But does that not hurt Sarma's personal interest?" asked Chandra.

"What is his personal interest now?"

"He wants to reach his wife Kamala"

"So let us stick to that story. We are helping him to reach his potential. We are all elders. Therefore, nobody would suspect our motives when we advise Sarma. We can use this situation for the benefit of both Sarma and our Mission Insiders." said Dr Sood.

Chandra's face lit up after understanding the plan. "Sarma coming to meet any of them would only be seen and understood by the onlookers that he is seeking help to reach his beloved. Nobody would suspect anything. It is a perfect confluence. An ideal diversion."

"Exactly. Now, go on. We've got much to do, and update me with any developments," Dr Sood concluded.

With a plan in place and his thoughts over the mission, Chandra made his way to Delhi domestic airport. The last plane to Hyderabad was boarding. Settling in his seat, he drifted off, waking only as the plane touched down in the early Hyderabad morning.

By sunrise, Chandra was at Begumpet Police station, where Vyas and his anti-terror squad were based. Vyas greeted him in the reception area, expression is grave. "We haven't captured Nayeem yet, but we've located his residence. He's not there," Vyas reported.

"Where has he gone?" Chandra asked, urgency threading his voice.

"They're saying he went to Saudi Arabia," Vyas replied.

"When did he leave?"

"Four days ago."

"And the airports? Any exit records?"

"He hasn't left through any known airports. It's possible he's still in India, or may be escaped by sea."

Chandra's mind raced. "Any other leads?"

Vyas's next words were heavier. "It's bad news. He's an illegal immigrant from Bangladesh."

"That makes sense. Maybe that is why he did not fly. Obviously, he would not be having a valid passport"

"That is not entirely accurate," Vyas interjected after a pause, his tone somber. "He somehow managed to obtain a passport."

"Incredible... Which country issued it?" Chandra's voice was a mix of disbelief and frustration.

With a heavy sigh, Vyas looked down. "We did... Our own country issued it."

Chandra was standing near a door. He had hit the door with his fist so hard in a burst of anger and cursed. "How... How could this happen? if the international community finds out we issued an illegal, that too a potential terrorist... a passport. Do you understand the implications?"

Vyas remained silent, absorbing the severity of the situation.

"Arrest everyone involved including the passport issuing officer immediately" Chandra commanded, his voice echoing down the corridor.

"Understood," Vyas replied, nodding.

"If he has already left our country then we must seek help from Interpol. But we will be ridiculed for issuing a passport to a terrorist. You know how international relations work. There is nothing for free out there on the high seas. They will exert a heavy price if they come to know. A great shame will befall on all of us." Chandra said.

"We have good diplomatic relations with Saudi Arabia. They are highly reasonable people. I am sure they will cooperate. Why don't we talk to them?" Vyas suggested hopefully.

"You know what it means? One of our political leaders has to take this initiative and call the Saudis. And you know politicians. They will ask for some kind of leverage. This mission is so critical, so vital for our national security. We must find a way to trace this terrorist Nayeem without generating any suspicions or expanding our circle" Chandra explained, strategizing their next move, "But first, even before we make any official moves, we must establish the fact that this terrorist is indeed in Saudi Arabia. Let us work on that."

After that there is nothing much can be done. They do not have the devices in their hands. The evidence that mind-controlling is involved is missing.

Vyas, though equipped with high-level security clearance, was taken aback by being kept in the dark about the mission specifics. "May I know why this person is so critical? What is the nature of the threat?"

Chandra met Vyas's gaze, his expression unreadable. "It's a mission of utmost secrecy involving our national security and potentially with huge implications for the security of many other countries. I do not have permission to divulge the details. But as you know we highly appreciate your cooperation."

Understanding the gravity of the mission, Vyas nodded. "Thank you for trusting me with this information". Little did he know in a distant future he would lose his life for knowing...

As they parted ways, Chandra felt the weight of the mission pressing down on him. The path ahead was fraught with secrecy and the potential for international repercussions. He stepped out into the morning light, ready to tackle the next phase of their critical endeavour.

4. NOW YOU SEE IT, NOW YOU DON'T

Year 1991, INT. ICU - PRIVATE ISLAND FACILITY, PACIFIC OCEAN

Lucian stood motionless beside the hospital bed. Frederick lay in silence, tethered to a web of humming machines. The room was cold, sterile–unnervingly quiet.

This wasn't just any hospital. It was a top-secret facility, buried deep within a private Pacific island, shielded from the outside world.

"You failed me," Lucian Wrathborne said coldly, his voice edged with contempt. "I tasked you with protecting Fred. And all you bring me is misery."

"But Father..." Paul hesitated. "You know Fred wasn't the same after Caroline died. He told us himself—he had no will to live."

"Which is exactly why I ordered you to watch him. And you failed," Lucian snapped.

Frederick had tried to end his life—swallowed a capsule laced with a potent neurotoxin. Paul managed to wrest it from his mouth just in time. But not before the damage was done. The poison had already plunged him into a coma. Lucian had him airlifted here—the best care money could buy.

Lucian's tone softened, almost imperceptibly. "What was he doing before the attempt?"

A flicker of something human passed behind his eyes. He didn't care for many. But Fred... Fred was different. Like a son.

Paul glanced away. "Batsinger002 told me Fred changed the BAT code."

BAT—Brain Activity Transformer. A powerful device that could manipulate minds from a distance. Fred had built it. He was Batsinger001, the original. Every expert since carried a numeric suffix.

Lucian's eyes narrowed. "Changed it? Why?"

"It looks like... he was trying to save a priest."

Lucian sighed, rubbing his temple. "Of course. He begged me not to kill that Jesuit Priest. When I refused... he must've tried to override me."

He turned back toward Fred, staring at the pale, unconscious face. "Do we know who the priest is?"

"No, Father. We're still trying to identify him."

Lucian nodded, slowly. "Keep digging. But do not harm the priest. Fred had an interesting attachment to him—someone he'd never even met. I need to know why."

"We can't track him right now—"

Lucian turned sharply. "Why not?"

"He's in a shielded zone. COMxBAT units short-circuit near it. BAT data becomes unreliable. And most of our operatives in India have been pulled—too much interference from rival factions. We're stretched thin."

"Who do we still have on the ground?"

"Bikku is prepping for extraction. Only two agents remain—Sajjad, near Kadapa, and Nayeem, who's assigned to Mission Schrödinger's Cat," said AIWAG, the network's **Air Wa**ter and **G**round (AIWAG) based operations central commander. The operatives under AIWAG had names—but they lived in the shadows, rarely using them.

"Who's coordinating both ops?"

"Bikku."

Lucian nodded. "Tell Bikku to finish Schrödinger's Cat. We've been paid. It must be completed. After that—clean up and pull out. No loose ends."

"You want to shut down all Indian operations?"

Lucian didn't look away from Fred. "Yes. Pull everyone out. Fred changed the BAT code while anchored near India—that was his final act before slipping into the coma. I need him conscious before we proceed further. Keep satellite surveillance running. I want real-time intel on all competitor activity."

He studied Fred one last time. Then, as he turned to leave, he whispered something that had never crossed his lips before.

"Fred... my son... I'm sorry."

His gaze caught the letters ICU on the glass wall. He said them aloud, almost like they meant something more.

"Fred... I see you. Wake up. We need to talk. You've been begging me to change... to be less ruthless. Maybe I'm finally listening. Wake up, Fred. Just wake up."

He turned to Paul. "Keep me informed."

Lucian stepped into the corridor. After a few paces, he stopped and looked back at AIWAG.

"You said Fred changed the BAT code to protect the priest."

"Yes, Father."

"And we still don't know who this priest is?"

"Not yet. I'm working on it."

Lucian nodded. "BAT can't hurt him anymore, correct?"

"Correct. Fred's override blocks any action that might harm the priest."

"But BAT can still detect stress patterns in his brain?"

"Yes. If he's attacked, BAT will register elevated stress levels. That could give us a trace."

Lucian allowed a faint smile–something calculating flickering behind it. A plan forming.

"Then we wait. If anyone lays a hand on him... we'll know. And we step in."

A beat.

"When BAT pings us, track whoever's threatening the priest—and neutralise them. Hunt them down if you must. No one touches him."

He looked one last time through the glass door at Fred.

"If he ever wakes up, I want to tell him I protected his priest. That'll be my gift to him—for everything he gave me."

"As you wish," AIWAG replied.

Year 1991, Johannesburg, South Africa: The study was dimly lit, with the last rays of daylight filtering through the heavy curtains, casting long shadows on the walls lined with bookshelves. The air was thick with the scent of aged paper and leather, the room exuding an aura of quiet power. At the centre of this sanctum, seated in a high-backed leather chair behind an imposing oak desk, was the Accountant—a man of unparalleled financial genius and cold calculation.

Seated at the desk was the planner, a man whose reputation for financial acumen was known in elite circles worldwide. He was in his early fifties, his sharp eyes hidden behind a pair of gold-rimmed spectacles. Every movement was deliberate, every action precise, a testament to his unparalleled expertise in the world of global finance and accounting. In front of him were two open reports.

Before him lay an A4 sheet of paper, freshly unfolded from a secure envelope marked with a wax seal bearing a cryptic symbol. The header on the sheet, printed in bold, stark letters, read:

HATE PERCENTAGE INDEX FOR BRAIN ACTIVITY TRANSFORMER (BAT) EXPLOITATION

The Accountant's sharp eyes, magnified by his gold-rimmed spectacles, narrowed as they scanned the list. The document, sent by his elusive and sinister boss, Lucian Wrathborne, was both disturbing and intriguing. Wrathborne was a shadowy figure, known only to a select few, and his motives were as dark as they were mysterious.

The list beneath the header was chilling in its simplicity:

1. Rwanda Tutsi vs Hutu - 90%

2. Middle East Jews vs Arabs - 93%

3. Bosnian vs Serb - 85%

4. INDIA Lower Caste vs Higher Caste - 90%

5. INDIA South Indian vs North Indians - 55%

6. INDIA Tamil vs Hindi - 82%

7. INDIA Sikhs vs Rest of India - 04%

8. INDIA Muslims vs Hindus - 92%

9. ...

The list contains 31 fault lines in India and continued further listing from around the world. "This is a serious amount of hate" thought the Accountant.

Each line was a stark reminder of the simmering tensions across the globe, meticulously quantified by Wrathborne's twisted algorithms. The percentages reflected the potential for igniting hatred, a measure of how easily these societal fault lines could be exploited through the mysterious "Brain Activity Transformer"—a device shrouded in secrecy, known to very few.

The Accountant leaned back in his chair, his mind racing as he considered the implications of the list. This wasn't just data; it was a blueprint for chaos, a map to trigger conflict in regions already teetering on the edge. The percentages were high, disturbingly so, and the Accountant knew that each number represented an opportunity for Wrathborne to further his inscrutable agenda.

On the left lay the 1992 IMF World Economic Outlook, its pages filled with data tables and economic forecasts. The planner's fingers moved swiftly over the figures, his mind calculating potential trade balances, currency fluctuations, and the fiscal health of various nations. He could see beyond the numbers, interpreting the data with the ease of a maestro conducting a symphony. His eyes sparkled as he recognized an emerging pattern—several Eastern European countries, struggling to stabilize after the collapse of the Soviet Union, had undervalued currencies and potential in raw commodities that could be leveraged in barter deals.

On the right was the SIPRI Yearbook, open to a detailed section on global military expenditures. The planner, with his unique blend of financial insight and strategic foresight, understood that money spent on arms was not just an expense, but an investment in power. He noted which countries were ramping up their defense budgets, linking this data with the economic insights from the IMF report. He knew that some nations, while cash-strapped, had abundant natural resources or industrial capacity that could be traded in lieu of currency—an opportunity ripe for exploitation by someone with the right knowledge.

The room was quiet except for the faint hum of a calculator, an advanced model for its time, its display glowing softly as the planner punched in numbers. He was calculating potential profit margins, factoring in not just the cost of goods but also the hidden value in the commodities that could be obtained through barter. His calculations were not just about money; they were about leverage, power, and influence. The planner leaned back in his leather chair, steepling his fingers as he considered the information in front of him. A sheet of paper on the desk was filled with notes written in a precise hand—an intricate plan was taking shape, one that would capitalize on the shifting economic and military landscape of the early 1990s.

The Accountant reached for his fountain pen, the gold nib glinting in the dim light as he made notes in the margins. His calculations were swift and precise, factoring in economic conditions, the availability of arms, and the potential profits to be reaped from the fallout of each conflict. Wrathborne had provided the fuel, and it was the Accountant's task to determine how best to ignite the fires of division.

As he worked, the Accountant's mind flashed back to previous instructions from Wrathborne—cryptic messages, each more unsettling than the last. This list was just the latest in a series of commands, all aimed at manipulating the darkest aspects of human nature for profit and power.

With a grim expression, the Accountant folded the list and slipped it back into the envelope, sealing it with deliberate care. He knew that Wrathborne's plans were not to be taken lightly; they required precision, discretion, and an unwavering commitment to the shadows.

Disturbing his deep study the telephone rang...

He reached for the telephone, an old rotary model that had seen countless confidential conversations.

As he lifted the phone he could hear the cold and calculative voice on the other side.

"You studied the list of fault lines I sent?," Lucian asked.

"Yes"

"How low are we on funds,"

"After we caused the collapse of the USSR our flow of funds went really down," replied the Accountant.

Nobody knows his real name. Like all the people assembled by Lucian, he has a nickname. They call him the Accountant. He is one of the greatest accounting geniuses. The country he belongs to tried to control him by playing crooked with his family life. His wife told him how she was brutally used and abused by the controllers in the Government before she died by killing herself. That has enraged the Accountant. He was about to become a whistle-blower but the controllers who work for the government knew. So they implicated the Accountant in a false charge and jailed him. It is at this time the Accountant was rescued by Lucian. Accountant is waiting for the opportunity to take his revenge on the country that made him suffer, he wants to wipe the country that drove his wife to despair off the map of the earth...

Love is an extremely powerful emotion. It is often misunderstood and ill judged. Love is a longing to give not to take. It is an inexplicable yearning to protect not to devour. Love is an act of self sacrifice. Wisemen never play wicked games with people in love. The people who played with the Accountant and the love of his life will find out soon.

"So you say wars are the only way to generate business?" Lucian questioned.

"Wars are the best way to move money, hide money behind war secrets, excuses and make more money. You only gave me Sri Lankan war to move money. You did not tell me you were planning to collapse the USSR," the Accountant said.

"It was a mistake. Our board of directors did not foresee the amount of longing world politicians have towards peace," Lucian admitted.

"But Father... hmm... I'm curious..." The Accountant interjected. "What was the real reason you collapsed the USSR?"

"The reason was simple. We attempted to provoke a conflict between the Soviets and America. It did not happen. Neither side took the bait. We expected the situation in Afghanistan would escalate tensions. But the emotions from the Soviets were not strong enough. Also the military is tightly controlled. We couldn't send many COMxBATs into the USSR because the CIA keeps watching them and the KGB keeps watching them in return. We have too little a wiggle room between them for us to play. It is too risky for us to establish our presence. So it is decided to break the USSR. We ignited the conflict in Kuwait and managed to get the Soviets to Kuwait. And you know... BAT took care of the rest." Lucian sighed, the weight of his decisions palpable.

"But Father... you know I've been using the old soviet networks to funnel our funds. It was a perfect iron curtain for our financial manoeuvres," the Accountant lamented, his frustration evident in his tone.

Lucian's voice crackled slightly through the receiver, the line hinting at the distance between them. "Looking back, it's clear, collapsing the USSR was a misstep. We were too fixated on orchestrating wars, obvious to how crucial the Soviet Union was for moving our funds. Imagine that."

The Accountant adjusted his phone carefully, intrigued. "Really?"

"Our initial plan was ambitious--top dollar was paid to bring down both China and the USSR simultaneously, wiping out both communist regimes," Lucian continued, his tone measured but edged with frustration. "We succeeded with the USSR for reasons I've mentioned before. But do you know why we stopped short in China?"

The Accountant leaned back in his chair, thoughtful. "I recall noticing that BAT driven mass protests in Tiananmen Square. For a moment, I thought you'd bring down both giants at once. But honestly, China was never ideal for our purposes. Their manipulated currency made fund transfers too complicated and risky."

Lucian exchanged slowly into the phone, "Precisely. Taking down two giants simultaneously seemed overly ambitious. We postponed the collapse of China."

The Accountant's tone sharpened slightly. "You mean China's downfall is still on the table?"

Lucian responded confidently, his voice clear through the static. "We can dismantle any nation we please, whenever we choose. But you've raised a critical point--if China is not useful to move our funds. What's your recommendation?"

The Accountant smiled faintly to himself. "Convert them into Capitalists. Full Fledged, Capitalists to the bone. Once they're deeply invested, they'll become ideal for our operations. Give me some time--I'll draft a detailed plan for you."

Lucian paused briefly before continuing, his voice warm with approval. "I'm glad we're having this conversation. Had we involved you sooner, we might have navigated the USSR situation differently. I've already recommended to the board that you be included in all future strategic discussions."

Accountant straightened, visibly pleased. "Thank you, Father. I really don't care which country you target next--they all deserve your wrath equally. Some, however, serve us best as useful pawns. I look forward to collaborating closely on your future plans."

Lucian's voice became slightly strained, as if revealing an unwelcome truth. "Yeah... There's a complication we need to factor into your scenarios. Aside from traditional mafias, we have a new rival."

"A rival?" The Accountant's voice sharpened immediately. "Who?"

"An unintended consequence of our actions," Lucian explained quietly. "After collapsing traditional powers like the USSR, corrupt and opportunistic government insiders formed their own cabal."

"But surely you can neutralise them easily?"

"Why would I?" Lucian asked calmly. "They're useful idiots, albeit dangerous ones. They operate from within governments, using official channels, military resources, and bureaucratic machinery for their protection"

The Accountant considered, carefully. "Where exactly is this new competitor most active?"

Lucian's voice lowered further, conveying the seriousness of the situation. "Asia, primarily, their activity is heavy inside India. We are tracking their activity in Asia. They're heavily investing in weaponizing microbiology. Keep that firmly in mind while designing your next strategies."

Lucian's voice crackled softly over the phone, "I realise microbiology isn't your field."

The Accountant hesitated slightly. "That's correct. I'm not familiar with microbiology at all."

Lucian's tone was patient, reassuring. "You don't need deep expertise. Just understand they're creating sports champions and talented individuals through advanced microbiological techniques."

"I'm not following you," the Accountant admitted.

"Imagine a cricket team," Lucian explained, his voice more animated. "Picture a batsman whose abilities are enhanced by microbiological engineering. Could we safely bet on him?"

A slow smile spread across the Accountant's face, though unseen. "Absolutely. Such syndicated betting would generate enormous profits."

Lucian chuckled softly, the sound sharp and clear. "Precisely. But here's the twist. We're closely monitoring these bioengineered individuals. Our competitors have already produced world-class chess champions. Yet, they're unaware we have the BAT system. They stake heavily on their engineered athletes, certain of victory. But at the crucial moment, we disrupt their carefully enhanced minds using BAT."

The Accountant laughed dryly, clearly impressed. "That's quite diabolical. The lengths people will go to for money–it's madness."

"Diabolical indeed," Lucian echoed, satisfaction evident in his voice. "Our competitors are baffled, wondering why their expensive creations suddenly self-destruct. They have no idea we're already exploiting some of their assets."

The Accountant's laughter echoed through the phone. "Brilliant. How can I assist you further?"

"For now, just quantify the financial potential our competitors have created with their bioengineered humans," Lucian instructed. "When the moment comes, we'll leverage their groundwork, trigger revolutions, and capitalise financially on their efforts."

"Understood. Returning to our immediate concerns–what specifically do you need from me now?" the Accountant asked.

Lucian paused briefly. "Assess opportunities in the Middle East. There's significant potential there. Any other suggestions?"

"Yes, several more avenues could be profitable," the Accountant replied confidently.

"Excellent. Fax me your detailed strategies. We'll run simulations to test these on a smaller scale first. Expect a yacht to collect you soon for our upcoming strategy session," Lucian explained.

"I'll look forward to these simulations," the Accountant responded eagerly, knowing it was a rare and valuable gathering.

Lucian concluded the call decisively. "I'll brief the board in the meantime. We'll reconvene during the simulations."

Several days later, the group assembled at the designated secret location, ready to strategise their next moves.

A sleek yacht bobbed gently, anchored off a lonely island somewhere in the vast South Atlantic Ocean, not far from the coast of South Africa. In the upper deck cabin, dimly lit by discreet lamps, the simulation plans are taking place. The Accountant sat opposite to Batsinger and Aiwag. A two-way radio crackled softly, carrying Father Lucian's disembodied voice into the hushed space.

"Accountant," Lucian began smoothly, his voice crackling through the radio, "we've decided to proceed with your advice.

We will create large scale war theatres. Congratulations--you are now a part of our Steering Committee."

The Accountant's eyes glittered in the half-light. "Thank you, Father," he replied softly, nodding respectfully even though Lucian could not see him. "I won't let you down."

Lucian hesitated briefly, an almost imperceptible pause, his thoughts momentarily drifting towards Frederick. Swiftly he returned to the present.

"My money is on the Middle East. The Arabs are flush with cash. Create a situation that pits them against the rest of the world, and our revenue stream remains secure indefinitely." the Accountant said.

"But for that to happen we must create a black Swan Event," Aiwag interjected cautiously.

"Exactly," Lucian said, a slight smile audible in his tone. "With the crazy communists out of the game, we must plan to provoke the American's again. They go absolutely batshit crazy when suitably triggered."

The word "batshit" seemed to ripple through the cabin, drawing knowing smiles from everyone present. To them, the term carried sinister significance, an inside joke soaked in deep-seated grudges against global powers. Very few people know the real meaning behind the word Batshit Crazy. They are the few who know it. BAT can make people go so absolutely crazy that it results in serious damage. Their smiles lingered, fuelled by the thrill of revenge. Grudge is an extremely strong human emotion. They are bathing in it.

"Yes," Aiwag agreed eagerly, eyes gleaming with excitement. "Let us do it. Let us drive America batshit crazy. Let us stage that Black Swan Event."

Lucian's voice hardened. "A Black swan event requires meticulous planning. Ruthless precision, beyond anything we've attempted before."

"We're with you completely, Father," Aiwag assured quickly. "Tell us your instructions."

Lucian's next words chilled the air. "So far, we've deployed BAT and COMxBAT for ground operations. It's time to take our operations airborne. To start with, we need to capture the brain activity of a pilot's brain in extreme distress."

"But Father," Aiwag stammered nervously, "loading a COMxBAT onto a civilian aircraft is practically impossible."

Lucian chuckled softly, unsettlingly calm. "We don't need an aircraft full of passengers. We only need to capture the activity of a Pilot's brain. Try a CARGO plane. Load COMxBAT disguised simply as cargo."

Aiwag stared blankly, the magnitude of Lucian's audacity settling heavily upon him. "How does Father get these kinds of ideas?... Lucian's imagination is both exhilarating and terrifying. Loading COMxBAT into an aircraft full of people is extremely difficult. But to capture the brain activity of a pilot we can simply courier it as a cargo," he thought, swallowing hard.

"We must capture the brain activity of a pilot flying into a tall building," Lucian continued relentlessly. "So that we can use and paste that brain activity for our future missions."

"That's incredibly risky," Aiwag murmured, sweat forming on his brow. "Our land based activities are easy to carry out. But Airlines are tightly controlled. They are surrounded by very high security. Any unusual activity draws immediate attention. Any eventuality gets thoroughly investigated. We risk exposure," said AIWAG. The nervousness in his voice is unsettling.

"Hmmm...yes, risky," Lucian admitted lightly, unfazed. "But BAT is our wild card. With BAT on our side we already have a huge advantage in this mind game. So let us proceed, but there is something else... Find me a pilot from Israel."

Aiwag's eyebrows shot upward, confusion evident. He sipped water nervously. "Israel? Why?"

"One of our clients has asked us to demonstrate our capabilities against Israeli interests. If we succeed, in pulling off this mission against Israel, it gives our client the necessary confidence. We secure substantial funding. Besides, we are getting paid to test the proof of concept."

Aiwag hesitated briefly, then nodded solemnly. "Understood, Father. Give me a few days. I will get our psych profilers to identify suitable pilots."

Several days later, Aiwag's anxious voice crackled through Lucian's receiver. "Father, we've identified pilots, preparing them with BATgoo-- but there is an issue."

"Go on."

"The pilots belong to El-Alim Cargo. And you know, El-Alim is the most secure airline in the world."

Lucian chuckled darkly. "Excellent. That is much better. The higher the security the better for us. It only sharpens our edge."

"But Father," Aiwag's voice quivered audibly, terror seeping through, "it's Mossad. They would burn us alive if they ever came to know we laid hands on them," Awag's lips quivered. His spine ran cold thinking of the possibility to get hunted down by the most dreaded intelligence agency in the world.

A long silence filled the radio channel, broken finally by Lucian's composed, ice-cold reply. "Then we'd better not be discovered. We always ran that risk. For decades we had been snatching food and conducting operations right under the noses of many highly reputed intelligence agencies. Did we ever fail?" asked Lucian. He answered his own question "We did not... So...Get on with it."

Aiwag took a day to get back to Lucian.

"We've successfully converted one of the pilots as BAPS. They are scheduled to fly on 12th September," Aiwag reported cautiously.

"No—shift it to 11th," Lucian interjected sharply.

"But Father, if we alter the schedule, Mossad will notice immediately. Their databases are monitored relentlessly; hacking into them is exactly what we were worried about," Aiwag replied anxiously.

Lucian's voice crackled irritably over the radio, "Who said anything about physically hacking their databases?"

Aiwag froze, his mind went blank. Without accessing El-Alim Cargo's databases directly, he saw no possible way to adjust the pilot's flight date. His eyes flicked desperately towards Batsinger, pleading silently for help. But Batsinger, equally confused, merely shrugged helplessly.

Lucian's impatience filled the silence. "No ideas? Nothing at all?" he snapped.

At that moment, Lucian deeply felt Frederick's absence. Frederick would have effortlessly solved this. But Lucian steeled himself, taking back control. "Use BAT's E-snatcher mode," he suggested firmly.

E-Snatcher stands for election snatcher. A sudden spark of recognition flashed across Batsinger's face, though Aiwag remained visibly puzzled.

"E-Snatcher?" Aiwag queried, bewildered. "How exactly can it help us infiltrate El=Alim's system without leaving footprints?"

"Batsinger," Lucian instructed, voice calmer now, "Perhaps, you should explain it clearly to Aiwag. I leave you both to get on with it. Let me know once you've sorted this," The radio crackled, signalling Lucian had left the conversation.

Aiwag turned to Batsinger, desperate for clarification.

"I'll demonstrate," Batsinger said simply, placing two playing cards before Aiwag: one a Black Joker, the other a Red Joker. "Look carefully. Decide which card you want to pick--but don't touch it yet."

"I'll choose the Black Joker," Aiwag announced confidently.

"Go ahead, pick it up," Batsinger encouraged.

Aiwag reached forward decisively, only to find himself staring in disbelief at the Red Joker in his hand. He blinked rapidly, jaw dropping in confusion. He was absolutely certain he'd chosen Black Joker.

"How...?" Aiwag stammered, shaken. "I know you used BAT, but without any initial preparation BAT does not work. But you just pulled the card trick effortlessly--how?"

"For something as simple as this," Batsinger explained patiently, "BAT needs no advance setup. That is why your ground ops were never involved."

"No wonder I had no idea," Aiwag murmured, astonished. "But how does it actually work?"

"It's straightforward," Batsinger elaborated calmly. "When you're presented with two choices, your brain momentarily holds both possibilities in your conscious mind. At that precise instant, BAT switches the action potential--the command signal--from one choice to the other. It's a seamless brain manipulation, entirely invisible to the subject."

Aiwag started thoughtfully at the playing cards, visibly disturbed yet fascinated by the demonstration.

"So," he murmured slowly, piecing it together, "When voting, suppose I'm presented with four or five parties. In my mind, I've clearly chosen one, and I'm certain that's how I've voted. Yet BAT may have silently switched the bioelectric pulse that sends commands to my hand which means my Brain voted for Party A but the command that went to my hand voted for Party B. Essentially I cast a vote without realising I've changed sides?" His voice rose slightly in astonishment.

"Exactly," Batsinger confirmed, a quiet satisfaction in his eyes. "This is precisely why Father says democracies are a sham.

We control elections, deciding who comes to power in whichever country we choose.'

"Incredible," Aiwag repeated, shaking his head in disbelief, trying desperately to process this revelation. "But here is a puzzle--What if the desired choice isn't already stored in my memory? Say I am choosing between two political parties, but imagine there is a 3rd choice--a third political party that I don't know about. How can Father make people vote for that?"

Batsinger leaned in, voice calm and assured. "Good question. In that case, we can't make the 3rd party win. This is why we use your ground network to create events which embed this third choice firmly into the voters' minds. Any memory--good, bad, or indifferent--can be leveraged."

Aiwag nodded slowly, understanding dawning. "Is this why Father always says 'No publicity is bad publicity?"

"Precisely," Batsinger replied, smiling knowingly. "It also extends beyond politics. We use BAT to control examination outcomes as well, pushing chosen individuals into positions of influence. We send the people of our choice into power positions in various countries".

Aiwag's brow furrowed with curiosity. "But exams aren't always multiple-choice questions, they involve essays too. How do we manipulate that?"

"Exams are designed by people, aren't they?" Batsinger said, eyes gleaming. "We copy the brain signals of the person setting the exam--their brain holds both the questions and answers. Then we imprint these memories onto our chosen candidates.

Copy pasting brain activity using BAT and COMxBAT is something you know very well."

Aiwag let out a low whistle of awe. "No wonder Father runs such flawless operations in any country that he lays his hands on. There's not a single country, no leader, no powerful individual beyond father's grasp." His voice brimmed with pride thinking of the master they serve and the formidable power he holds.

"Right," Aiwag continued briskly, refocusing. "Back to our immediate plan--Father insists we switch the flight date from 12th to the 11th of September using the BAT E-snatcher mode."

"Understood," said Batsinger, his expression suddenly thoughtful. "But why specifically the 11th of September"

Aiwag smiled faintly, a brief flash of insight crossing his face. Yet almost immediately, his expression darkened again into puzzled anxiety. "Hold on--actually, we might have a serious problem," he stared at Batsinger, anxiety flickering in his eyes.

"What?" Batsinger asked sharply.

"BAT can switch the date when the date is predetermined," Aiwag explained slowly, voice taut with uncertainty. "But once the aircraft is airborne, the pilot is constantly checking dynamic flight data. How on earth can we maintain control in real-time under those circumstances?"

Batsinger smiled calmly, his confidence unwavering. Adjusting the BAT device on the table, he leaned forward. "Let me demo you."

"Check your watch. What's the time?"

Glancing down, Aiwag replied confidently "9:02."

Batsinger's eyes glinted mischievously. "Are you sure?"

Frowning, Aiwag looked again, his certainty vanishing. His face paled, disbelief etched deeply into his features. His watch now clearly displayed "8:46". "How...?" he muttered weakly.

Batsinger leaned back, savouring Aiwag's confusion. "Are you absolutely certain?"

Now thoroughly rattled, Aiwag stared again at his watch, his mouth falling open. It showed "9:37". Thinking that the watch may have some issues, he patted his watch again... But it still shows "9:37". Hastily he glanced at the large digital clock on the cabin wall, it too read "9:37". He breathed out shakily, regaining composure. "Two clocks can't both be wrong," he insisted more confidently. "Yes, I'm sure--it's 9:37."

Batsinger paused dramatically before repeating softly, "Are you really sure?"

Aiwag threw his hands up helplessly, overwhelmed. "Fine, I give up. Explain what's going on."

Batsinger rose from his chair and approached Aiwag. "Earlier, BAT switched the command from your brain to your hand when picking the playing card, correct?"

"Yes," Aiwag confirmed hesitantly. "You said BAT can alter the action potentials, fooling the brain to think it picked up one card while the muscle actually picked up another card."

"Precisely," said Batsinger, eyes gleaming with intensity. "We humans have both action organs and sense organs. BAT doesn't just manipulate actions--it also changes perceptions. What you're seeing right now is not reality, but what BAT wants your brain to perceive."

Aiwag's eyes widened, horror settling into his expression. "You're telling me the actual time is different, but BAT has changed inside my brain what I am seeing? Is it distorting my perception?"

"Exactly," Batsinger nodded, his tone matter-of-fact. "There's just one catch—we can trick a pilot's perception, but we can't fool the Flight Data Recorder."

Colour drained from Aiwag's face. "Then what do we do?" he asked, voice barely above a whisper.

"Simple. You already have ground operations in multiple countries, correct?" Batsinger asked calmly.

"Yes," Aiwag confirmed warily.

"Then use your teams to recover the flight data recorder before any investigators arrive," suggested Batsinger smoothly.

Aiwag's breathing quickened, panic edging into his voice. "Are you mad? I can't plan like that... We risk exposure. Sending someone into a crash site will put our people under intense scrutiny. It's too risky." Aiwag composed his thoughts "This is a no-go mission."

"This is only a temporary solution," Batsinger reassured him gently. "I'm already working on something permanent. But just this once, can you make the flight data recorder vanish from a cargo crash?"

After a long pause, Aiwag took a shaky sip of water, meeting Batsinger's gaze reluctantly. "Alright," he conceded finally, voice firming slightly. "Just this once. But until you provide a foolproof method, I'm not risking my people in another BAT operation involving aircraft."

"Understood," Batsinger agreed, his voice reassuring. "Next time, I promise a method that keeps your ground teams safely hidden."

Aiwag shook his head slowly, awe filling his eyes. "That's extraordinary. We can manipulate altitude readings, instrumentation–show the pilot anything we choose. Incredible." With spontaneous delight, he hugged Batsinger tightly. "You know," he said, pulling away slightly, "I've been involved in some dark plots, but when Father first tasked us to target Israel, I was terrified. Now, after your demonstration, I feel certain we can pull this off without a hitch." Dramatically, he snapped to attention and raised his arm in a mocking Nazi salute. "Hail Father!"

Batsinger grinned broadly, mimicking Aiwag's gesture. "Hail Father!"

From across the room, the Accountant finally broke his silence, observing them closely. "Do you know who you remind me of?" he asked dryly. "Reincarnated Nazi commanders."

Amused, Aiwag and Batsinger shared a glance, their playful mood shifting swiftly into theatrical seriousness. Stiffening their backs like disciplined soldiers, they saluted once more in exaggerated unison. "Hail Father!"

"Stop it, both of you!" snapped the Accountant, irritation creeping into his voice. "You may behave like reincarnated Nazis, but Father is no Hitler. He doesn't hate Jews or anyone else–he does what's necessary."

Chastened, Aiwag and Batsinger dropped back into their chairs, the brief humour subsiding. Both men had endured lifetimes filled with suffering, betrayal, and humiliation before Father found them. He had offered them freedom, purpose, and the chance to feel human again. Moments like these were rare glimpses into their buried innocence.

Breaking the silence, Batsinger reminded quietly, "You still haven't explained–why specifically the 11th of September?"

Aiwag's expression tightened, growing serious. "I'll explain later. Remind me when things settle down." He rose abruptly. "I need to return to my yacht urgently and send information to Father." With that, he swiftly exited the cabin, closing the door firmly behind him.

Outside, Aiwag's mind raced. Thoughts crowded his consciousness, questions spiralling about BAT's staggering implications. Preoccupied, he nearly stumbled off the edge of the fishing trawler towards the rope ladder. A sudden, pressing question halted him sharply. He knew chances to speak face-to-face with Batsinger were few and far between. Once BAT synchronised operations through SANI satellites with COMxBATs and MEDxBATs, their interactions would vanish altogether.

Determined not to miss his opportunity, Aiwag spun back, reopened the cabin door, and stepped inside. The Accountant and Batsinger glanced up, surprised by his quick return.

Aiwag took a step into the cabin, his face a blend of urgency and apology. "Sorry... just one last question. After this, I promise I'll leave you both in peace." He looked directly at Batsinger.

"Go on," Batsinger said, settling back into his chair.

"I've been thinking about examination systems," Aiwag began, his voice tinged with curiosity. "It's thrilling to know Father has people in governments across various countries."

"Not just governments," Batsinger interjected. "Private sectors too."

"Yes, of course," Aiwag nodded, waving a hand. "But it can't be that simple. There are people out there–truly brilliant minds–whose intellect alone earns them their positions. Their cognitive abilities are exceptional. They don't need BAT to pass exams. Replacing all of them with our people would be a Herculean task."

Batsinger stood and stretched, giving Aiwag a puzzled look. "I'm not sure I follow."

"I wasn't finished," Aiwag said. "As someone in operations, I understand how difficult it would be to infiltrate every system. That's why I assume Father only places a select few in each organisation. A handful, just enough to influence outcomes without drawing attention." He glanced at Batsinger for confirmation.

Batsinger nodded. "You're right. We don't replace everyone. There are genuine talents in those positions. Our strategy is to embed a small percentage–around twenty out of every hundred. It's about balance, not saturation."

"That makes sense," Aiwag replied, his brow furrowed. "And I assume those twenty don't even know who they really work for?"

"Correct."

"That brings me to my real question," Aiwag said with a faint smile. "If they're unaware of Father's role, and we can't keep constant tabs on them, how do we actually identify who's ours and who isn't? It must be incredibly difficult to track."

Batsinger raised his eyebrows and shrugged. "That, I genuinely don't know."

"I do," the Accountant interjected calmly, folding his hands on the table. "Education, placement, and tracking of Father's people is an entirely separate division. I know because I account for them as part of our income sources."

"Who runs it?" Aiwag asked, intrigued.

"Tedbatter," replied the Accountant simply. "He's the one who manages the invisible map of our influence."

Both Batsinger and Aiwag turned to the Accountant with identical looks of confusion.

The Accountant raised an eyebrow, surprised. "You mean to say neither of you knows about Tedbatter?"

They glanced at each other, then replied in unison, "No."

"Well, that explains it," the Accountant said with a knowing nod. "You've been mipered."

"Mipered?" Aiwag echoed, frowning.

"A memory wipe," the Accountant clarified. "BAT selectively erases information to maintain operational secrecy. If you don't need to know something for your specific function, it gets removed."

Aiwag blinked, then nodded slowly. "That actually makes perfect sense. We may have been mipered. But still—I want to know the answer to my question. Just for now. How do we recognise our people inside governments?"

"I'll tell you," the Accountant said, leaning back slightly. "But I doubt you'll remember it by the end of the week. Miper is automated–it runs in cycles, clearing unnecessary details from memory."

"I know," Aiwag said with a faint smile. "But let me have the knowledge while I can."

"Tedbatter is the head of TEDxBAT operations," said the Accountant.

"BAT I know," Aiwag said, "but what's TED?"

"Theoretical Education Distribution," the Accountant explained, "crossed with Brain Activity Transformer. TEDxBAT is responsible for identifying, selecting, and embedding cognitive profiles into candidates. Tedbatter oversees the whole process."

"And how does he track them? That's what I'm really asking," Aiwag pressed. "Ever since Father tasked me with the Israel mission, my anxiety's been through the roof. I need to understand the tools and strengths we've got at our disposal."

The Accountant gave a slight nod. "Governments use all kinds of subtle identifiers–code names, wearable tokens, even symbolic tattoos. These tags help distinguish the embedded operatives. Mafias and secret networks use similar systems."

Batsinger raised a hand, interrupting. "Wait–are you saying we're not the only ones doing this? That mafias are placing people in government too?" His eyes widened with fascination.

"Absolutely," said the Accountant. "Governments place covert agents under official secrets acts. Mafias—old-school, ruthless thieves—embed their own. And then there's us. We are the sharpest of them all. Apex predators, as Father likes to say. But make no mistake, it's crowded in there."

He paused, his tone darkening. "And not everyone plays by the same rules. Some of those mafia-aligned agents use appalling coercive methods. I've seen what they're capable of. My wife... she was compromised. Broken. And the so-called authorities turned a blind eye."

He fell silent for a moment, wiping his brow with the back of his hand, trying to shake off the memory. The room hung heavy with that truth, even Batsinger now subdued.

Aiwag spoke softly, "We may be monsters, but at least we're precise monsters."

Aiwag leaned in slightly, his curiosity still burning. "I understand how governments keep track of their inner circle. But how does Father track ours?"

"Oh, that's straightforward," the Accountant replied. "Tedbatter edits their genes. He gives them subtle physical characteristics—markers only we can identify."

Aiwag blinked, taken aback. The idea was both thrilling and disturbing.

"Gene-edited babies aren't Father's invention," the Accountant continued. "It was the governments who first crossed that ethical line. They've been breeding bespoke humans for years. Father simply rescued one of the scientists from that dark programme. She works for us now, still running her operations under Father's command. When she identifies gene-edited assets working for governments, they're... removed. We use them in BAPS fieldwork, then replace them with our own."

Aiwag frowned, struggling to digest the implications. "I can believe governments would do something so monstrous. They've always been able to bury their crimes. But the private sector?" He paused, collecting his thoughts. "Gene editing would never fly there. Regulators would catch on immediately." He turned to Batsinger for support.

But Batsinger only grinned, tapping the face of his watch. "Are you sure?"

Aiwag froze. The earlier demonstration came flooding back–how BAT had made him misread the time.

"So... BAT deceives the regulators too," he murmured. "It feeds them false data."

"Exactly," Batsinger confirmed. "They only see what we want them to see. If we need to throw them off the scent, we'll sacrifice a few of our rivals–those working for mafias or other networks. Never our own."

The Accountant gave a small nod, then added, "Father once said something that's stuck with me. "When government operatives seduce, it's called diplomacy. When we outsiders do the same, it's labelled prostitution. The act is the same–it just depends which side of the fence you're on.'"

Aiwag nodded slowly. That was all he needed to hear.

"I'll ask Father not to Miper this particular conversation. I'll need it for the airborne mission we're about to plan." With that, he turned and exited the room.

He made his way to the edge of the fishing trawler, descended the rope ladder, and climbed into the waiting motorboat. As the boat sped across the waves, Aiwag's gaze remained fixed on the large, ominous silhouette of the yacht ahead. He had work to do—and now, he had the knowledge to do it well.

Aiwag's mind buzzed with possibility as the boat drew closer to the yacht. The BAT demonstration had not only stunned him, it had opened new doors—some exciting, others dangerous. But one thing was clear: they needed funds. And fast.

Once back on board, he wasted no time. Grabbing the two-way receiver, he called across to Batsinger, whose vessel was still within range.

"Batsinger, I've got another question," Aiwag said.

"Go on," came the static-laced reply.

"You showed me how BAT's E-snatcher mode can influence elections."

"That's right."

"How confident are we in its effectiveness?"

"Oh, we're very confident," Batsinger said. "You remember your operation in Southern India a few months back?"

"I do."

"Then tell me—what stood out to you about the political scene there?"

Aiwag paused, thinking. "Most of the politicians were former film stars. Their faces were everywhere–posters at every corner, walls plastered with their grinning images."

"Exactly," Batsinger said. "The human brain is constantly consuming TEA."

"Tea?" Aiwag frowned. "I don't follow."

"Thought. Emotion. Action. BAT's E-snatcher is calibrated to hijack all three."

Aiwag, once a master chess player, quickly caught on. "A movie poster introduces a thought into the viewer's mind. Based on the type of visual it evokes emotion. A desire to watch the movie results in watching the movie."

"Spot on," Batsinger said. "Our human brain once it sees something it can not unsee it. Imagine a movie actor as a hero vanquishing all bad folks. Though it is just a movie the brain does not know it is a movie. That is why we identify with emotions shown in the movie. If it is a depressing movie, we stay depressed for a few days. We have to use a conscious discernment to tell ourselves that it is just a movie and that it is unreal... But not all people are capable of such discernment."

"So you can make a movie hero win the election much easier than a regular honest politician who genuinely craves to help his constituents," Aiwag mused "No wonder film stars win elections in Southern India."

"Correct," Batsinger confirmed. "Using BAT's E-snatcher mode we can make the viewers of the movie vote for their movie hero in a real-life election."

"But not everyone goes to the cinema," Aiwag pointed out.

"Why do you think you see so many posters of the politicians on the streetsides?" Batsinger asked.

"So, you force the brains of passers by to see it. Once they see it, they cannot unsee it?" Aiwag said.

"Precisely. We don't know how the neurons in the brain store this information or where they store it. But we know the particular pattern the brain's bio-electrical circuits light up when seeing a particular image. We use it to switch and snatch the vote." Batsinger said. "Why do you ask? What have you in mind?"

Aiwag was silent for a moment. Then, "Is the Accountant still in the conference room?"

"Yes. One moment."

A few seconds later, the Accountant's voice crackled through. "What is it?"

"I've got a list of cloned and genetically modified singers maintained by our competitors," Aiwag said.

"And?"

"We're strapped for cash. Why not use one of them to generate income? Our ground crew could get paid properly."

"Concerts don't make much money," the Accountant replied. "Not enough for what we need."

"I will make you a billion. Is that enough?" Asked Aiwag.

"That would do nicely," the Accountant admitted. "How?"

"Put Batsinger back on."

A moment passed. "I'm here," Batsinger said.

"If I engineer a terror event–one somehow tied to a specific singer–can BAT manipulate people into buying concert tickets?" Aiwag asked.

"Absolutely. For BAT, there's no such thing as bad publicity. You embed the name and face into the public mind, and I'll take it from there. BAT will make them buy."

"Wicked," Aiwag said with a grin. "We can legally siphon off insane amounts of money."

"I like it," the Accountant cut in. "We could even form companies, manipulate markets the same way."

"Perfect," said Aiwag.

"I'll need a few days to write BAT modules for this. What name should we give to this special program?" asked Batsinger

"Call it 'The Devil's Concert,'" the Accountant replied. "I'll brief Father. We're about to create a whole new breed of money-making, fame-fuelled devils who will fund our operations."

"And what about the market traders we control?" Batsinger asked.

"Call that one 'Vampires of the World Trade,'" said the Accountant with a smirk.

Year 1991, Bombay Dockyard, Bombay, India:

An old, weather-beaten fishing trawler sat idle near the shore, shrouded in a large tarpaulin. To a casual onlooker, it appeared abandoned or under repair–nothing more than a relic of the sea.

It was late evening. A rumbling BEST bus pulled up at the dockyard stop. From among the weary commuters, Bikku stepped off. His appearance was deliberately unremarkable—plain trousers, a buttoned shirt, and his long hair tied back. Cradled under one arm was a scorched COMxBAT unit. He scanned the area briefly, then approached the covered vessel. Picking up a loose stone from the ground, he tapped the hull three times—sharp, deliberate knocks. A signal.

Moments later, the tarpaulin shifted. Nayeemuddin's head emerged cautiously. He recognised Bikku and lowered a rope ladder. Bikku climbed aboard.

Inside the dim belly of the boat, Bikku dropped onto a wooden crate and exhaled. "We're shutting down operations in India," he said. "Did you recover the COMxBATs from Karjat?"

Nayeem nodded, pulling aside a cloth to reveal three black suitcases. "All three. One's burnt out. The other two are intact."

Bikku added his own charred unit beside them. "That makes four—two functional, two destroyed. I'll file the report with Aiwag."

"What's next?" Nayeem asked.

"We've received confirmation. Mission Schrödinger's Cat must be completed."

Nayeem's expression tightened. "There's a complication."

Bikku's eyes narrowed. "What sort?"

"Circle Inspector John saw one of the burnt COMxBATs," Nayeem said. "I don't know how. By the time I arrived, he and Dr Priya from the sleep research lab were examining it. They were also discussing that they are going to inform the head of the sleep research Lab Dr Avasthi."

"So we have Mission Shroendinger's cat to complete and there are two others who eyeballed our COMxBAT?" asked Bikku.

"Correct," said Nayeem "Interestingly all three of them travelled to Bangalore. They're returning tomorrow evening on a late flight to Bombay. I've been monitoring their travel plans. Figured Father might want them... dealt with."

"Well done. We got instructions to complete Mission Shroendinger's cat. Tie up any loose ends and exit India."

"Should we take them out tomorrow night? They'll likely travel by road to Karjat after landing."

"Proceed," Bikku said firmly. "I'll send the COMxBAT coordinates to Aiwag and inform him the mission will be completed. We'll request extraction once it's done."

"Understood. See you tomorrow night."

With that, Nayeem picked up one of the functioning COMxBAT cases and descended the rope ladder. Bikku watched him disappear into the evening haze before pulling the ladder back in and resecuring the tarpaulin. The shadows deepened around the boat, silent as the mission moved closer to its deadly end.

5. CONSCIOUS INTERGALACTIC ENTITIES (KIES)

Year 1991, Kedarnath, India. The towering Himalayan peaks, wrapped in a ghostly mist, stood as silent witnesses to the eternal cycle of life and death. The ancient Kedarnath temple, dedicated to Lord Shiva, loomed in the background, its timeworn stone walls glowing dimly under the flickering flames of the temple lamps. The temple's sacred energy pulsed in the crisp mountain air, the scent of burning camphor, ghee, and sandalwood incense mingling with the raw, untouched cold of the altitude.

Aghora stood barefoot near the edge of the Mandakini River, his dark robes heavy with the evening dew. The river, flowing with icy, glacial waters, whispered through the rocky terrain, its currents carrying the echoes of thousands of prayers offered here since time immemorial. Nearby, the snow-dusted valley stretched into the horizon, its silence punctuated only by the distant ringing of temple bells and the soft murmuring of wandering sadhus.

In front of Aghora, a small sacrificial fire (homa) burned inside a havan kund made of rough-hewn stone. He sat cross-legged before it, his eyes closed, his mind attuned to the energies beyond the material realm. Around him, he had arranged sacred offerings: a copper vessel filled with holy water from the river, fragrant bel leaves, and a small mound of ash from a funeral pyre—a reminder of life's impermanence.

The moon, partially hidden behind a veil of drifting clouds, cast a silver glow over the snow-laden peaks, bathing Aghora in an ethereal light. His rudraksha beads swayed rhythmically as he chanted ancient mantras, his voice merging with the howling winds, a haunting yet serene invocation calling upon Lord Shiva to guide Ranga's soul.

A chill breeze swept through the valley, causing the flames to flicker wildly, as if acknowledging the presence of the departed spirit. Aghora opened his eyes, gazing into the fire, searching for omens in the dancing embers. He knew Ranga's journey was not over—it had merely shifted to another plane.

Aghora took the copper vessel in which Ranganna's ashes were kept. He removed the cloth covering on the vessel. He took a little bit of Ranganna's ashes and drew a very small circle on the ground in front of the fire. He created a small doll made of rice flour mixed with Ranganna's ashes. A doll that resembles a human with two legs, two hands, a head and a body. He placed the doll inside the circle. He took a little bit of sacred water in his hand and sprinkled it lightly on the doll.

Then he called "Ranga... you are safe. You are safe from the prying forces like Śākini, Dhakini, bhrahma rakshasa etc.... I command thee... Ranganna... Wherever you are hiding. Come forth... Come forth..." Aghora's chanting reached the ethers and gently knocked on the doors of a dimension called "Preta Loka". The departed souls which are lucky, who are not yet captured by forces like Śākini and Dakini, take temporary shelter there. They can stay there for 12 lunar months.

"Ranga's ghost emerged like a smoke. First unsure of his surroundings but the ashes of his deadbody burned with proper funeral ritual performed by Aghora have maintained the connection to his soul. His soul automatically got attracted towards the doll inside the circle. He appeared as a ghost right above the doll. The fire in the background is providing smoke though which one can make up his body.

A cold mist coiled from the circle, forming an indistinct smoky silhouette. Aghora watched as the spectral form of Ranganna hesitated, wavering like a dying ember, before taking shape above the doll. His features–half-formed and shifting–became visible through the thickening smoke of the fire.

Then, in a voice laden with sorrow, he spoke. "Aadesh, Gurudev..." Ranganna's spectral form bowed slightly, his voice hollow, drained–like a man who had lost everything in a wager.

Aghora's heart weighed heavy with grief. He sighed. "Times have passed... You have crossed over. I can no longer ask how you are, for I already know. But still... I ask–How are you, Ranga?"

The wind whispered in response. Ranganna remained silent. Some answers are too heavy to be spoken.

Aghora's expression darkened. "Tell me what happened. Did Kaamini push you into the realm of the dead?" His voice was sharp, edged with unspoken accusation.

Before Ranganna could respond, the air shifted.

A presence.

Aghora did not turn, for he knew she was here.

From the shadows, Kaamini stepped forward–a vision of spectral grace, draped in dark ethereal mist. Her form was solid yet translucent, her eyes gleaming like embers beneath a veil of sorrow.

"Why would I do that, Gurudev?" she asked, her voice laced with something between amusement and pain.

Aghora was not surprised. Sometimes, in death, guilt binds the suspect to the victim. If someone is accused in life, they become karmically entangled with the soul they are believed to have wronged. If the suspect has also perished, they remain together–tethered by unfinished fate.

Aghora's piercing gaze locked onto Kaamini. "So, you did not cause his death?" His voice was cold, scrutinizing.

Kaamini folded her arms, tilting her head. "Gurudev, why would I kill him? He was far more useful to me alive than dead."

Aghora narrowed his eyes. "Yet you made him open the gates of hell."

Kaamini flinched, her lips pressing into a tight line. She did not deny it.

Aghora's voice thundered through the valley. "You bear partial responsibility for his end! Therefore, it is now your duty to protect him. You will guard Ranganna's soul and ensure he does not fall into the hands of Śākini, Dakini, or any other imps!"

Kaamini let out a sharp laugh, though there was no humor in it. "I refuse," she said flatly.

Aghora's eyes blazed with divine fury. "You dare defy me, Kaamini?"

She sighed, shaking her head. "I spent my entire living years looking after adult children—men who couldn't handle their own destinies. I will not carry that burden in death. I cannot babysit him." She turned to Ranganna, rolling her eyes. "He's a man. He's a ghost. Let him handle his own shit."

Ranganna lowered his gaze.

"But if he is left unprotected in the realm of the dead, Śākini will capture him," said Aghora.

Kaamini smirked, amusement flickering in her eyes. "Oh, there is no such fear, Gurudev," she said. "Your Ranganna has become somewhat of a celebrity in the realm of the dead."

Aghora's brow furrowed. "What?"

Kaamini chuckled. "Ranganna had a friendly encounter with the Sun-worshipping priest. Śākini has no desire to touch him. None of the minions want to touch Ranganna even with a barge pole"

Aghora's mind raced. "Explain."

Ranganna spoke softly. "It is true, Gurudev. I had Upadesh–a spiritual conversation–with Sarma Ji a few hours before I died. Two days later, I saw him again, even from the realm of the dead. I called out to him, but Sakini–who was haunting me–fled the moment I uttered his name."

Aghora's breath caught. "She fled?"

"Yes," Ranganna nodded. "She refuses to come near me, as long as I do not utter Sarma Ji's name in her presence."

Aghora's fingers tightened around his rudraksha beads. "Whatever Sarma has done, it has troubled Śākini deeply." He exhaled slowly. "She does not wish to invite that trouble again."

A silence stretched between them.

Aghora studied Ranganna and Kaamini, his mind already calculating the weight of destiny.

"Something greater is at play here... Sarma's connection to the other side is deeper than I imagined. If even a creature like Śākini fears him... what does that make him?"

But this was not the time for questions.

Aghora took a deep breath, centered himself, and spoke the final rites.

"May you be free, Ranga. May you walk the path unhindered. May your soul find its way back to the eternal source."

A single black raven, perched on a nearby rock, let out a low, throaty caw–a sign that the ritual had been received in the unseen realms.

Aghora folded his hands in final prayer, then took a handful of sacred ash and let it slip through his fingers into the Mandakini River, watching as it dissolved into the icy waters.

Ranganna's spirit flickered. Kaamini's form dimmed.

And then–they were gone.

The next day Aghora called the phone number Chandra gave. They are all busy. But after a few attempts finally Chandra came online.

"Hello Gorak. How are you?" Chandra asked "Have you completed the funeral rituals of your disciple?"

"All is done. My Ranganna is now in the protected realm of Preta Lok" replied Aghora. "I am now ready to travel back to wherever you want me to be. Please let me know"

"Plans changed. Sarma helped us with vital information which gave us a lot of answers." said Chandra.

Aghora is happy and feels elated that Sarma was able to help. "I know, I know... My gurudev Param Aghora spoke highly of the sun-worshipping priest. If you have his help, you don't need me at all" replied Aghora.

"Nothing as such. You are highly praised and revered by Rao saheb, so you are also equally important for us to the Police as a spiritual consultant" said Chandra "Do you want me to give you the address of the Sun worshipping priest?"

"Yes please..."

"Priest Sarma is no longer working at the place where you found him near Tirupati. He is now moved. He is now working for a company in Karjat. You may want to travel to Karjat in case you want to meet him." Chandra gave the address of the and put down the phone.

Aghora is now in no hurry to rush back to South India. He decided to wander around the Himalayas to calm his soul which is still reeling under grief of losing Ranganna.

A few days later one evening while Aghora was in his prayers suddenly Karnika appeared.

Normally Karnika appears only when called.

"What is it?" asked Aghora.

"Aadesh Gurudev. You asked me to keep an eye on the Sun-worshipping priest. I can see him now."

Aghora's eyes widened, his head tilting slightly as he stared in disbelief. "But... you said you couldn't see him. He's inside a protective shield!" His voice wavered, the unspoken question hanging between them.

"That is true. But since the day your priest is married his shield is terribly weakened. We all from the realm of the dead can see him. He has become highly vulnerable" replied Kaamini.

Aghora did not believe what he was hearing. "Sarma is married?! When did this happen?" asked Aghora.

"A few days before Ranganna's departure. It happened suddenly. Myself, Karkotaka and a few others from the realm of the dead were the witnesses." replied Karnika.

"Explain," said Aghora.

"The priest and this woman who is deeply connected to him from his previous life reincarnation went up the hill. He has lowered his shield. Cupid god shot an arrow and they are married. Because he lowered his shield, I was able to witness his marriage" said Karnika.

"I can understand you as a witness. But how come Karkotaka was a witness? His ruthless soul is far away from such events." asked Aghora.

"Karkotaka now is a fan of Priest Sarma. His soul hovers around Sarma whenever he comes out of the realm of the dead. He seeks to listen to the voice of Sarma." replied Karnika.

"This Sun worshipping priest is surpassing everything in spiritual realms." thought Aghora. His heart flooded with emotion of pride knowing Sarma.

"Okay... Now what news have you brought for me?" asked Aghora.

"Your Sarma is in danger. He is poisoned" replied Karnika.

"What? Poisoned? Why didn't you tell me this news the moment you appeared before me?"

Karnika did not reply. She is a spirit that gives hour-long downloads. One has to guide her with proper questioning otherwise the point is lost somewhere in her conversations.

Aghora emerged from his trance, his breath steady but shallow, as though reality had reluctantly taken him back. He pulled out the slip of paper Chandra had given him and stared at the phone number scribbled in haste. Without hesitation, he dialled.

"Sleep Research Laboratory," answered a woman briskly, her voice clipped and professional.

"Yes, hello," Aghora said, forcing calm into his tone. "Could I speak with Siddhanta Sarma, please?"

"He's away at a conference," she replied. "May I ask who's calling?"

"I'm his brother. It's urgent," Aghora said, his voice laced with quiet intensity.

There was a pause. "He's attending a conference in Bangalore. You could try reaching him at the venue."

"Please–could you give me the address and contact details?"

After a short silence, she rattled off the information. Aghora jotted it down, thanked her, and ended the call.

He sat still, gripping the receiver, his mind racing. Bangalore. That's nearly two days by train. Karnika's warning echoed in his thoughts–Sarma is poisoned. He's in danger. The words didn't just worry him. They churned his gut.

He had to act. But how?

A sudden thought lit up his mind like a flash of lightning–Jeeva.

His disciple. A Naga Sadhu. Still in Bangalore, attending spiritual lectures by a wandering saint. Aghora quickly dialled the number.

"Jeeva," he said, the moment the line connected.

A warm, reverent voice answered, "Ādesh, Gurudev."

"Jeeva, do you remember our search for the Sun-worshipping priest near Tirupati?"

"How could I forget, Gurudev? We lost Ranganna on that path."

Aghora's voice dropped. "That priest is in danger. Karnika says he's been poisoned."

A breath caught on the other end.

"This," Aghora continued, "is what my Gurudev, Param Aghora, tasked me with–protecting the Sun-worshipper."

"Tell me what I must do," Jeeva said, already steadying himself.

"I'll give you an address. Go there. Find the priest–Sarma. He may still be at the conference. Warn him that his life is at risk. Tell him to fast for five days–no food at all, only water. Not a morsel, not a drop of anything else. Then tell him I'll come to him soon. In the meantime, he must admit himself to the nearest hospital. They'll cleanse his system. It's the only chance he has."

"As you command, Gurudev. I'll go right away."

Jeeva moved like a man possessed. He reached the conference centre in no time, navigating swiftly through the crowd of delegates and security staff. Near the reception desk, slumped in a chair like a marionette whose strings had been severed, sat Sarma–his eyes half-lidded, his skin ashen, his lips dry and cracked.

Jeeva paused.

He's already slipping...

Without wasting another moment, he surged forward.

Earlier that week, Rashmi and Sarma had travelled together to Bangalore. Throughout the journey, Sarma had been haunted by a gnawing ache—the quiet sorrow of not having been by Kamala's side when she needed him most. The guilt clung to him like a shadow, never letting go.

The conference had drawn to a close. Rashmi, flying higher in rank and privilege, took a flight to Bombay. Sarma, newly recruited and still at a junior grade, had to settle for a sleeper berth on a night train back to Karjat.

After a simple lunch, he sat on a chair near the conference reception, idly watching delegates disperse. A strange fog was creeping into his mind—thoughts scattered, responses delayed. The usual sharpness of his intellect was dulled, like a knife long neglected.

As a seasoned spiritual practitioner, he could sense something was amiss. His awareness, usually crystal-clear, now flickered like a failing lamp. But he couldn't quite name the feeling. It was as if something foreign had entered his body, quietly rewiring his brain.

"Aadesh..."

The voice stirred him.

He turned towards the source and blinked at the figure standing before him. "That's an Aghori greeting," he muttered.

"Aadesh," the stranger repeated, bowing slightly. "You may not know me, sir. I am the disciple of the great Gorak Aghora."

Sarma's brows knit. "Ah... You must be a fellow disciple of Ranganna?"

"Yes, sir. And I am truly sorry for what happened to him," said Jeeva, his voice carrying the weight of shared grief.

Sarma nodded solemnly. "He was brave. A seeker to the end."

"Indeed," said Jeeva. "But today, Gurudev has sent me on another task. He is deeply concerned about your well-being. He instructed me to find you and alert you immediately."

Sarma's gaze sharpened slightly. "Alert me? About what?"

"It appears you've been poisoned," Jeeva said gravely. "It's already affecting your mind."

Sarma blinked, but said nothing.

Jeeva stepped closer and quietly explained the cleansing protocol that his teacher, Gorak Aghora, had advised. A five-day fast—only water. Immediate hospital admission. No delay.

"I'll take you myself," Jeeva added. "There's a hospital nearby."

Sarma didn't question it. His connection to spiritual teachings ran deep. When messages arrived through such channels, he knew better than to ignore them.

Without another word, he rose to his feet and walked out of the conference hall. Jeeva followed closely.

They hailed an auto-rickshaw. As the three-wheeler rattled its way through the streets, the drowsiness in Sarma grew heavier. His head lolled slightly. His breath slowed.

By the time they reached the hospital gates, Sarma was barely conscious.

A stretcher was wheeled out. He felt himself being lifted, his body weightless, his senses slipping. His final memory was the ceiling above him blurring into darkness.

Then—nothing.

Sarma drifted in and out of consciousness for the next three days. His mind floated somewhere between dreams and wakefulness, like a leaf caught in slow-moving water. On the third day, he opened his eyes fully. The hospital ceiling came into focus, and for the first time since his admission, he felt the clarity of full awareness return.

He sat up slowly, supported by pillows. His body felt lighter, but fragile—as if still recovering from a storm. In the corner of the room, someone sat peeling oranges with deliberate care, the scent of citrus hanging gently in the air.

As soon as Sarma stirred, the man turned and offered a peeled orange segment, wordlessly.

Sarma blinked and accepted it, still looking around, expecting to see a familiar face. "Where's Jeeva?"

"If you're looking for Jeeva," the man replied with a kind smile, "he's gone to the market. I sent him to fetch some fresh fruit for you."

Sarma frowned slightly. "I don't believe we've met. Do I know you?"

"I'm afraid not," the man said. "But I know you. I am Gorak Aghora—the one who sent Jeeva to find you."

Sarma's eyes widened with recognition. He had heard the name whispered with reverence. Ranganna, Jeeva, and others had spoken of this enigmatic figure—a living legend among the elusive Aghori mystics.

"Oh..." Sarma murmured, absorbing the moment. "So, you're Gorak Aghora. An honour to meet you."

"The honour is mine," Gorak said, his voice gentle. "I've been hoping to meet you for some time."

Sarma looked at him, still unsure. "But why? Why were you searching for me at Tirupati? Why are you trying to help me?"

Gorak Aghora leaned forward, resting his hands on his knees, his gaze steady. "My teacher—blessed Param Aghora—recognised your incarnation. He saw it clearly. He instructed me to find you and offer you guidance and protection. This has been my duty ever since."

Sarma listened silently. A long breath escaped him.

"I've been battling with this idea of reincarnation for months," he said. "Ever since someone told me I might be a reincarnated master. But I still struggle to believe it. I grew up in a dysfunctional family... I was abused, traumatised. Sometimes I wonder if I've just created a fantasy of spiritual significance to escape from it all—to make sense of a broken past."

Gorak's gaze softened. "I understand. But you are not deluded, Sarma. You are a reincarnated master. I've had more than enough confirmation. You mustn't doubt that part of yourself."

The two spoke for a while—about reincarnation, destiny, the burden of spiritual memory. Gorak described how, one evening in Karjat, a small circle of seekers had discussed Sarma's life, piecing together signs that pointed to his past lives and deeper purpose.

A few minutes later, Jeeva returned, carrying a bag of fresh fruit. He greeted Gorak with reverence and offered Sarma a tender smile.

Sarma's eyes were already growing heavy again. The effort of sitting up, the emotional intensity of the conversation—it was all too much. His body, still in recovery, called him back to rest.

He lay down and drifted back into sleep, the smell of fresh mangoes and oranges still lingering in the air.

News of Sarma's hospitalisation in Bangalore travelled swiftly. As soon as the Sleep Research Lab was informed, Dr. Priya wasted no time. She rang Dr. Avasthi—now fully recovered—and CI John. Within hours, the three of them boarded a flight to Bangalore.

They arrived at the hospital without fanfare, anxious and tired, their hearts burdened with worry.

The next morning, as sunlight filtered gently through the curtains, Sarma slowly opened his eyes. The first thing he saw was Aghora, sitting quietly at his bedside, watching over him with a serene intensity. Beside him stood Dr. Avasthi, Dr. Priya, and CI John—their expressions a mixture of concern, relief, and quiet affection.

Sarma's heart swelled. A surge of emotion rose within him, unexpected and overwhelming.

These people... they came all the way for me.

Never in his life had he imagined such a moment–surrounded not by status or wealth, but by genuine care. The kind of love that asked nothing in return.

"I would do anything for these people," he thought, the tears welling unbidden. Anything.

After exchanging pleasantries, the conversation gradually turned to the question that had been quietly haunting them both–Who had poisoned Sarma? And why?

"Did you see who mixed the poison into your food?" Aghora asked, his voice calm but probing.

Sarma shook his head slowly. "No..."

Aghora's eyes narrowed slightly. "Do you never question the intentions of those who approach you?"

Sarma's gaze drifted toward the window. "No. I don't begin with doubt. Even when people deceive me... I grieve, yes–I mourn the betrayal–but then I let it go. I move on." He paused, the sorrow in his voice unmistakable. "But I never imagined someone would go so far... to erase my memory... to poison my food..."

His words faded into silence. A shadow passed across his face–more pain than anger.

"I know," Aghora said softly. "Rao Saheb warned us–you're too trusting. He said the ones you believe in the most... they'll be the ones to hurt you."

Sarma shifted uneasily in his bed, his fingers tracing the edge of the blanket. "I am not designed to hate," he said, almost as if reminding himself. "I am designed as Prem–which means love. That is all I've ever known. But... thank you, Gorakh. Truly. Thank you for sending the Naga Sadhu to warn me before it was too late. And thank you for being here, for coming all this way..."

His voice cracked slightly.

He had thought he was attending a gathering of noble minds—people convening to discuss saving the world. He hadn't expected betrayal. He hadn't expected poison.

"Karnika warned me," Aghora replied. "She told me you were in danger—that you had been poisoned. I was in the Himalayas when the message came. So I rang Jeeva. He was already in Bangalore and could reach you quickly. By Mahakali's grace, we were not too late."

Sarma lowered his head in gratitude. "I truly don't know what good karma from a past life has earned me such friends. But to answer your question—I don't know who my enemies are. I don't see the world through suspicion. Suspicion corrodes the spirit—it makes you paranoid. It robs life of its ease and beauty. So, by conscious choice, I refuse to be suspicious of the people I interact with."

"That's exactly your problem," Priya interjected gently, her voice breaking the stillness. "You have these... abilities. You could know what people intend, but you choose not to."

By now, Priya had grown certain that Sarma wasn't ordinary. She had seen too many signs—his calm foresight, his inexplicable intuition. He was something else—and she was quietly determined to understand him better, to stay close and study whatever power lay beneath his gentle surface.

"True," Aghora said, nodding in agreement.

Sarma gave a faint smile. "That's not entirely fair. I can't stop birds and animals from gossiping. They chatter constantly. Sometimes they reveal the intentions of those around me."

He looked at Aghora, his expression solemn. "In fact, it was a crow that told me Ranganna had passed on into the other world."

A hush fell over the room.

The weight of that simple statement–the natural world conspiring to protect him, to mourn with him–was not lost on anyone present.

"I've requested a list of everyone who served food at the conference," said John, his tone firm and purposeful. "Chandra informed me that you're under our protection now. No one should be able to harm you again. We'll get to the bottom of this."

Sarma shook his head gently, a faint trace of resignation in his expression. "It won't help, John. Even if you find the names, I won't be able to identify the culprit. I never saw who poisoned me. And there were no birds around to warn me either."

Dr Avasthi, standing near the foot of the bed, clenched his fists. The tension in his body was unmistakable–his outrage barely contained. "Can't you perform any rituals, something to find out who your enemies are?"

"There are rituals," Sarma replied calmly. "But I don't practise them. I don't walk through life assuming I have enemies."

"But you do," Avasthi pressed. "You may not think you have enemies, but they may very well see you as one. You're not the only one writing truth. We're all being watched, hunted. How can you protect yourself if you don't even want to know?"

Sarma looked at him with serene eyes. "If someone believes I am their enemy, then that is their karma, not mine. I haven't harmed them. I haven't returned their hatred. I didn't see who gave me the poison. That's all I know."

There was a brief silence–until Aghora spoke.

"But I saw him."

Everyone turned.

Aghora's face had darkened, his eyes reflecting something far older than mere memory. "I saw the one who poisoned you. After Karnika warned me, I asked her to take me to him. He walks in human form–but what resides within him is no man. The demon Apasmāra has taken hold of him."

A hush fell across the room.

"I don't know how," Aghora continued. "I was taught–we all were–that Apasmāra was cursed by Adi Shankara never to enter the human body again. That curse was supposed to be eternal. And yet, I saw it. I felt it. Apasmāra is inside him. And that unsettles me deeply. How could this happen?"

Apasmāra. The name alone carried weight–an ancient demon of ignorance, known to inflict confusion, memory loss, and disease through subtle poisons of the mind and body. He was the one who danced beneath Shiva's feet, crushed in the Nataraja's cosmic rhythm. And ever since the curse of Adi Shankara, it was said he had been banished from human vessels.

Sarma stared into the distance, his mind already drawing threads together. "You said the person who poisoned me was possessed by Apasmāra?"

"Yes."

"But we both know that Apasmāra was forbidden from entering human bodies. That curse hasn't been broken for millennia."

"Exactly. That's why it confounded me. I didn't expect it at all," said Aghora.

A faint glimmer passed through Sarma's eyes.

"I see how it's possible," he said slowly. "The one who poisoned me... is not fully human. He is a Conscious Intergalactic Entity—from a different timeline altogether."

"Conscious Intergalactic Entity?" Priya echoed, her brow arched with amusement. "Sounds like something from a science fiction novel."

She chuckled, but her curiosity was unmistakable. "But seriously, what is a Conscious Intergalactic Entity?"

Sarma smiled gently. "The Bhagavad Gita says: 'Beings emerge from the unknown, and into the unknown they dissolve. They appear only momentarily... therefore, do not grieve.'"

Priya's eyes lit up. "That's Chapter 2, verse 28, isn't it?"

Sarma looked at her, visibly impressed. "That's incredible. You even remember the chapter and verse. Yes—that's exactly the śloka I'm referring to."

"I remember it because it always struck me as something that borders on quantum physics," Priya said. "Though, I must admit, many find that verse quite confusing."

"It is confusing to the mind," Sarma agreed, "but only because it's pointing to something beyond the mind. That verse doesn't describe poetic sentiment–it speaks of the absolute truth."

He paused, allowing his words to sink in.

"We appear and disappear to one another at an astonishing speed," he continued. "Like frames in a film reel–when flicked quickly, they create the illusion of continuity. But in truth, what we call life is merely a rapid sequence of impermanent glimpses. This world, as we know it, is not a steady flow, but a succession of flickering moments."

Everyone around the hospital bed leaned in, drawn into the quiet gravity of his voice.

"Beings exist in all forms," Sarma went on. "In animals, yes. In trees, certainly. But also in what we consider inanimate. Stones. Stars. Even the void. All of them–every single one–are Conscious Intergalactic Entities. Each one stands like a Shiva Linga in the vast expanse of Chidākāsha–the space of pure conscious awareness."

He raised his hand slightly and gestured upward.

"At night, when we look up, we see billions of stars scattered across the sky. To most, they are just stars. But to the awakened eye, they are sentient presences–silent witnesses to the great cosmic unfolding. Each one, a luminous pillar of intelligence suspended in the void."

"So… these Conscious Intergalactic Entities are like stars?" asked Dr Avasthi, his voice low, cautious, curious.

"In a sense, yes," Sarma replied. "But more than that. The space of conscious-awareness is not empty—it is densely packed, more than we can possibly imagine. It holds trillions—perhaps an infinite number—of these Chi, or Keys. That's how they're pronounced: Chi. Not born, not dying. They simply are. Eternal. Unbound. Witnesses and participants in the play of existence."

He turned to Priya. "That is what the Gita means when it says 'beings appear from the unknown.' They are not truly coming into being—they are revealing themselves momentarily. Just long enough for us to catch a glimpse."

"Fascinating…" John murmured, eyes wide, as though seeing the night sky anew.

"You know what's even more fascinating?" Sarma asked, his eyes brightening. "Just imagine yourselves as stars—solitary sovereigns of vast galaxies, drifting billions of light years apart in the expanse of space. Alone. Ancient. Watching."

He leaned forward slightly, lowering his voice as though sharing a secret with the cosmos itself.

"And let's say, after eons of solitude, you grew restless… longing to see others. To feel something beyond yourself. And just like that—you became entangled. With me. With each other. With all the other CIEs—Conscious Intergalactic Entities—gathered in this very room."

Dr Avasthi tilted his head, intrigued. "But what is the force that makes such entanglement possible?"

Sarma responded without hesitation. "Karma. That overwhelming gravitational pull–not of physics, but of emotion. Karma draws my CIE and your CIE into communication, projecting this interaction onto a stage we call 'planet Earth'."

He looked around the room, slowly. "But in truth... you are not real. Nor am I. This hospital, these walls, this city–they may not even exist. There may never have been such a thing as planet Earth."

A hushed silence settled over the room.

"We are merely CIEs," Sarma continued. "Alone, yet tethered–like radiant pillars standing in the vastness of Chidākāsha, the space of consciousness. Through some mysterious process, we become entangled–and thus, we see each other, hear each other, speak to each other."

Dr Priya folded her arms thoughtfully. "But we're not just appearing... we're thinking too. Right? Cogito, ergo sum. I think, therefore I am."

Sarma nodded, visibly pleased. "Yes. But what you call 'thinking' is just electric fluctuation in the field. And your feelings–your grief, your joy, your rage–those are magnetic fields created by those fluctuations."

He paused.

"These magnetic emotional fields create a binding agent. A glue. That glue... is karma. It pulls CIEs into forms. Into appearances."

He turned to them all. "Let's say overwhelming love and trust accumulate in one CIE. What happens? It takes the form of a dog. That's how it manifests to us. When that emotion fades or transmutes, that same CIE may disappear–only to reappear elsewhere, as something else entirely. Hatred, for example, may cause it to appear as a rattlesnake. A CIE of violence becomes a tiger. A CIE of cunning becomes a fox. A CIE of surrender becomes a deer. You see? Every creature you encounter is a pure expression of a CIE's emotional field–its deepest desire, its unmet need. It may be having a solitary existence a billion light years away from you, the observer, but a mysterious force entangled your CIE with that CIE. It appears and it disappears."

He gestured to the window. "Open your eyes and look at the world–not as a zoo of species, but as a theatre of desires. What you are seeing are quantum projections of karmic emotion. Every appearance is a birth. Every disappearance, a death. Every reappearance... a reincarnation."

He took a breath.

"That is how we must understand Chapter 2, Verse 28 of the Bhagavad Gita."

"So you're saying there's consciousness... and then there's matter?" asked Dr Avasthi.

"In the beginning," Sarma said, "there was only consciousness. Then, through some mysterious process, consciousness turned into or appeared as matter. Like Shiva becoming Shakti. Like father becoming mother. The One became two. Then many. Like the Big Bang. A splintering of a homogeneous mass of awareness–scattered across the universe. Each fragment became a Conscious Intergalactic Entity. Each one still connected to the Whole."

Dr Priya leaned forward, eyes gleaming. "Is that mysterious force–the one that makes consciousness appear as matter–what we call Vishnu Māyā?"

Sarma smiled. "Yes."

"And what about space and time?" asked Dr Avasthi. "Do you mean to say everything is illusion? What about physical distance? The passage of time?"

Sarma nodded slowly. "Einstein's spacetime collapses at extremes. Below 10^{-33} centimetres, space itself loses structure–it becomes probabilistic, governed by quantum mechanics. And time? It dissolves at 10^{-44} seconds. Beyond these limits, classical physics breaks down. At that scale, our notions of distance and duration are no longer valid. What remains... is consciousness. So yes, to perceive the CIEs, we need an entirely new mathematics. A new language."

Dr Priya hesitated. Then she asked what everyone else was thinking.

"But is there any proof? Any evidence to support what you're saying–that Conscious Intergalactic Entities even exist?"

Sarma smiled again–the way a mountain might smile in the wind: silent, ancient, and deeply amused.

"Evidence?" he repeated, almost in a whisper. "The proof is everywhere. In the way your cat watches empty space, as if it sees something you cannot. In a baby's laughter that arrives without cause. In the quiet pull of déjà vu. In dreams that remember lives you've never lived. In a bird that appears just as you think of someone long gone."

He paused, letting the silence deepen.

"The only visible proof," Sarma continued, his voice soft yet unwavering, "is the sheer uniqueness each CIE carries–a uniqueness so absolute, it leaves fingerprints in the physical world. Your retinal pattern. Your thumbprint. The brainwaves dancing in your head. No two alike, anywhere on Earth. That uniqueness is not random–it's a message. A signature."

He looked directly into the eyes of his questioner.

"You are not me. And yet, we are entangled. You and I could be separated by a billion light years, but the connection remains. Silent. Unbroken."

He looked at her with the warmth of a teacher who sees a spark in his student.

"Tell me, Dr Priya. Have you never felt the presence of something far older than yourself... something watching you... not with judgement, but with recognition?"

Priya didn't answer. But her silence said enough.

He turned to Aghora. "You've heard of penguin colonies?"

The question was so abrupt it gently shook Aghora out of the quiet reverie he'd been floating in. He had been absorbing Sarma's words like sacred mantras.

"Of course," Aghora replied. "They gather by the millions, enduring brutal winters, huddled together for warmth."

Sarma's eyes twinkled. "Can you tell one penguin from another?"

Aghora chuckled. "No. They all look identical."

"Ah, but this is where the CIE reveals itself in nature," Sarma said. "A mother penguin, amidst millions, recognises her baby. She knows. She hears a cry that resonates deep within her being. Not with her ears–but with something older, deeper."

"How does she do that?" Aghora asked.

"Love," Sarma replied. "Each CIE carries the force of love–it resonates at the level of origin. It binds us. Even if your CIE is currently located a billion light-years away from mine, love creates the bridge. It entangles us."

"But love is just an emotion," Priya interjected gently. "What about hate, then?"

"Love is the CIE's effort to entangle. Hate is the effort to disentangle," said Sarma. "Imagine you're a star. A planet drifts into your orbit–you feel its pull. That is love. Then, the planet begins to break away–that is hate. The magnetic repulsion of two fields that once harmonised."

He looked around the room.

"Of course, I might be reaching for metaphors too big to hold. But I hope you see what I see. We are all CIEs. Potential stars. Radiant beings in an infinite cosmos. Our emotional fields–like magnets–draw others to us or push them away."

Aghora nodded slowly. "I see your point. Lord Shiva created a galaxy for each of us. We just have to recognise it. Each of us is luminous. Resplendent. Independent."

John, who had been silent, finally spoke. "How does this concept of CIEs apply to other religions? To the faiths of the world?"

Sarma turned to him, his tone now gentle and inclusive. "All religions are valid, John. Each one originates from the emotional resonance of a powerful CIE. A prophet, a mystic, a godform—these are intensely bright CIEs who pulled others into their orbits. What follows is the galaxy—the religion—that forms around them. Christianity, Islam, Judaism, the six branches of Hinduism, indigenous traditions... All of them are expressions of spiritual entanglement."

"There are millions of such forgotten CIEs," he continued, "especially among the lost gods of the European continent. Their power still exists in the conscious intergalactic space. We can still tap into them. They are not gone—only unremembered."

John's brow furrowed. "What about Christianity, specifically?" His voice carried the weight of sincerity. For him, this was personal. "How do I reconcile faith when others oppose or dismiss it?"

"Imagine Jesus Christ as a Conscious Intergalactic Entity," Sarma said. "So bright... so powerful... His resplendent love, his gravitational pull drew countless others toward him. That radiant pull became Christianity. It's the same for all faiths. The heavens imagined by each religion are real—because they are manifestations of entangled emotional fields."

He paused.

"When someone converts from one faith to another, it's like redirecting a satellite. You're breaking the gravitational bond with one CIE and establishing a new entanglement with another. That takes immense karmic energy."

"But whatever your path," Sarma said, now looking around at each face, "you must remember this: you are a CIE. The master of your universe. Everything you do—every word, every intention, every bond—is your karma."

Aghora, intrigued, leaned forward. "I know you follow Advaita. How do you reconcile the concept of CIEs with the non-dual philosophy?"

Sarma smiled. "In the beginning, there is only Brahman—infinite, indivisible consciousness without attributes. Nirguna. Brahman does not create or differentiate. It simply is."

"But when reflected through Māyā—the great illusion—it appears as Īshwara, the lord of the manifest universe. Īshwara becomes Hiranyagarbha—the cosmic womb—the dreamer of creation. And from that womb arise individual waves of awareness... the CIEs."

"CIEs," he said, "are nothing but unique currents within Hiranyagarbha. Individualised expressions of the same undivided field. They appear separate, scattered across galaxies and timelines. But fundamentally, they are one."

"And when this cosmic intelligence condenses into form, it becomes Virāt—the manifested universe. Stars, planets, trees, bodies... But even in form, the CIEs remain connected. Like a dreamer's many characters, all living within the same dream."

Everyone fell silent.

There was no rebuttal. No restlessness. Only the stillness that follows the sound of truth.

Just then, a nurse stepped in quietly, clipboard in hand, to check Sarma's vitals. The beep of a monitor filled the silence like a soft bell, reminding them all that, for now, they were still playing their parts in this earthly theatre.

But in the space between those beeps, they all felt it—what Sarma had said wasn't theory. It was a memory, faint but undeniable.

Something older than time, whispering across the stars.

"So, you mean," Priya asked, "this is how we go through birth after birth?"

"Yes," said Sarma. "To our naked eyes, people seem to be born and die. But from the perspective of the CIE, we are like stars. Constantly vibrating. Our thoughts are like solar flares—coronal ejections."

Dr Avasthi nodded. "I see the metaphor. Thoughts become emotions, and emotions become actions. Actions become karma."

"Exactly," said Sarma. "When actions hurt others or ourselves, that karma forces reincarnation. It's like two soldiers fighting. They run out of bullets and begin to brawl. They exhaust themselves, fall asleep, wake up—and fight again. Until one day, someone decides to stop."

Gorak spoke thoughtfully. "So, being non-violent in thought, emotion, and action... reduces karma?"

"Partially," Sarma replied. "But each CIE is driven by three primal forces: the desire to know, to survive, and to be happy. All three produce karma. Even love causes karma—because attachment leads to action. The key is equilibrium. When desire no longer distorts the vibration, karma loses its grip. Entanglement ends."

He paused. "Nothing truly dies. Every CIE that ever existed still vibrates in Chidākāsha. Each is an OM—a primordial vibration. When that OM becomes disturbed, it becomes Hata–a movement away from its original stillness."

Aghora's eyes widened. "That's why we call it Anāhata–the unstruck sound."

"Not just us," Sarma added. "Christians say Amen. Muslims say Ameen. All unknowingly refer to the same primal vibration–the CIE in its pure, pre-vibrational state."

"Where does this knowledge take us?" Aghora asked, his voice hushed.

Sarma's eyes narrowed. "To the knowledge that nothing ceases to exist. And if it doesn't cease, it can be brought back."

"You said the person who poisoned you came from a different timeline," said Dr Priya, her brows knit. "Because they are a CIE? What exactly do you mean by 'timeline' in this context?"

Sarma nodded slowly. "Adi Shankara lived in the 8th century. The demon Apasmāra was cursed by him–prevented from ever possessing a human body again. That curse binds this timeline. So, the only way Apasmāra could re-enter the human realm... is through a body from before that timeline."

"You mean," Aghora leaned in, "someone used a body that predates the 8th century?"

"Exactly," said Sarma. "They must have unearthed a corpse buried before Shankara's time. Then, through some ancient science–or magic–they fused the CIE of a contemporary being with the remnants of that old body. That allowed Apasmāra to bypass the curse and possess it."

"You mean... we can resurrect entities?" Aghora asked. "Using... dirt?"

"Yes," said Sarma. "That's the idea behind Mrittika Suktam–the Vedic hymn glorifying Mother Earth. There are esoteric methods described where dirt–charged with the residual vibration of a being–is fused with a dormant CIE. The fused essence is then consumed, usually as fruit. When a man and woman engage in union after ingesting it, they give birth to that CIE."

John looked both amazed and alarmed. "So... to create a warrior, you'd find the burial site of ancient warriors, fuse the dirt with a CIE, and let it reincarnate?"

"Yes," Sarma replied. "But beware–not all humans may have lived their life in a noble way. Some are very seriously dangerous and damaged people! If they died of thinking to kill people or they died in violent confusion then their Conscious Intergalactic Entity holds the killing intention of that moment of terror in its invisible vibrational form. Their CIEs died with rage, bloodlust, and confusion. If you resurrect them, you risk reviving those very impulses."

Dr Avasthi's eyes gleamed, caught between wonder and dread.

"So... if someone unearthed the grave of a psychopath and revived them, that CIE would carry the violent blueprint of its death?"

"Yes," said Sarma calmly. "That's precisely why we Hindus only bury Saints and Children–those whose Conscious Intergalactic Entity departs without violent or corrupt intent.

Their vibrations are pure. Safe. The rest, we burn. Cremation ensures the physical residue–flesh, bones, blood, dirt–is turned to ash. It severs the link. If such a soul reincarnates, it may still carry karmic scars... but not the murderous momentum of its final breath."

He leaned in slightly, lowering his voice.

"If the body remains intact, the CIE can be drawn back into this world with the very intention it died with. And if that intention was hatred... bloodlust... delusion... then what returns may look human, but carries the ghost of something else."

"Egyptian mummies," said Priya slowly, her voice a mix of awe and fear.

"Yes," said Sarma, nodding. "Their bodies are still here–preserved, waiting. If someone has found a way to reintroduce their CIEs into living bodies... the implications are catastrophic."

He let the silence stretch, then added:

"Remember–they lived four thousand years ago. Long before Christianity. Before Islam. Their vibrational memory contains no moral reference to those faiths. No concept of 'Thou shalt not kill' as we understand it today. If such entities return... they will not discriminate. They will not feel remorse. They will act from a primal script, unfiltered by the ethics of any living tradition."

"So the person who gave you poison must be an Alien. A time travelling Terminator? Somebody somewhere fused the physical body of a dead person who died some thousands of years ago with CIE. That person, because the CIE is from the time before Adi Shankara, is not bound to his curse. Therefore, he was able to give you poison?" Dr Priya asked.

"I see Sarma's point. I buy into it." said John while looking at Priya. "This also explains how the demon was able to poison Father Francis!" said John... "It makes total sense. The body his attacker Stephen's CIE wearing must have been fused with a mummified body before 2000 years. For that CIE the CIE of Jesus's or the associated emotional magnetic fields which is known as two billion Christians is unknown! So Stephen was truly an alien... A terminator who travelled from a timeline before the world came to know about a messiah called Christ!"

"Exactly," Sarma said. "To him, Christians were unknown. He was an alien. A terminator from another timeline. The demon that you don't know or can't name is an alien to you. The demon that attacked Father Francis that was inside the body of Stephen is from pre-Christian era. They had a rage towards Christians. That is why the demon was able to over power. I am no exception either... Apasmāra attacked me." Said Sarma

"I see it now," John murmured. "That's why Father Francis said the demon had to be named–because without knowing it, we have no power over it. What we cannot name, we cannot control."

"Precisely," said Sarma. "That's why we say in Hinduism–knowledge makes a man immortal."

Avasthi exhaled deeply. "That explains why sometimes Muslims kill Muslims, or Christians kill Christians–with extraordinary cruelty. Their CIEs may not even come from the Islamic or Christian timeline."

"Correct," said Sarma. "Islam began in the 6th century, as a response to the militaristic narrative of the Roman Empire. So, any mummified body that predates the 6th century cannot technically be a Muslim. The collective consciousness had not yet breathed Islam into existence."

"Sorry... I lost you there," Avasthi admitted.

Sarma nodded gently. "Let me explain. Every Conscious Intergalactic Entity–or CIE–holds four inherent potentials. In Tantra, we call them Para, Pashyanti, Madhyama, and Vaikhari.

"Initially, a CIE exists in a pure, formless transcendental state–Para. From there, it enters the state of vibration, where it becomes aware of itself. This is Pashyanti. In Sanskrit, Pashyanti means 'that which sees'. It is the state of inner vision–the creative impulse.

"Imagine standing in front of a mirror. You are in the Para state. The reflection you see is Pashyanti–you see yourself. This state is sometimes misunderstood in the West as narcissism. But it's deeper than that–it's the soul beginning to witness itself.

"Now, suppose you want to change what you see. You apply colour to the reflection. That act of transformation is called Madhyama–the process of shaping thought into form. Then you step back, observe, and articulate what you've created. That is Vaikhari–the expressed word, the manifest world."

"I think I follow the four stages," said John. "But how does that relate to Islam?"

"Take Prophet Muhammad," said Sarma. "Until the age of forty, he wasn't known as a Muslim. Just as Jesus was born into Judaism and known as a rabbi. Until their defining revelations, their CIEs were still in the Para state—witnessing the world, feeling a disconnect, a deep discontent with prevailing religious practices.

"When the Prophet began to receive revelations, his CIE moved into Pashyanti—the visionary and creative state. He sought to transform the world he saw. Islam, as a vibrational construct within the collective consciousness, was born after that point.

"So, any CIE that existed before the 6th century wouldn't carry the vibrational memory of Islam. If such a being were brought back or reincarnated, it would have no resonance with Islamic values or identity. That's why, in certain extreme cases, you may see what appears as Muslims slaughtering Muslims. The body might carry a label, but the CIE inside it may be from a time when Islam didn't yet exist. The same applies to Christians killing Christians. Brother against brother."

"But reincarnation is an ongoing process," said Priya, her voice barely above a whisper.

"Correct... That is why conflicts also are an ongoing process. We call the result as duḥkham. A state of misery. But in this case, some mad scientist found out about the process of reincarnation and now creating Psychopaths in the laboratory and releasing them in our midst..." Sarma said.

"Okay," said Avasthi, finally leaning back, "I'll admit... it's far-fetched. But the pattern makes sense."

"You can recreate a being with mantra?" Avasthi asked, his voice sceptical, yet laced with curiosity.

"Of course," Sarma replied. "Lord Rama's wife–Sita–was born of the earth. King Janaka knew the ancient science. That knowledge still exists... if one dares to seek it."

There was a quiet certainty in his tone–like the calm before a storm–and it sent a ripple through the room. An unspoken energy. Everyone felt it.

"That's... a lot," Priya murmured, her eyes still fixed on him. "We'll have to continue this. But not now. You need rest, Sarma. We've got a flight to catch. We'll resume when you're back in Karjat."

One by one, the group rose, reluctant to leave but bound by the obligations of the day. Each paused at the doorway, casting a final glance at Sarma–each gaze marked by a subtle shift, as if they were leaving with a weight they hadn't arrived with.

Sarma lay back, his eyes half-closed. The soft hum of the monitors filled the room, merging with the echo of retreating footsteps.

The battle has only just begun, he thought.

Late evening.

A flight from Bangalore touched down at Bombay airport. Dr Priya, Dr Avasthi, and CI John disembarked, walking silently through the terminal. A car from the Sleep Research Lab awaited them. All three got in.

The vehicle moved steadily through the dimming outskirts of the city, heading toward Karjat. The night was quiet. A chill rode on the wind.

Then came the bend.

The car swerved. The tyres screeched, lost grip. The driver panicked—too late. The vehicle veered off the road and plunged into the valley below.

A brutal descent. Metal against rock. Windows shattering. Gravity claiming its due.

It was a death roll.

There were no survivors. All four—Priya, Avasthi, John, and the driver—died instantly.

Elsewhere, Nayeemuddin returned to the Bombay dockyard. Bikku was already there, waiting in the shadows.

"Well done," Bikku said with a nod. "Mission accomplished."

They boarded a small boat and drifted out to sea, slipping quietly into the darkness beyond India's shores.

Hours later, their boat reached a yacht anchored in open waters.

AIWAG stood waiting on deck.

Thus, within less than ten days of its inception, the ultra-secret operation known as Mission Insiders lost twenty-five percent of its team.

And no one on the outside even knew it had begun.

6. FLIP THE TABLES

Mid 1991, Bangalore, India.

It was morning. There is a storm brewing outside. The coconut trees outside swayed like possessed dancers, their fronds thrashing against the storm-bent sky. A distant clap of thunder made the small birds on the window sill flutter in nervous bursts, their chirps sharp with unease. Sarma lay still in his hospital bed, his eyes locked onto the restless world outside, as if the storm carried a message only he could decipher. Aghora was sitting on the ground near the east side wall meditating.

"There seems to be some tension," said Sarma.

Aghora opened his eyes. "Did you say something?" Aghora asked.

"The birds. They are not liking the weather outside. They are discussing a strategy on how to gather their daily grains in case there is a storm."

Aghora looked at the birds and sighed. "I am still recollecting the discussion we had about CIEs yesterday," said Aghora. "Now I can't see the birds the same as I saw them yesterday. I can't unsee them now. They are CIEs reincarnated as birds for a certain amount of time to fulfil certain destiny."

"You know, I heard scientists are working on a hypothesis that memories work on their own without any agency," said Sarma. "These birds remind me of that hypothesis"

"I don't understand," said Aghora.

"Let me explain, Suppose, you create a new game. A game that was never known or played before. Teach that game to a bird. The brain neurons in that bird if you collect them in a laboratory dish and leave them there, the brain neurons continue playing the game." said Sarma.

"What even after the bird is dead? The neurons outside the body in a laboratory dish?" asked Aghora. "Unbelievable".

"Correct. But if such a hypothesis is true then it only validates what I see as CIEs which are entangled appearing and disappearing in the space of consciousness. Suddenly the whole creation makes perfect sense." said Sarma.

"But bad people don't make sense to me," said Aghora, frowning. "Why would anyone choose to harm others? What compels someone to behave that way? What explanation would you give, looking from the perspective of galaxies, stars, and planets?"

"Bad people," Sarma said quietly, "are like black holes. Their gravity pulls you in, and once caught, your light–the light of your Conscious Intergalactic Entity–no longer shines outward. It gets trapped. Invisible. That's why human effort, all our rituals, our disciplines–they exist to help us stay outside the pull of such black holes."

He paused, his voice steady, almost reverent.

"The food we consume–Virat–also plays a role. Everything in the visible universe is potentially divine. Even the human sperm cell, one of the smallest cells in the body–just about 5 micrometres long, barely 2.5 to 3.5 micrometres wide–carries a kind of knowing. But how? The memory isn't stored within it. It's held in the magnetic field around it–an invisible force.

"Just as a magnet attracts iron, a growing human cell attracts karma. That's what likes and dislikes really are–magnetic fields shaped by karmic attraction and repulsion. Karma is not abstract. It's all-pervading. It wraps itself around every moment, every atom."

Aghora leaned forward, eyes narrowed. "What is the force that moves a CIE?"

Sarma's gaze turned inward. "The Conscious Intergalactic Entity does not move in the way we think of motion. It is held in place by Ātma Shakti–the force of the Self. It is the surrounding dark matter–Ākāśa–that carries energy. A thought is simply energy attracted by the CIE. Perception is a thought. Sound, sight, taste, touch, smell–they're all waves of energy making contact with the CIE. And it responds through that subtle force."

"I still don't understand where hatred fits into this," said Aghora.

"Hate," Sarma said slowly, "is an emotion. A bio-electromagnetic field created in conscious space. But what happens when you hate someone who does not deserve your hatred?"

Aghora looked uncertain. "What does happen to such a person?"

"Their CIE no longer computes," Sarma replied. "It tries to destroy another CIE, but there is no true opposition. The hatred is baseless. It's like a star trying to collide with a phantom. The other star isn't even there–it's an illusion."

He paused, voice darkening.

"Such a CIE collapses in on itself. Its entanglement is annihilated. It reincarnates into the darkest corners of existence–places where the Sun doesn't shine. Solitary confinement. Millions of lifetimes in shadows. And eventually, something stirs... a longing for light. Some of them create their own bioluminescence, a desperate imitation of light, just to remember what it felt like. From there, they begin the long journey of reincarnations, slowly crawling back toward some constellation of hope."

Aghora sat silently for a while, then spoke.

"And what is the recourse... if we don't want such incarnations?"

"Simple," said Sarma, his voice calm as still water. "Forgive thy enemy. Anchor yourself to the truth. Even if your enemy hurts you, you do no such thing in return. Because you understand–every step away from truth pulls your CIE into incarnations unknown.

"That's the path of passion shown by the Christ. Prophet Jesus. And it is the very same path followed by our ancient Hindu seers. Compassion is not submission–it is navigation."

"Is this learning in any way tied to why people fear death?" asked Aghora.

"The fear of death," said Sarma, "is the memory of reincarnation. Each incarnation carries a cost. Our CIE intuitively remembers the pain endured in previous lives. That's why we resist returning. People know that burns from fire cause intense pain–just the memory of that suffering can make someone weep if threatened with flame.

"In the same way, the fear of death is not about ending. It's about beginning again–the CIE's dread of yet another cycle. The whole arc of human life is shaped by a desire to escape reincarnation."

"Is that state what we call liberation?" Aghora asked.

"Yes," Sarma nodded. "We know it as Brahma Nirvana. In that state, the CIE ceases to exist. It stops vibrating. And without vibration, there is no creation–no form, no desire, no return."

A quiet moment followed, broken by the creak of the door.

A hospital ward boy stepped in. "Who is Sarma?" he asked.

Sarma turned his head slightly. "I am."

The boy handed him a folded telegram. "This just arrived." Without waiting for a response, he left.

Sarma's fingers trembled as he opened it.

Priya, Avasthi, John died in an accident. DO NOT TRAVEL. STAY IN BANGALORE. I AM ON MY WAY - Chandra.

The words swam. His vision blurred. His grip on the paper tightened.

A hollow ache spread through his chest, like an implosion—breath fleeing his lungs, replaced by a silence deeper than thought.

“Priya...” His voice cracked.

He looked up at Aghora, the paper crushed in his trembling hands.

“They're dead.”

The room tilted. The sterile white walls closed in. Only yesterday, they were here—laughing, breathing, alive.

Now—nothing.

Aghora froze. The wind outside howled through the half-open window, rattling the glass like a wounded spirit mourning the dead.

“Oh God... Only yesterday they were all here,” Aghora whispered. “I feel so sorry.”

Sarma's voice was low, hollow. “I remember Priya saying they were being targeted. She feared for her life. But I... I thought they’d be alright. I kept thinking the situation would sort itself out.”

A bitter silence followed. He had clung to that hope like a child clings to a dream. And now it lay shattered.

The next day, Chandra arrived at the hospital. His face was drawn, his eyes carrying the weight of unwelcome truth.

He explained the accident in a few quiet words. How the car had swerved. The bodies. The instant deaths.

"Why, sir?" Sarma asked, his voice cracking under the weight of grief. "Why would anyone kill them?"

Chandra sighed, his expression hardening. "Money."

"Money?" Sarma echoed, stunned.

"There are people in this world," Chandra said, "who will do anything for it. We believe Priya's family was targeted because her father was a pioneer in nuclear research. Someone, somewhere, must have paid a shadowy organisation a fortune to wipe them out. The whole family."

"That's so... cruel," Sarma murmured.

"Yes. It's cruel. But that's the world we live in. It runs on money. Not logic. Not justice."

Chandra paused, studying Sarma. "You know the Sleep Research Lab isn't safe. Four people saw the COMxBAT suitcase–first-hand. Dr Priya, Dr Avasthi, Circle Inspector John... and you. Now, only you remain."

Sarma looked down. The weight of it sank in like cold iron.

"I don't think it's safe for you to continue working there," Chandra said, his voice firm. "You've already been poisoned once. Your confidence didn't protect you from that. You're too important to us now. We can't afford to lose you. So, I'll inform them–you're not returning to Karjat."

"But... where will I go?" Sarma asked, crestfallen. He had just begun this new path—and now even that was slipping away.

Chandra looked at him carefully.

"Do you want to go to the United States?"

Sarma didn't hesitate.

"Of course."

Chandra nodded, then changed the subject. "Tell me something. You can sense people when they're mind-controlled, right? I mean—like some sort of devil's possession?"

"I can," said Sarma. "But that premonition only works when my mind is at peace. If I'm distracted or disturbed, it might not function. But... about eighty percent of the time, yes—I can feel it. I can sense when someone is under control."

"Eighty percent is good enough," said Chandra thoughtfully. He turned to Aghora. "What about you, Gorak? Can you sense when someone is possessed?"

"I can't sense it directly," Aghora replied. "But I can use Karnika—my seashells. With my divination tools, I can find the truth."

Chandra rubbed his chin. "Right... so we can't drop you into a room full of people and expect you to pick out the mind-controlled one instantly."

"Obviously not," said Aghora. "But if you bring me a photo of the person, I can work with that. My tools will tell me."

"Good... good..." Chandra muttered, half to himself. "You'll be our back-up plan."

He turned to Sarma, eyes sharp with intention.

"Here's what we'll do. Sarma—listen to me carefully. Go to Hyderabad. Just like you found that job in Karjat, find another one there. I'll help you from the background as much as I can. But more importantly, use your divine intuition. Find a path that leads you closer to your true purpose. I know, for now, that purpose is reaching your wife. That's good enough. Let it guide you. Just go to Hyderabad."

"Alright, sir. If you say so... but how exactly do you want me to help you once I'm there?" asked Sarma.

"What we've found—these mind-controlling suitcases—is a clear and present threat to national security. We want you and Aghora to operate from the shadows. From the very outermost layer. You'll observe, quietly. From time to time, you'll receive invitations to certain gatherings—parties, events involving defence personnel, nuclear scientists, researchers. You'll be introduced as you are—a spiritual man. Nothing more. Just attend. Feel the room. If your intuition detects anything off... anyone under influence... let us know."

He turned to Aghora.

"Gorak—if Sarma senses someone is compromised, I'll bring you their photo. You'll help us confirm what's going on."

"But if I show up at these events," Sarma said, "they'll immediately become suspicious. Someone will ask me, 'Who invited you to this party?' What would I even say?"

"That's true," Chandra admitted. "But what other choice do we have? This is a risk we must take."

Sarma smiled faintly, almost cryptically.

"I don't have to be there in person," he said. "One of my gifts—astral travel—can take me there in an instant. My spiritual body travels while my physical body remains untouched. It's like remote viewing, only clearer... more direct."

Chandra stared at him. "You mean you could actually enter those spaces, unseen?"

"I can," Sarma said calmly. "I've done it before."

Aghora's eyes lit up. "Can you really do that?"

"I don't understand," said Chandra, glancing between them.

"It's one of the eight superpowers," Aghora explained eagerly. "Lord Hanuman grants these Ashta Siddhis to his true disciples.This one is called Prapti (प्राप्ति)—the ability to obtain or access anything, anywhere, including the power to reach distant places instantly."

"Yes, I've heard of the Ashta Siddhis," said Chandra slowly. "So this is one of them?"

"Yes," Sarma nodded. "So here's my suggestion. Whenever you need me to observe something discreetly, carry an object I give you. It could be anything—a book, a pen, a necklace, a ring. As long as that object is present at the location, my soul can travel there astrally. I'll be able to see, hear, and sense what's happening—without physically being there."

Chandra's expression shifted from curiosity to strategy.

"That's brilliant," he said. "It mitigates the risk even further. We won't need to expose you at all."

He stood, decisive now.

“Right then. Travel to Hyderabad as soon as you can. Find a place, settle in. Once you’re ready, give me a call.”

After that Chandra left for Delhi. Gorak and Sarma are left alone.

“Gorak, I am grief stricken by the fact that our friends and wellwishers are mercilessly killed by a group because they felt money is more important.” said Sarma. He started calling Aghora by his first name upon Aghora’s insistence.

“True, Sarma ji... I do not understand the money mindedness. Love, attachment, living a peaceful family life, helping the community all these are so good. They give us satisfaction. I do not think Money should be given that kind of importance. But they are really running mad after money. They are sacrificing the peace of the weak and vulnerable in their mad pursuit of money.”

Sarma did not reply. Sarma’s gaze drifted to the framed portrait of Jesus Christ, a dull glow from the hospital light casting shadows on His solemn face. The wounds on His hands, the sorrow in His eyes—they weren’t just relics of the past.

For a moment, the air around Sarma grew electric, charged with an unseen force. His breath hitched. The image of Christ seemed to shift, the lips unmoving yet whispering words into his bones—

"Follow my lead."

His fingers clenched the bedsheet -- “Flip the tables.”

Sarma sat up, breathless, pulse racing. The realization hit him like lightning: The meek must reclaim the world, and trust must not be bound to any single human.

"Let us flip their tables," Sarma said.

"What? Flip the tables? What do you mean? Whose tables?" asked Aghora.

The very first thing Jesus Christ did when he entered the house of his God was to flip the money brokers' tables. We need to take that inspiration from Jesus. Let us break the financial controlling chokehold. They are abusing the trust of the meek and vulnerable. They sacrificed our friends to earn money. So, we will do something radical, money that is spent by anyone must be visible for everyone else to see. But money is a necessary evil. Without it we cannot function. We should not allow anyone to weaponize our weakness. We will establish trust which is not bound to any single human." said Sarma.

Aghora drew a blank. He understood Sarma is thinking of creating alternative finance but not sure how that will help.

"We have two problems at hand," said Sarma. "Problem one: Mind-controlled people like Apasmāra. Problem Two: Providing necessary substance to people who wake-up. I mean those who are no more mind controlled."

"How to solve it? What do you think we must do?" asked Aghora.

"The harsh truth is descending upon me after listening to the death news of our friends. There is a very high chance that none of us will survive this mission. None." said Sarma as a matter of fact...

Aghora fell silent... The heaviness of the tense room became unbearable as they both contemplated the death that seemed inevitable to escape...

"But you and I both know that the fear of death will not deter us from doing what is right..." Sarma broke the silence and looked at Aghora...

"Right..." said Aghora "I am so angry at the people who lured my gullible Ranganna into opening the gates of hell. They killed him..." his voice was trembling.

"And I am so angry at the people who killed my student Manasi who had life ahead of her. And my anger increased after listening to the death news of Priya, Avasthi and John. They are innocent people" said Sarma "You see you and I we both are connected to righteous anger... We can use this energy. This would suffice to power a new generation who are awakened"

"So, you suggest we create people who are awakened?"

"Yes... Because we cannot allow evil forces run rampant and take over the world in case we do not survive this battle"

"So?"

"So, we must create a hidden army...A holy army... We breathe life into them... They will avenge us..." said Sarma "but not with bullets and bombs... An Eye for an eye will make the whole world blind... But they will avenge us by being born free." Sarma looked at Aghora.

Aghora's eyes burned with frustration. His fists clenched at his sides. "I don't understand... You're saying we create an army, but they won't fight back? They won't strike? Won't take revenge?" His voice rose, raw with fury.

Sarma got off the hospital cot. He stepped forward, his eyes dark and unyielding. "Not with bullets. Not with bombs. That's their game."

Aghora stared at him, breath heavy, waiting.

Sarma's voice dropped to a whisper, heavy as iron.

"We will avenge them by being born free."

Aghora blinked.

Sarma's expression softened, just for a moment.

"Think. What is the one thing they fear the most?"

Aghora's lips parted, the realisation creeping in like dawn breaking over a long, silent night.

"People... who cannot be controlled."

Sarma nodded, the flicker of fire in his eyes unmistakable.

"We create an army," he said. "An army of people who wake up. Who think for themselves. Who stand up to the mind-controlling psychopaths. Slowly, we push the boundaries. One liberated CIE will awaken another... and so it begins."

He looked beyond the room, as if seeing years unfold.

"If we start now–it's 1991. By the time these awakened souls take their place in society... it will be thirty years from now. They'll begin to do what is right. What is just."

Aghora's excitement faltered. Doubt crept in.

"We'll need money. Resources. A lot of both. You and I–we're dirt poor."

Sarma didn't flinch.

"Fortunately, we don't need to arm this holy army with bullets. Today's governments run on violence–buying it, selling it, justifying it. Our people won't be part of that machinery. But they will need livelihoods. Jobs. Stability. Right now, most resources go to those who conform—who serve the madness of mind-controlling systems. But our people... they are born free, they think free, and they must die free."

"But how do we support them, then?" Aghora asked, still hesitant.

Sarma's voice deepened, almost solemn.

"As I said—we'll flip the tables of those who hoard the wealth. We'll create our own currency. Our own system. We cannot stand on the same financial platforms and expect to do justice to people shackled by this grotesque control."

He paused. "The meek are crying for justice. And it is God who guides us to answer that cry. The meek... must inherit the Earth."

"But how?" Aghora whispered.

"When intentions are right," said Sarma, "the universe responds with perfect mathematical precision. And when the time comes—I will find a way to earn billions to support our cause. If becoming a billionaire is what it takes... then I will become one. If I'm still alive."

Aghora met his gaze.

"I trust you."

Sarma looked at Aghora and asked "You trust me. But can you trust the people who are ready to kill others for the sake of money?!"

"No way... But how will an ordinary person know who to trust who not to trust? The world is seeming to be run by people who are mad about money. How to trust anyone?" asked Aghora.

Sarma exhaled sharply, his mind racing. The problem wasn't just money–it was trust. Money had become a weapon, wielded by the powerful against the weak.

"We must... rewrite the rules," he murmured.

Aghora raised an eyebrow. "Rewrite how?"

Sarma's gaze turned sharp, determined. "A system where trust is not placed in men. Where no one–not a king, not a banker, not a politician–can twist it to their will."

Aghora frowned. "Impossible. Trust is built on people."

Sarma's lips curled into a knowing smile. "Not if trust is written into numbers."

"Why numbers?"

"Because the creator of this universe used mathematical precision behind all this. Have you heard of the Fibonacci sequence? We find those numbers in nature. Similarly we will use God's lead and put our trust in a code."

Aghora inhaled sharply. "A code?"

Sarma nodded. "A perfect mathematical solution. When the time comes, it will reveal itself. Trust... We must find a way to establish trust in the system without involving any human. I already have an idea. I will start working on it," said Sarma. "But let us take this challenge step by step."

The confidence in Sarma that they could find money and resources reassured Aghora.

The hospital nurse came and checked Sarma's vitals.

After a few minutes a Doctor came. He checked Sarma's vitals chart "You are doing perfectly well. We can discharge you now," the Doctor said.

Gorak took leave and returned to the Himalayas. Sarma reached Hyderabad in search of a job which could take him to his destination -- the USA.

The person in Indore received a call from Mayur Vihar, Delhi. The information he received unsettled the person in Indore. He dialled the Bali Islands.

"Shikhandi here," said the voice from the other side.

He glanced nervously around before whispering into the receiver. "I received a call from Delhi. It's about Sarma."

Shikhandi exhaled, eyes narrowing. "Did we administer the memory-wiping poison?"

The person in Indore wiped his forehead with a trembling hand. "We did. But... he survived. He seems to be working and remembering okay."

"How?"

"Someone called Aghora alerted him"

"But only few of us know, who is this Aghora? How did he know?"

"We don't know. We are trying to find out."

"Okay. The drug will take some time to affect." said Shikhandi.

"But he is recollecting perfectly well"

"Hmm... Has the hospital collected blood samples of Sarma?" asked Shikhandi.

"Yes, as you have asked I got them by medical courier." said the person in Indore.

"Make sure you leave no trail. If anyone comes to know we are messing with the confidential records of the hospital we will be in big trouble," said Shikhandi.

"No problem with that, we have already eliminated the person who gave us a portion of Sarma's blood samples," said the person in Indore. "What do you want me to do with them?"

"Send them to me"

7. ṬUYŪRUN WAḤSHIYYA – SAVAGE BIRDS

October 1992, Hyderabad, India:

Sarma sat on a bench in the park, staring into the distance. Life had become unbearably difficult. Struggles were nothing new to him, but the thought of Kamala and their separation gnawed at his mind, leaving him anxious and despondent.

As Chandra had advised, he had found a job in Hyderabad. However, he quickly realized that his knowledge of computers was insufficient to secure a better future in the United States. Determined to change his fate, he enrolled in an advanced computing course. He studies systems engineering during the morning hours, from late afternoon to late night he works at an office as Systems analyst.

"If I have to work for a living, why not aim to be the best in the industry?" Sarma thought. But the sheer intensity of his ambition unsettled him. At times, his own thoughts frightened him–thoughts driven by an insatiable hunger for success.

Sarma had once believed he was heading to Karjat. Little did he know, his life had taken a dimensional shift, pushing him into a living hell. A hell from which escape seemed nearly impossible. His mind wandered to Dante's Inferno–"Abandon hope, all ye who enter here."

Another image flashed in his mind: Maharshi Dadhichi, the seer who sacrificed his life so the gods could forge a weapon from his spine to vanquish the demons. Sacrifice. That was the key. Sarma, too, had nothing left to lose.

His mind echoed a verse from the Bhagavad Gita:

hato vā prāpsyasi swargaṁ jitvā vā bhokṣhyase mahīm

tasmād uttiṣhṭha kaunteya yuddhāya kṛita-niśhchayaḥ (2.37)

"If you fight, you will either attain the celestial realms or emerge victorious to enjoy the kingdom on Earth. Therefore, rise with determination, O son of Kunti, and prepare to fight."

Sarma's thoughts were abruptly interrupted. On a nearby bench, a young man and woman were sharing lunch. The man's voice carried over to him.

"Didi, it's so good that you came to see me. I missed home-cooked meals."

"Ammi asked me to take care of you," the woman smiled. "Eat well so you can study properly."

"You're flying back to Pakistan in two days. What will I do then? Who will cook for me?"

She laughed, her smile radiant. The way sunlight danced across her pearl-white teeth made her look otherworldly.

"But I'll only be gone for a few days," she reassured him.

"Don't go, Aapa."

"I promise I'll return soon. And I'll tell Ammi to find you a wife, so you can enjoy home-cooked meals forever!" she teased.

Sarma watched them, captivated. The love between them—so pure, so divine—tugged at something deep within him. He sighed heavily, his heart aching for the love he had never known in his own family.

The priest in him instinctively offered a silent blessing. God bless them.

Shaking off his emotions, Sarma rose and made his way to the computing institute, where he was studying advanced systems engineering.

Sarma sat near the reception, closing his eyes. Behind him is the computer system lab. Students are seated in front of the monitors. Sarma agreed to work as a Computer lab assistant to get a discount on the school fees. He will have to assist If students who are practising their C++ scripts face any difficulty. Dust off computers, keep the lab environment clean etc., are some of his duties. Exhaustion weighed down on him like a heavy fog. He had never felt this level of lethargy before. Since arriving in Hyderabad, something alien had started gnawing at his psyche. Most of the priestly stuff he memorised he started losing them. He is feeling sad and exhausted about slowly losing his brain power. He has to do something about it. He thought.

Just then, a voice cut through his thoughts.

"Hello, Ma'am. I'm here to join the music computing classes."

The voice was familiar. Sarma opened his eyes. It was her—the young woman from the park. Her brother stood right behind her.

A course in Music Computing focused on the intersection of music, technology, and computing—using digital tools, programming, and artificial intelligence to create and manipulate music.

"Sure," the receptionist replied. "Can I have your name to pull up your application?"

"Noor. I'm Noor Khan," the young woman said.

The receptionist glanced at the screen and nodded. "Your application has been approved. Let me introduce you to the computer lab assistant. He'll guide you through the systems and with the initial programming. Your classes begin tomorrow morning."

With that, the receptionist called for Sarma.

"Mr. Sarma, this is a new student, Ms. Noor Khan."

Sarma stood up and smiled. "Hello, welcome. Please follow me—I'll show you the lab."

As Noor turned toward him, her eyes caught his attention. They shone with an innocence that was almost hypnotic—captivating, otherworldly. She wore a soft rose-colored dupatta, draped lightly over her head, and long earrings that swayed gently as she moved, like ripples in a quiet lake.

God has made her supremely beautiful, Sarma thought, steadying himself against the sudden rush of emotions.

He had already developed a certain fondness for her—watching the tenderness with which she treated her younger brother had left an impression. Meeting her now, as a fellow student, felt like serendipity. The exhaustion clouding his mind faded, replaced by a strange sense of familiarity, as if a long-lost friend from another life had returned.

"You like music?" Sarma asked, breaking the silence.

"Who doesn't?" Noor replied with a slight smile.

"True. Me too. I love music," Sarma said.

Noor's expression shifted to concern. "I have to leave for my hometown for a week. I might miss some classes. I expected the semester to start in ten days, but I got a sudden call from the institute asking me to complete the lab admission today. That's why I'm here." She hesitated. "I just hope I don't fall too far behind."

"A professor fell ill, so they had to reschedule the classes," Sarma explained. "Don't worry—the institute knows this will affect some students. They'll accommodate you. And if you ever need help, I'm here."

Noor's shoulders relaxed slightly. "So, are you a full-time employee?"

"Not really," Sarma chuckled. "I'm a student too, but I work as a Teaching and Systems Lab assistant."

He then walked Noor through the basics, showing her how to navigate the system and introducing her to the compiler she would use to edit and synthesize music.

An Airbus A310 touched down at Karachi Airport.

There were no direct flights from Hyderabad, India, to Karachi, Pakistan, so Noor had to travel via Delhi. After a long journey, she finally emerged from the arrivals hall.

Her father, Imran, was waiting for her just beyond the customs checkpoint.

“Salaam Alekum, Baba,” Noor greeted him warmly as she approached.

“Waalekum Assalam, beti,” Imran replied, gently touching her forehead in affection. “How was your flight?”

“It was boring, Baba. Too long. You should arrange a direct flight so it’s easier for us to travel,” Noor said, sighing.

They stepped out of the airport. A black government car, its red beacon flashing, with a green license plate reading "Pakistan Government," was waiting for them.

The driver saluted Imran and quickly opened the door. They got in.

Imran smiled as he settled into his seat. “I’ll speak to our government about it. Perhaps they can arrange a special flight between Karachi and Hyderabad–just for my dearest daughter.”

Noor giggled. “Yes! That’s exactly what I want.”

Imran chuckled. “Pakistan can’t afford such luxuries. But I have a better idea–I’ll find you a wonderful husband who is also rich. Then you can ask your future husband to fly you in private jets.”

Noor’s cheeks flushed a deep red. At the mention of marriage, she fell silent.

After a moment, she spoke softly. “Baba... I do want to marry. I don’t care if my future husband is rich or poor. But pray to Allah that he is as loving and caring as you. Someone who will never break my trust. Someone I can rely on, like a rock, for as long as Allah wills me to live.”

Imran looked at her with pride. “Insha Allah,” he said, his voice filled with emotion.

Their conversation flowed effortlessly as the car made its way through the bustling streets of Karachi.

Soon, they arrived at their relatives' home, where they were staying temporarily. Imran had some official work in Karachi, which he had completed while waiting for Noor’s arrival.

The next day, they began their journey to Kharan. By the time they arrived, the evening sky had turned deep indigo, and the air carried the coolness of the desert night.

As soon as Noor stepped inside, excited laughter and tiny footsteps filled the courtyard. Her younger siblings rushed toward her, their eyes gleaming with joy.

"Noor Baji is here!" one of them squealed.

Her mother, Fatima, watched with a radiant smile as Noor embraced them all.

"Alhamdulillah, you have arrived safely, beti," Fatima said, placing a loving hand on Noor's head.

Noor had brought sweets from Hyderabad, a small treat for her siblings. They gathered around her, sharing stories and laughter late into the night. The warmth of family made the fatigue of travel disappear. Eventually, they drifted off to sleep, their voices fading into the quiet of the night.

The Next Morning, Noor woke up to the familiar voice of Ruksana in the kitchen, speaking to her mother.

"Ammi, has Noor Baji arrived?"

Smiling, Noor got up and made her way to the kitchen.

"Assalamu Alaikum," she greeted.

"Wa Alaikum Assalam, Noor. It's so good to see you!" Ruksana beamed.

"It's great to see you too, Ruksana," Noor replied warmly. "I brought the things your mother sent, but I haven't unpacked yet. I'll come by in the afternoon to give them to you."

"No rush, and jazakAllah for bringing them," Ruksana said gratefully.

The package Noor carried was from Ruksana's mother, Begum, who had sent homemade sweets for her daughter through a student from their hometown studying in Hyderabad.

Breaking the silence, "We are going to Sheikh Adil's home after tea for blessings," Ruksana said. "Would you like to join?"

"Of course, I'd love to," Noor agreed.

Fatima, who had been listening quietly, spoke up. "Ask Sheikh Adil to make dua for Adam. He is struggling in England."

Noor's expression changed. "What happened to my brother? What kind of struggle?"

Fatima sighed. "Nothing serious, but he is questioning everything–faith, traditions, people... The Imam of the local masjid in London spoke to your father. He's concerned that Adam is becoming... too much like the English."

Noor frowned. "But what's wrong with that? Allah has blessed Adam with a sharp mind. He is a thinker! Perhaps the Imam just doesn't understand him."

Fatima looked at Noor with caution. "Be careful how you speak in front of Sheikh Adil. You don't want him to have concerns about you as well."

Noor sighed. "Oh, is Sheikh Adil still upset with Adam?"

Fatima smiled knowingly. "Sheikh Adil holds on to his anger tightly, but aside from that, he is a good man. Insha Allah, his prayers will guide Adam toward clarity and peace."

After some more conversation, Ruksana took her leave to return home.

After unpacking, Noor picked up the package from her bag and made her way to Ruksana's home, the afternoon sun casting long shadows on the streets of Kharan.

"How is Asma?" Noor asked. Asma is Sajjad's sister. A year younger than Noor. She and Noor studied in the same college. They are good friends.

"She is continuing her education in Lahore, you know. She is excited you are back. She will arrive tomorrow morning. She is looking forward to spending a few days with you." said Ruksana.

"Oh! how I wish Asma studied with us in India," said Noor.

"I know. It is her deep desire to go to India with you and study there. But you know we cannot afford that kind of money. Allah has blessed you with abundance." said Ruksana.

"I told Asma that I can speak to my father. We can easily get her a loan to study in Hyderabad," said Noor.

"I know... But Sajjad does not want to send her to India." said Ruksana.

"Is it because of Mustafa?" asked Noor.

Mustafa and Asma became close. But the conservative society in Pakistan does not allow such closeness. Sajjad did not appreciate his sister getting close to Mustafa. Since Mustafa is now studying in India, Sajjad suspects that his sister is looking to go to India to be close to Mustafa.

Just then, Sajjad entered, dragging a green suitcase–the COMxBAT.

Ruksana, a little annoyed, said, "Why do you always keep that suitcase so close? I swear, it feels like my co-wife. You give it more attention than me."

Sajjad did not reply. He said a simple hello to Noor as if to acknowledge her presence and went into the home.

He went upstairs into the attic. It is a locked room. He opened the attic door. He carried the COMxBAT into there. He left it there in the attic and there is a similar colour green COMxBAT which is connected to an electric socket. He unplugged it. He plugged in the COMxBAT that he brought in with him. COMxBATs are designed to work for months without any battery recharge. But to be on safeside AIWAG instructs all his ground crew to charge the battery of COMxBAT whenever possible. Sajjad is a ground crew member.

While unplugging the COMxBAT he felt someone was watching him closely. The hairs in his neck raised and quickly turned around and saw Noor. They have all grown up together since their childhood. So they have freedom to roam freely in each other's homes. She followed him to ask him about Asma.

Noor temporarily forgot that she followed Sajjad to ask for Noor. But curiously looking at the green colour suitcases in the attic. One is plugged into the electric socket and the other Sajjad is holding in his hand.

“What are those suitcases? Don’t you carry medical stuff for Sheik Adil in them? Why is that suitcase plugged into the electric socket?” Asma asked.

Sajjad froze. He did not know what to reply.

“You know Sheik Adil has a heart condition. We have a monitor in the suitcase that requires charging.” replied Sajjad. “Why are you here?”

“Oh... right. I almost forgot. Sajjad bhai, I wanted to ask if you’ll allow Asma to study in India. With me.”

He knew Noor had seen too much. He couldn’t risk exposure.

"Fine. Take her. But, she is in the middle of her college year. She has her holidays in January. You can speak to her tomorrow when she arrives to see you. Book your tickets." Sajjad said quickly.

Noor lit up. "Really? You're saying yes without an argument?"

"I'm serious. Take her. Ruksana said you're leaving next weekend?"

"Yes! Thank you! I will tell my father to book tickets for Asma" Noor beamed, then left the attic.

Sajjad locked the door behind her, opened a hidden cupboard, and pulled out a briefcase. Inside was a satellite phone–only to be used in emergencies.

He dialed a number. Nayeem answered. The line was on speaker, as per Aiwag's strict protocol aboard his yacht.

Nayeem sat in the main office cabin of the yacht. In front of him lay a black A5 notebook. On its front page, he had just written the Arabic title: Ṭuyūrun Waḥshiyya – Savage Birds.

He was compiling a list. Names of people unafraid of heights. Those who might be interested in pilot training. And most importantly, those who were Islamic. The source? A massive dataset pirated from Shikhandi's lab – The Terminators Book.

Ṭuyūrun Waḥshiyya was ready.

Nayeem was just about to rise and goto Aiwag's cabin to hand it over when the satellite phone rang.

"I am Sajjad speaking"

"What's up?" Nayeem asked.

"Your sister Noor spotted the COMxBATs," Sajjad said, voice tense.

Sajjad owed everything to Nayeem, who had given him this job after his father died. His role: keep the COMxBAT near Sheikh Adil. He was paid well.

"What did you tell her?" Nayeem asked.

"The usual–heart monitor. I also approved Asma's trip to India to distract her."

"Good move. Let me know if Noor asks anything further about COMxBATs."

Sajjad hung up. He went and handed over the book to Aiwag. Bikku was also present in Aiwag's cabin. After Nayeem left.

Aiwag turned to Bikku. "You heard the phone call. Nayeem's sister spotted the COMxBAT. Keep tabs on her."

"But she lives in India. We pulled our crew out," Bikku replied.

"We'll outsource. Leave it to me."

An hour later, Aiwag contacted Lucian–"Father."

"One of our agents' sisters saw the COMxBAT," Aiwag explained.

"Is she a threat?"

"Yes. Nayeem and Noor's father is a senior Pakistani official. That's why we radicalised and hired Nayeem and through him we developed a team. He recruited his team. If

Noor talks, her father might question Sheikh Adil—and he doesn't even have a heart condition."

Lucian nodded. "Do two things. First, give Sheikh Adil a mild heart attack—nothing fatal or debilitating. Just enough to sell the story."

"What's the second?"

"Let Shikhandi know. Do not directly contact him. He has a good network within Hyderabad. Make him think that she is a valuable asset. He will take the bait. He is a businessman. If my guess is right, Shikandi drools over the opportunity because of the business he is planning in the Middle East."

"Understood, Father. I'll make the arrangements. I will send someone to casually drop the information with Sulfikar about Noor. I am sure he would inform Shikhandi about her."

"That should take care of it. We will know what he does after that." said Lucian.

Aiwag looked at the black colour A5 book in front of him on the table. He opened the book the second page onwards names, addresses of Savage Birds - potential list of hijackers.

The top row contained the name "Mohammed Attatayi" in Egypt.

8. ATTATAYIS

December 1992, Ayodhya – temple town, Uttar Pradesh, India

Cold air enveloped the town in the middle of winter. People assembled fireplaces by the roadside. They sat around them in silence, huddled under worn blankets, letting the flames lick warmth into their fingers.

It was 2 a.m. local time. The town was fast asleep. Even the stray dogs had curled into themselves, quiet beneath shuttered tea stalls.

High above, a massive military-grade tanker aircraft entered Indian airspace. No radar noticed its intrusion. It moved deliberately, smoothly—too quiet for its size.

The aircraft flew directly over Ayodhya. In its hold: a large chemical payload. With practised precision, it released the substance into the clouds below. No lights. No noise. Just mist dissolving into vapour.

Once the delivery was complete, it banked and vanished into the sky, slipping back across the border without leaving a trace.

A few hours later, the clouds began to rain.

By morning, people across a fifty-kilometre radius drank from their usual sources—wells, ponds, hand pumps. Water, as always. But now, something else was inside it. The chemical spread. Quietly. Invisibly. Human bodies absorbed it without resistance.

Somewhere in the Atlantic Ocean.

The sea outside was restless, but inside the upper cabin of the large yacht, everything was still.

Lucian Wrathborne's team sat around a wide metallic desk bolted to the floor. Charts, screens, and steaming mugs were scattered across its surface. Above them, soft LED lighting hummed. A speaker crackled to life.

Lucian's voice came through the two-way radio. Calm. Distant. Authoritative.

"Have they delivered the payload?"

"Yes, Father..." Aiwag responded, glancing towards the communicator. "But Father, I do not think this will work. You know we failed to ignite many times in the past."

"I know," Lucian said, from wherever he was. His tone didn't shift. "But do it anyway."

"Set the stopwatch for twelve hours. Our research team is clear—the bioengineered humans, created by our competitors, will begin to turn. They'll start responding to commands. From both sides. After twelve hours, they will be under our control."

He paused. A subtle hiss followed—a breath, a signal, a moment.

"Meanwhile, continue with the rest of the simulation meetings."

Lucian's voice returned a moment later, sharp as a scalpel.

"Accountant."

"Yes, Father," the man said, leaning forward in his seat.

"It is now final. The board reviewed your recommendations. You identified three opportunities—three conflicts. We agree. All three have been greenlit. The teams are in place to exploit the pre-existing fault lines."

Around the table, shoulders tensed. The room was quiet.

"This team—right here—will function as the centre. You oversee the other three. If one of them fails, you act. You take over. Immediately."

"What are the three?" Batsinger asked, eyes narrowing.

Lucian didn't hesitate. "First, we activate the BAT. Tutsi versus Hutu in Rwanda."

He paused long enough to let it land.

"Accountant, you claimed this would weaken British influence. Clarify."

"That is correct, Father," said the Accountant. "All former British colonies are saturated with engineered divisions. Divide and Rule was not just a strategy–it was a legacy. They left behind borders drawn in blood and bone. To this day, the local rulers feed on those divisions."

He leaned back slightly. "We don't need to dismantle that system. We simply insert ourselves into it. Rwanda is perfect. It allows us to generate and circulate wealth–quietly, cleanly, beneath the noise of European guilt and international bureaucracy."

"And you suggest we take payment in the form of mining contracts–diamonds, gold, that sort of thing?" Lucian asked over the radio.

"Correct," said the Accountant. "I've already charted out how to extract money using this conflict."

"Father, we understand your plan to exploit Rwanda," Batsinger said, leaning forward on the desk. "What are the other two conflicts?"

Lucian didn't hesitate. "Let us exploit the fault lines between Bosnians and Serbs."

A pause.

"I liked this suggestion. It offers two main advantages. First, it will draw NATO into the fight. Since Muslims are involved in a European conflict, the Middle East will pour funds into it–sentiment will be too strong to ignore. For many gullible Muslims, this will seem like a holy cause. Perfect cover."

"But Father," Aiwag interjected, "how does that help us? We're looking for money, not sentiment."

"Correct," Lucian said, his voice sharper now. "I'll let the Accountant explain. Listen carefully, Aiwag. Your role in this is going to be critical. Memorise every detail. As you may have guessed from our previous discussions, I'll be sending you soon into the Middle East."

Aiwag didn't reply. But beneath the calm surface, his heart pounded. Despite Batsinger's reassurances, his instincts screamed warning. If the operation touched Israel, it was a hornet's nest. One wrong move, and Mossad would bury them before breakfast.

He couldn't hold it in.

"Father... Please tell me we're not involving Israel in this Middle East planning. You know how difficult it was to pull off the cargo airline op. I still tremble at the thought that Mossad might have spotted us... might be watching us, waiting for our next move. I can't operate under that anxiety. Don't put me in that position again. I can't risk it."

"I understand," Lucian replied coolly. "For now, we will stay out of Israel as much as possible."

Batsinger glanced at Aiwag, then spoke thoughtfully. "You know, your fear of Israel reminds me of The Art of War."

"How?" Aiwag asked, wary.

"Sun Tzu wrote, 'The supreme art of war is to subdue the enemy without fighting.' Without knowing the full context, without even confronting Father or the formidable shadow organisation he commands–Mossad had already won. Without setting foot on the battlefield."

He paused.

"You, Aiwag, are one of our most formidable team members. You work directly for Father. And yet... you're afraid. That alone proves the point–subdue the enemy without fighting."

The room fell into an awkward silence. The only sound was the soft hum of the cabin's systems and the faint creaking of the yacht.

Finally, the Accountant broke it.

"We expect good funding from the Balkan conflict," he said. "NATO may present itself as a purely military alliance, but it has deep economic implications. Defence contractors make billions when a new country joins. They encourage these new members to discard their old Soviet or regional arms and switch entirely to NATO-standard weaponry."

"I heard that's how they make their money?" Batsinger asked, eyes narrowing.

"Yup... that's how they make their money," said the Accountant. "Any spare part made for a NATO tank can be used in another NATO country's tank. Standardisation across all member states. While NATO doesn't operate as a commercial entity, its policies directly contribute to the profitability of defence contractors in member nations."

He leaned back slightly, his tone darkening. "But the real kicker? The funding for those weapons–the procurement budgets that fuel the war machines–comes largely from the Middle East."

"How so?" asked Batsinger.

"Muslims worldwide function as an Ummah–a collective bonded by faith. They may be scattered across borders, but when it comes to attacks on Muslims, they unite. That's the sentiment we ride on," said the Accountant.

"How?" Aiwag asked, eyes narrowing.

Lucian's voice cut in through the radio. Steady. Unmoved.

"We learn the commercial intricacies of every NATO supplier. And we trace the channels of funding from the Middle East. That's your task, Aiwag. I expect you to know the names–every wealthy backer, every funder. Their names are important."

"But... many of these people funding the wars from Islamic countries probably have good intentions," Aiwag said hesitantly. "They believe they're protecting fellow believers."

"Does that matter?" the Accountant snapped. "Neither NATO, nor the funders, nor the politicians care. They'll send their sons and daughters to die, sell weapons by the tonne, and call it honour. So why should we care?"

"I agree," Batsinger chimed in, almost too quickly. "We know how to hijack faith. Faith was meant to bring people closer to their own hearts–to inner peace, to awakening. But everywhere you look, the first thing they throw away is their faith. God has become optional. They slaughter one another for profit. We didn't create the fault lines. They did. They don't know how to live in peace. So why should we care? We have our own agenda–our own way of life. Independent. Unapologetic."

"But aren't we the ones instigating the conflict?" Aiwag asked, voice rising just slightly.

"Not just us," said the Accountant. "We're the ApeX, yes–but there are others. Politicians, investment bankers, arms dealers, energy lobbyists... all salivating at the chance to fund the next war."

He leaned forward, voice low. "Tell me, Aiwag... even if a brother suspects a third party is stirring the conflict, why does he still raise the knife against his own blood? They don't care. They choose not to see."

"So... you're saying man has no free will?"

"Of course he does," said the Accountant. "Even when our BAT zaps their brains, it can't touch their witnessing self. That inner observer. The soul. The divine spark. That self is God, in many religions. If they connect with that, they'll see what's right and wrong. But they won't. So they pay. You see? We're not to blame. Just because the other fellow is stupid, doesn't mean we must stoop to his level to argue."

The room fell silent. Only the soft creak of the yacht and the rhythmic sway of the sea filled the space.

The point about faith–how easily it was sacrificed for material gain–weighed heavily in the air. Each person around the table had lived through their own abusive systems, until Lucian's organisation rescued them. And yet, here they were, building their own.

"Okay, Father," Batsinger finally said, breaking the silence. "So, as I understand, we have teams in Rwanda and the Balkans ready to exploit the fault lines. What is the third one?"

"The third one," said Lucian, "we've already discussed in a previous simulation. We're going to make the USA go BATshit crazy. We can generate enough capital from Rwanda and the Balkans to fund our global teams. But the third conflict—this one—is different. It must be executed slowly. Strategically."

"This isn't our plan," he continued. "Our Accountant pointed it out, and our research team followed up. Turns out, our competitors already have a full-blown plan in motion. They intend to push the USA into full psychological fragmentation. Our task is simple—we piggyback on what they've already established."

"What's the conflict?" asked Aiwag.

"Islamic fundamentalism versus the rest of the world," Lucian replied. "The Middle East is brimming with wealth. To extract it, our competitors have engineered elaborate schemes. They've seeded ideological, economic, and cultural traps. All in motion. We don't need to start from scratch. We only step in where it suits us. Where they need assistance, we become their suppliers."

"But, Father... won't they suspect us?" Batsinger asked, his voice calm but firm.

"So what?" the Accountant interjected. "Who said there has to be honour among thieves?"

Lucian didn't respond.

They took a five-minute break.

Afterwards, the team reassembled in the upper cabin, coffee cups replaced, notes in hand. The ocean rocked the yacht gently, like a lull before the next storm.

Lucian joined them again, as always, through the two-way radio.

"Aiwag," said Lucian.

"Yes, Father."

"I'm going through the list of FBs from various faiths and political parties. But I don't see the list of FBs from the Islamic world," Lucian said.

FB stands for Fire Breathers—individuals who breathe fire of discontent into their followers and the networks around them.

"Hmm... Father... the list isn't there because we found there are too many. It stopped being a list—it's become a volume. I'm in the process of compiling a book. At this rate, it'll be as thick as the Oxford English Dictionary," said Aiwag.

Lucian paused for a moment. Then laughter crackled through the two-way radio—measured, layered, rising in waves. Aiwag allowed himself a slight smile, proud to have amused his elusive master, even briefly.

"Fine. Compile your book if you must. But I don't need a book—I need a list. A hundred individuals. Forget the standard criteria you used for influencers from other faiths or from among the Socialists. I want you to follow up with Madrasas that endorse active violence. Start there. Find the teachers. Identify and filter a list of FBs from that pool," Lucian said. "And make sure to cross-verify with the lists we've received from our competitors."

"We're already doing that, Father. I've completed the earlier list you asked for," said Aiwag.

"The one for operatives we can programme to carry out airline attacks?"

"Correct, Father. That's the list."

"Send it to me."

"Father, I have a question. Why did you want us to draw that list from the genetically modified and cloned individuals maintained by our competitors?"

"Our research team informs me these individuals are no longer human. They look human–but they are brain-programmed," Lucian replied.

"You mean like our BAPS, Father?" Aiwag asked.

"Oh no. We operate with a certain grace in our methods. We can wake up our BAPS–we can release them from their programming whenever we choose. But the ones our competitors manage? Those are Terminators. Their genetic and biological programming is embedded, irreversible. They don't require activation. They just switch on. Instantly," said Lucian.

"How is that even possible?"

"We don't know yet. That's why the programme we launched in Ayodhya today is critical. It will help us determine whether we've succeeded in hijacking their resources," Lucian said.

"But why is that important, Father? We already have our BAPS. Why go after our competitors' assets?" asked Batsinger.

"There's a good reason," said Lucian. "As you know, not all missions involving our BAPS succeed. Some of them wake up in the middle of a mission–conscious of who they are, what they're doing. But the Terminators maintained by our competitors? They don't fail."

"You know how we found that out?"

"How?" Aiwag asked.

"Our researchers were reviewing BAPS biomarker data and behavioural reports. While comparing sources, they discovered something. Any BAPS who is also on our competitors' Terminators list never wakes up. Not even mid-mission. Every mission involving such operatives has a 100% success rate. We still don't know why."

"In that case, Father," said Aiwag, "I'll extract the top hundred from their Terminators list and send it to you."

"Good. Do that by tomorrow," said Lucian. "Also, we need a new name for this group. Something that will inflame sentiment–something that resonates with Muslims. We can't call them BAPS. This has to be a separate unit. What name do you suggest?"

"Recently, I was speaking with our satellite communications engineer–the one who named our LEO as SANI. He mentioned that in Hinduism, zombies are referred to as Attatayis. It's a term found in their holy book, the Bhagavad Gita. Perhaps we can use that?"

"Perfect. Call this new group Attatayis. And send me the list by tomorrow."

The radio crackled. Silence. Father had left the conversation.

"What are Madrasas?" Batsinger asked.

"They're schools that teach religious texts. We're interested in the ones that promote violence in the name of faith," said Aiwag.

"Are these the same kind of Fire Breathers we used to incite the riots in Punjab? I remember—that was when I came on board. I was tasked with compiling a list of influencers who advocated violence as their first response to conflict. I'm the one who coined the term Fire Breathers," Batsinger added.

Aiwag turned and looked at him—really looked at him. There was a stillness in his gaze. He was trying to understand why Lucian had chosen this particular man for the current mission.

It made sense now.

Batsinger already had experience finding Fire Breathers.

"It's great to know you're the original creator of that list. The list you compiled was incredibly helpful for COMxBAT to tag BAPS for the assassination," said Aiwag.

"But I heard the mission in India was a failure?" asked the Accountant.

"We managed to carry out the assassination and incite riots. But we didn't reach our full objective. Still, that event gave us an interesting insight," said Aiwag.

"What kind of insight?" asked Batsinger.

"We assumed that people who carry Buddha or Gandhi in their minds would be incapable of violence. But we found a staggering number of hypocrites. They were using Gandhi and Buddha merely as political mascots. When the moment came, they turned violent with ease–committed mass murder without hesitation. That surprised us," said Aiwag.

"But isn't that what we wanted?" asked Batsinger.

"What–mass murder? No. That wasn't the objective. It was just a fault-line test. A simulation. It got out of control. Father expected the Sikhs–who wear swords publicly–to be the first to escalate," said Aiwag.

"What happened then?"

"We expected a Black Swan event to spiral India into civil war. But the Sikhs... they only appear aggressive. Underneath, they have a huge appetite for empathy. They were the first to try restoring peace. And we lacked enough ground power to sustain the operation. So, in that sense, it was only a partial success," Aiwag said.

"So, what now?" asked Batsinger.

"Father assigned one of the AIWAGs to design a programme to erase Gandhi from the Indian psyche. But that too failed. The operation is on hold for now–we pulled our resources from India. However, what we're experimenting with today in Ayodhya might offer a new direction," said the Accountant.

"But why did it fail? With BAT on our side, we should've succeeded..." said Aiwag.

"Gandhi is lodged too deeply in the Indian conscience. You already understand how our E-snatcher works," said Batsinger.

"I do. The image in the brain matters," Aiwag replied.

"Exactly. Indian currency has Gandhi printed on it. We pay people to work for us. But when the BAT-controlled subjects look at the money—and see Gandhi's face—they begin to wake up, right in the middle of missions," Batsinger said. "That's why the programme failed. BAT relies on the messages stored in the mind. Ahimsa—non-violence—is the antithesis of what we want. Our paymasters want blood. They want people to drop like flies. How can we achieve that when forgiveness is glorified and peace is preached?"

"So, what was the ground plan?" asked Aiwag.

"We want to erase Gandhi from the Indian psyche," said the Accountant.

"How?"

"We identify Fire Breathers—unemployed, insecure, political rejects. They're naturally volatile. We feed their ego. We give them a mission: hate Gandhi," said Batsinger. "Then we use BAT to help them pass exams, succeed in life, become visible. AI will push them into prominence."

"AI... as in Artificial Intelligence?" Aiwag asked.

"No. In this context, AI stands for Augmented Intelligence. We amplify their reach. Make them famous. Make them rich. You know BAT can make even a donkey go viral," said Batsinger. "So, these Gandhi-hating FBs start pulling crowds."

"And then?" Aiwag prompted.

"These FBs will gradually indoctrinate the public. They'll nationalise violence. Rebrand it as heroism. The narrative will flip: violence becomes glory. Peace becomes cowardice. And by then, many of their followers will already be BAPS. All we'll need is a spark. We'll ignite India," Batsinger said, eyes glinting with calculated certainty.

"What happens after that?" Aiwag asked .

"We can use the Rwanda or Balkan model we've already tested," said the Accountant. "If our plans work, we replicate it in India. Trigger chaos, then send in international peacekeepers. By that point, the economy would have collapsed due to excessive violence. It would be a golden opportunity–for us to loot under the guise of aid."

"The plan is essentially this," said Aiwag. "Identify all the useful idiots who believe Gandhi was wrong and violence is right. Promote them. Amplify them. Then sit back and watch. When we ignite them, they'll fight. They'll slaughter each other. That's our roadmap."

He paused. "A question."

"Shoot."

"I heard Gandhi approved of killing rabid dogs. Is that true?" Aiwag asked.

"Correct."

"Then Gandhi wasn't truly non-violent."

"He was," said Batsinger. "But he used non-violence as a strategy. A very calculated one."

"I'm not following."

"The Fire Breathers who rage against Gandhi and his so-called hypocrisy have no understanding of colonial history," Batsinger said. "The British were masters of violence. Ruthless. Cold. Efficient. Just look at how Europe colonised the rest of the world–it took more than just ambition. It required an intimate relationship with gore."

The Accountant nodded. "Show me one armed Indian freedom fighter who survived after taking on the British. Just one. You won't find any."

"Were the British really that ruthless?" Aiwag asked.

"They had to be," said Batsinger. "Otherwise, how would they maintain such a sprawling empire?"

"Exactly," said the Accountant. "The British actually wanted Indian freedom fighters to resort to violence. It justified stationing more troops. It gave them reasons to wage battle after battle. Their army wasn't idle–they were refining their methods, testing their propaganda, perfecting clandestine operations."

"Every act of violent rebellion gave them a new excuse to tighten their grip," added Batsinger. "Take the 1857 rebellion. The British crushed it with unimaginable brutality. They exiled the last Mughal emperor. Slaughtered civilians. Stamped out resistance for the next century. It was a violent uprising–and they used it to legitimise total control."

"For ninety years after that," the Accountant said, "no armed rebel survived long enough to make a difference. Prove me wrong."

"So... what did Gandhi do differently?" Aiwag asked.

"Gandhi understood the British," said Batsinger. "He knew they were prepared for violence. But they weren't prepared for defiance without violence. He gave them no reason to unleash their strength. But he kept provoking them. Quietly. Persistently."

"After losing loved ones in two World Wars," the Accountant said, "the British were exhausted. Gandhi's methods forced them to recognise the power of non-violence—something they couldn't fight with guns or armies."

"I see it now," said Aiwag. "If we want a war theatre inside India, we need an endless supply of BAPS. Fire Breathers are the key—they turn their students or followers into aggressive, emotionally charged tools. The more rage inside a BAPS, the better for us. But the problem is—Bapu and Buddha are lodged too deeply in the Indian brain. Their memory of non-violence is waking up our BAPS mid-operation."

He looked up.

"That's why we need to erase them—from the public conscience."

"Is that the reason for this special project in Ayodhya?" Batsinger asked.

"Correct," said Aiwag. "We can't ignite India unless we erase Mahatma Gandhi from their minds. And that's not going to happen anytime soon. So, we're activating a contingency plan."

He leaned forward slightly.

"The Terminators maintained by our competitors—when we convert them into BAPS, their success rate is 100%. We're testing it now. We'll have the results by tomorrow. If it works... then erasing Gandhi from the Indian psyche becomes irrelevant. We'll be able to ignite Indians whenever we want."

9. SHIKHANDI

December 1992 - Deep within the Bali Islands. Among the countless fragments of land scattered across the Indonesian seas, this particular island was forgotten by most. But it had a purpose now.

Inside a dimly lit study, a large portrait of the Mahābhārata loomed on the wall. In it, the great warrior Bhīshma stood helpless, arrows piercing his body, as Shikhandi—once a woman, now a man—faced him with a bow in hand. Behind Shikhandi stood Arjuna, using the situation cleverly to defeat the otherwise invincible Bhīshma.

On the desk below the portrait, several telephones sat neatly arranged. One of them—red—rang.

The man behind the desk picked it up and answered calmly, "Shikhandi here."

Very few knew his real name.

Publicly, Shikhandi was the chairman of a pharmaceutical company based in Indore, India. But in truth, he spent most of his time on this island, overseeing a state-of-the-art biological research facility.

The caller was Gupta—his personal secretary.

"When are you sending Dubey over?" Shikhandi asked.

Dubey was an astrologer. A man who read birth charts and interpreted destinies. Shikhandi believed in astrology. Deeply. For him, knowing the future wasn't just comfort—it was a necessity.

Depression comes from dwelling on the past. Anxiety, from fearing the future. Tarot, astrology, tea leaf reading—they're all tools to silence that fear. Dubey, one of the best in the trade, charged heavily. Apart from money, his other craving was women.

Shikhandi could afford both.

He had no shortage of wealth. Running illegal human trials for foreign pharmaceutical giants had made him rich. He offered what they couldn't get in the West: fast, unregulated results. India, with its teeming population and blind spots in record-keeping, was his playground. Every day, lakhs of people died in the country—many from gross medical negligence. Nobody kept count. Nobody dared to question. The system was a cartel of cartels—judicial, medical, pharmaceutical. Shikhandi simply greased what needed greasing. And it worked.

"I'm sending Dubey," said Gupta. "But he's asking to fly first-class."

"Send him. We know the cravings of his flesh. He's useful," said Shikhandi.

"There's a problem with that," Gupta hesitated. "He uses the flight to market his astrology. Chats up everyone in the cabin. My concern is—his loose talk might let someone know you're his client. But he refuses to fly economy. Says it messes with his planetary alignment."

Shikhandi rolled his eyes. "Tell him he'll be flying in a private jet. That should align his chakras."

Gupta smirked. "He'll be thrilled. The man loves his luxuries nearly as much as he loves predicting doom."

"Send him with Vinay. He has his own jet. Ask him to bring Dubey along. Dubey will be ecstatic once he finds out."

"Sure," said Gupta.

Shikhandi rose from his chair and walked out of the study. His private island estate spanned fifty acres, encircled by a high-security perimeter. At the far end of the property stood a cutting-edge biological research lab. Just beyond the fence, a private runway. A jet sat ready, gleaming in the morning light.

Shikhandi took a deep breath. He loved his opulence.

Inside the lab, a few scientists were hard at work. Shikhandi moved past them and entered a secure conference room, where two scientists were already seated.

"Good morning," he greeted.

"Good morning, Mr Shikhandi," they replied in unison.

A shift passed through him—a quiet internal switch. You are not Shikhandi. You are Shikhandi, a voice whispered. He raised his arms slowly, as if embracing the identity fully.

"Please, be seated," he said. "Any progress with the cross-verification?"

Dr Reinschmidt, a German microbiologist, adjusted his thick-rimmed glasses. "Specimen 000013 was incubated from a Luxor-based genome. We reconstructed his biological matrix with 94.7% fidelity. Fascinating, isn't it?"

Reinschmidt wasn't here for the money. He was here for the science. His early career involved research on reviving Egyptian mummies. After German authorities discovered the potentially dangerous implications, they shut down his lab. But before they could destroy everything, Reinschmidt salvaged the essential data and went underground. When Shikhandi approached him, he agreed without hesitation.

"We know Stephen was born in 1965." Reinschmidt opened a massive, leather-bound catalogue titled Terminators 1960–1965. He flipped to a marked page and pushed it towards Shikhandi.

Each row in the book detailed a name, year of inception, geo-location, and a unique identifier. The "Terminators" were humans born from an experiment—an attempt to inject the essence of Egyptian mummies into pregnant women worldwide. Over a million women gave birth during that window. Healthy babies. Unknowing experiments. Stephen was one of them. Terminator ID: 000013.

“What does this mean for our immortality research?” asked Shikhandi.

They were chasing immortality—not through technology, but biology. The working hypothesis: memories could be transferred from one body to another. So far, only traits had transferred. Like scent on the hand after touching dead fish—persistent but shallow. Skills passed on. Instincts. But not memories. A great singer could be reborn as a gifted vocalist, but would not recall the songs of her past life—unless taught anew.

“You tracked Stephen’s growth?” Shikhandi asked, eyeing the entry.

“Karjat,” Reinschmidt confirmed. “Status: Terminated.”

Dr Gottlieb, a Swiss psychiatrist, exhaled a ribbon of cigar smoke. “Ah, Stephen. A masterpiece in dysfunction. Self-awareness ruined him. He spiralled—addiction, paranoia, homicide. In the end, he became what all tragic constructs become—a killer.”

“He killed his own mother. Then Father Francis. Then himself,” said Shikhandi. “Why? Is something going wrong with our experiments?”

“I wouldn’t say that. In fact, it confirms the potential. We’ve already harvested Stephen’s essence. A fresh batch of Terminator babies—designed to be killers like him—are on the way,” said Reinschmidt.

“But that will take twenty years,” said Shikhandi. “I need marketable product now. I want proof that we already have killers in our current database—so I can start selling.”

"We're working on it," Gottlieb said. "Ayodhya is the test ground. We've placed Terminators in both Hindu and Muslim households. The programme has been running for a year and a half since Stephen's death."

"No results yet?"

"Not the kind we want," said Gottlieb. "They hate each other, shout, provoke–but no outbreak of Stephen-level violence. It's... disappointing."

"Alright. Continue your experiments," said Shikhandi, rising from his seat.

He walked out, past the lab, across the estate–his mind already on the next move. Ayodhya would tell him whether the world was ready for what he had to offer.

Delhi Airport.

A sleek private jet stood ready for take-off. It belonged to Vinay–a mining magnate who had become obscenely rich by playing the system. His empire spanned Africa and Latin America, where he acquired copper, manganese, and precious metal ore through highly lucrative contracts.

The only catch? These mines were often located in unstable countries–ruled by warlords, dictators, or megalomaniacs. It served the interests of a global cabal to keep these regions in poverty. Under the guise of humanitarian aid, they looted resources. Vinay had mastered this global game. But in making his fortune, he'd made a deal with the devil. Part of that deal involved satisfying the peculiar demands of some of these rulers—tasks for which he often turned to his associate, Shikhandi.

It was a small ten-seater jet. Inside, Dubey the astrologer relaxed in plush leather seating, soaking in the luxury. He marvelled at the private jet, silently thanking his stars for answering his lifelong wish.

Two others were onboard. One was Mamadou, tall and dark-skinned, the Director of Security Services for a private mining firm in Zambia. The other was DeSantos, a liaison for a Mexican drug cartel.

Air traffic control gave the green light. The jet roared into the sky, bound for Shikhandi's private island—a three-and-a-half-hour flight over the ocean.

The Island.

Upon landing, a golf cart awaited to take them to the guest quarters adjacent to the lab. The rooms were luxurious—designed with every conceivable comfort. Each guest had access to a personal chef.

Dubey entered his suite and was instantly spellbound by the decor. He pulled back the curtains to find a breathtaking ocean view. Just then, a knock at the door.

"Enter," said Dubey.

A young woman in a fitted suit stepped in. "Mr Dubey?"

"Yes."

"Shikhandi sir would like to meet you at 4 PM. I'll escort you to the meeting room when it's time."

She left. Dubey napped for a few hours. At precisely 4 PM, another knock. The same woman stood waiting. He splashed water on his face, wiped off the sleep, and nodded that he was ready.

They walked along a concrete path to the rear entrance of the lab. The woman opened the door and led him to a conference room, then silently left.

After a few minutes, Shikhandi entered.

"How are you, Dubey?" he asked.

"I'm doing well, sir. Thank you for your trust in my astrological services," Dubey replied, already calculating what to charge. A man with an island and a lab? He won't flinch at six figures.

"Let's get straight to it," said Shikhandi, placing a birth chart on the table. "Read this. Use whatever tools you need. Tell me everything you can about this person."

Dubey pulled out a Casio pocket calculator and began his work. Shikhandi watched, patient and unreadable.

"This individual was born during a rare planetary alignment," Dubey said finally.

"What's special about it?" Shikhandi leaned forward, eyebrows raised.

"There are two life paths available to this person. One path leads him to become a great spiritual master—perhaps the founder of a new religion. A unifying path, one that brings peace across faiths."

Shikhandi gave a slight nod. "Interesting. But I don't care for saints. What's the other possibility?"

"He will become immensely powerful and wealthy. By 2005, he will earn his first hundred million dollars. He could easily be one of the ten richest men in the world."

"Now that's something," said Shikhandi. "What else?"

"He was born in Kataka Lagna," said Dubey.

"What does that mean?"

"It's the same astrological configuration as Lord Śrīrām's. Known for marital sorrow. His wife was taken from him. Gandhi and Vivekananda were also born in this Lagna—neither enjoyed a peaceful married life."

Dubey hesitated. "Who is this person?"

"You'll know soon enough. But he just got married."

"I see. And you believe you're the demon in his life?" Dubey asked cautiously.

"I don't believe. I know. I'm in the process of destroying his marriage," said Shikhandi, his voice disturbingly calm. "Does his chart confirm I'm the one?"

"I'd need to see your chart too—for comparison," Dubey said. His voice had softened. Shikhandi's calculated cruelty had unsettled him.

"I must warn you," Dubey continued, choosing his words carefully. "This chart is powerful. If you interfere, you may succeed temporarily—but the consequences will be devastating. You'll trigger a cosmic backlash. Because you'd be knowingly destabilising someone marked for greatness."

"But he was born in Kataka Lagna, you said. Isn't suffering part of his fate?" Shikhandi asked.

"Yes. But that's the point. If fate plays its part, it's natural. If you intervene knowingly, it invites destruction upon yourself."

"I'm warning you—as your astrologer—do not tamper with destinies like his."

Shikhandi gave a slow smirk.

"I've already sent someone to the US to gather intel on the person he married," he said.

"Oh?"

"His name is Sarma."

"Sarma?" Dubey echoed. "A Brahmin... Like me."

"No. He is nothing like you. You Brahmins have tribes, right?" asked Shikhandi.

"We identify our tribes as Gotrams," said Dubey.

"We don't think this Sarma belongs to any of your known tribes. That's what's perplexed us for a long time. He seems to be a lone Brahmin—descended from some long-lost lineage."

"How do you know?"

"We consulted a palmist"

"What did he say?"

"I will show you," Shikhandi had push forward a paper on which an eye was drawn. Dubey recognised the photo.

"Is this not a symbol from Egypt?"

"Correct. It is called the Eye of Ra"

"Eye of Ra?"

"It is the Eye of Sun, logic and action. He is a sun worshipping priest. Sarma has this eye in his right palm. Dr Gottlieb, our resident psychiatrist and scientist thinks it gives Sarma some kind of superpowers. We are still trying to find what those are. But he seems to be carrying the guardianship of sacred knowledge," Shikhandi said.

"That is interesting. I will look into it more when I meet him. You said you're sending someone to the USA to meet the person Sarma married. What exactly are they meant to do?"

"To test the waters," said Shikhandi, smiling cryptically.

"I don't understand..." Dubey said.

"Let me tell you a joke," said Shikhandi, leaning back. "There was this famous film producer–very wealthy, but not very good-looking. One day, at a party, he saw one of the most gorgeous actresses and started flirting with her. She got annoyed and said, 'Why are you flirting with me? I wouldn't sleep with you even for a million dollars!'"

Dubey blinked, unsure where this was going. "That must have hurt. I feel sorry for the producer."

"On the contrary," said Shikhandi with a wink, "he replied, 'So now we have a price... Let's negotiate.'"

He burst out laughing. Dubey didn't get the humour, but he understood the message: Shikhandi, being the cold strategist he was, wanted to throw money at Sarma's loved ones–to see who could be bought. And whether anyone would sell Sarma out.

In that moment, Dubey thought: This man really is the devil incarnate.

"Who is this person?" he asked. "This Sarma you're trying to destabilise?"

"Someone of no consequence," said Shikhandi.

"A man like you wouldn't waste his time unless the person was important. Come on, tell me. Who is he? And why do you want to become the demon in his life?"

Shikhandi didn't answer immediately. After a moment's pause, he changed the subject.

"Dubey, how much money do you make?"

Dubey shifted uneasily in his seat. He calculated carefully before answering. "Roughly two thousand dollars a month."

(In truth, that was only during good seasons when rich clients were abundant. Most months, he earned half that.)

"Are you satisfied with that?" asked Shikhandi.

"Not at all. If I had the chance, I'd love to earn far more. Much, much more," Dubey admitted.

"Alright then," said Shikhandi. "Here's a deal. I want you to move close to the person whose chart you're studying. Befriend him. Observe him. I'll pay you double what you earn now, plus expenses."

Money—the oldest seduction. For Dubey, it struck like a spotlight on a deer. He froze. His mind raced. He'd lied about his income, and now, Shikhandi was offering a sum he couldn't refuse.

"Alright," Dubey said cautiously. "If you promise that much... I'll do it. But what exactly do I have to do?"

"Walk with me," said Shikhandi, rising from his chair.

They walked down the corridor to a smoke-filled office where Dr Gottlieb sat reading a thick psychology manuscript, puffing on a cigar.

"Dr Gottlieb, meet Dubey," said Shikhandi. "My personal astrologer from India. He's very skilled."

Gottlieb glanced at Dubey over the rim of his gold-framed glasses. "Ah, Dubey. How do you do? Has Shikhandi briefed you?"

"He told me you want me to get close to the person in the birth chart," said Dubey.

"His name is Sarma," said Gottlieb. "He's been my test subject for years. Now he's reached the next phase of his journey–and we want you to assist us."

"What sort of assistance?" asked Dubey.

"We want to do a psychological experiment. Based on the chart you read. We'll destabilise his path in multiple ways–to observe how he navigates the riddles of his destiny."

"So you're testing a birth chart through real-world experiments?" Dubey asked.

"Exactly. And we already know he's destined for greatness," said Gottlieb.

Shikhandi cut in. "Let me give you a bit of background. My father was a politician. His biggest rival? Dr Rao."

"You mean Dr Rao, the former Home Minister of India?" asked Dubey.

"Yes," said Shikhandi. "Rao took a personal interest in Sarma. And at the time, Rao and my father were at political war. My father died of a heart attack, and our family has always believed that if he hadn't crossed Rao, he'd still be alive."

His eyes hardened.

"So I took it upon myself to destroy everything Rao cared for. Rao was like Bhishma—the wise old commander. So I became Shikhandi—his nemesis."

"Is Sarma related to Dr Rao?" asked Dubey.

"There's a distant relation. But it doesn't matter," said Shikhandi. "What matters is—Dr Rao believes Sarma is destined for greatness. Ever since we discovered that, we've been working to destabilise him."

As they spoke, Vinay walked into Dr Gottlieb's office, where the room still lingered with cigar smoke and shadows.

"Hello, all. Nice to see everyone in one place," said Vinay.

"Vinay, come in..." smiled Shikhandi. "We were just talking about Sarma."

Vinay turned to Dubey and grinned. "Dubey, you've hit the jackpot. Welcome to Mission Destabilised Destiny."

Dubey couldn't believe what he was hearing—or seeing. Three powerful men, united with a single mission: to ruin one man's life.

"What's the reason for your rivalry with Sarma?" Dubey asked.

"Oh, I've got no rivalry," said Vinay, waving the idea away. "It's purely business. I was paid to track and report on Sarma during his childhood. Later, Shikhandi joined the mission–for personal reasons."

"So... Shikhandi joined to destabilise Sarma's destiny?" Dubey asked, turning back.

"Initially, we outsourced the job to his relatives," said Vinay. "We paid them regularly–to fail him. They drugged him whenever he was close to achieving something significant. Gave him brain fog. Made him look unstable in front of potential mentors."

Shikhandi nodded. "We underestimated him. We didn't expect such genius."

"What do you mean?"

"He started attracting people of influence," said Vinay. "We knew Dr Rao wasn't directly mentoring him, just watching over him from afar. But our tactics worked–we planted enough doubt in the minds of those who cared about Sarma."

"But now," Shikhandi added, "we know he's widened his circle. He's grown. He's connected to some very powerful people. That's where we failed. We didn't see his rise."

"Which is why we're changing our tactics," said Vinay. "From now on, our people will be placed directly in his inner circle. This is where you come in."

"What exactly do you want me to do?" Dubey asked, steadying his breath.

"Go to wherever he lives. Move there. If he relocates, you follow," said Vinay. "You'll become his friend. His confidant. He loves spiritual sciences–he'll warm to you quickly. He never had proper friends, so even small talk makes a big impact. Show him affection, and he'll let you in."

"Sarma knows a bit of astrology," added Shikhandi. "It won't be hard for you to win his trust."

Vinay leaned forward. "And you'll get a front-row seat to how his Kataka Lagna destiny unfolds in real time."

"But we'll need something from you," said Shikhandi with a mischievous smile. "We need you to steal a pair of Sarma's clothes."

"What?" Dubey asked. "Why?"

"Because Sarma is going to appear in front of a judge–and act completely mad," said Shikhandi. "The judge will then declare him legally incompetent. The marriage will be nullified."

"But I've read his chart–he's extremely intelligent. Why would any judge believe he's insane?" Dubey asked.

"Exactly. That's where the clothes come in," said Vinay. "We'll have a lookalike wear them and impersonate him."

"Why his clothes?" Dubey asked, eyes narrowing.

"Because if the judge gets suspicious and asks for a scent test with a police dog, the scent will match. The dog will confirm it's Sarma," said Shikhandi. "Not that it matters–the judge is already on our payroll. He's part of our judicial cartel."

Dubey stared at them, stunned. "That's... diabolical. You have no respect for the law?"

Vinay laughed. "You think men like us became billionaires without mastering the cartels? Government, judiciary, pharma, mining—it's all a system. We just play it better than others."

"Sarma will be divorced," said Shikhandi. "If we succeed, his wife will join our side. If she resists, we'll use the divorce to turn her against him. Tell her he's a fraud. A liar. A madman."

"And if all else fails..." said Vinay, his voice lowering. "We'll escalate. Some of our plans involve real violence. We'll threaten him. Break him."

"Now that you know what to do, my secretary Gupta from Indore will coordinate with you," said Shikhandi, signalling the end of the conversation.

Dubey took his leave and returned to his room. He poured himself a glass of fresh water and drank slowly. Then he turned to the window.

Outside, the vast ocean churned restlessly, waves crashing against the shore.

The shore always maintains a barrier against the mighty ocean, he thought. God is a protective barrier for certain destinies. These madmen want to breach that barrier. And now I've joined them. Will I succeed—or will I be swallowed?

He looked once more at the birth chart in his hand and whispered, "Sarma, who are you?"

After Dubey left, Dr Gottlieb also left the room. Vinay turned to Shikhandi, his expression laced with concern.

"What's wrong?" Shikhandi asked.

"We can't just parachute Dubey–a loudmouth from another state–into Sarma's inner circle."

"Why not? What are you getting at?"

"Have you forgotten? Sarma is now consulting for Chandra. And Chandra, as you well know, is the acting head of state intelligence."

"So?" Shikhandi said, unfazed.

Vinay leaned in. "What if Chandra starts digging into Dubey's background? If he connects the dots, we're finished. Also... we can't ignore Aghora."

Shikhandi's eyes narrowed. "What about him?"

"He's the one who warned Sarma about our poisoning attempt a year and a half ago, remember?" Vinay said, staring hard.

"Ah... now I see your point," Shikhandi murmured. "Both Chandra and Aghora are in Sarma's support circle. So, what do we do–destabilise them?"

"No," Vinay said quietly. "We may need to go further. What if we remove them entirely?"

"You mean... kill them?" Shikhandi asked. Then, after a brief pause, he added calmly, "Yes. We can arrange that."

"Chandra already has enemies. Some of them operate well outside the law. We just need to point the right group in his direction–and pay. They'll package the hit as something noble. Patriotism. Justice. Vengeance. Take your pick."

Shikhandi smirked. "India has no shortage of groups willing to justify violence in the name of ideals."

And just like that, the cold-blooded assassination of a senior law enforcement officer was being set in motion.

"We can use Dengrwn Hagrama to organise the hit," Shikhandi suggested.

"Hagrama? From the Bodo insurgency?" Vinay raised an eyebrow.

Dengrwn Hagrama—exiled, stateless, and volatile—had once been the fiery leader of a Bodo nationalist faction in Assam. Once a champion of Bodoland's independence, now a shadow on the run. But still very capable. Still dangerous.

"They're desperate for funding," said Shikhandi. "I've already been providing support. You'll meet him—tell him this comes directly from me. Don't negotiate. Don't ask questions. Pay whatever he asks."

Vinay nodded slowly. "He's efficient."

"He is," Shikhandi confirmed. "He'll keep it clean. And if he does it his way, the blowback will never touch us."

"And what about Aghora?" Shikhandi asked. "Dengrwn isn't the right person for that kind of hit."

"There are others," Vinay said. "India's full of hypocrites with blood on their hands—murderers dressed in saffron robes. I know one who moves around as a sadhu. He'll do it cleanly. I'll handle that from my side."

The private jet had earlier dropped off its two passengers—Mamadou and DeSantos—at their respective destinations. Vinay, however, had chosen to stay behind. He remained on

Shikhandi's private island, indulging in further discussions–and the extravagant hospitality Shikhandi was known for. Wine flowed freely, and beautiful women were never in short supply.

A few days later, the jet returned to the Bali Islands. Vinay was already waiting on the tarmac as the engines cooled and the cabin crew made preparations.

He stepped aboard.

The pilot turned to him and asked, "Where would you like to go, sir?"

Vinay answered without hesitation. "Kathmandu."

"To Nepal? Understood," the pilot replied with a crisp nod. "I'll initiate the clearance request with Tribhuvan International and file the flight plan now."

He moved swiftly toward the cockpit, already speaking into his headset as the cabin doors sealed shut behind them.

The jet began to hum with anticipation–ready to take Vinay deeper into the shadows of conspiracy.

Kathmandu, Nepal. It has long been a hotspot for clandestine meetings. Many insurgents and intelligence agents from India have operated out of Nepal due to the open border and weak enforcement. Dengrwn is living in Nepal under a fake identity using Nepal as a neutral ground.

A dimly lit teahouse in Patan, Kathmandu. Late evening. The air smells of smoke, damp earth, and betrayal.

The old copper bell above the door barely jingled as Vinay stepped into the teahouse. A lazy ceiling fan creaked above. Tourists had long disappeared from this part of town, replaced by men who spoke in low tones and always watched the door.

He spotted Dengrwn Hagrama at a corner table, sipping salt tea from a chipped ceramic cup, his eyes obscured by aviator glasses even in the dim light. Dressed in a faded military jacket over civilian clothes, he looked like a man between identities--part of revolutionary, part ghost.

Vinay sat opposite him without a word.

"Shikhandi asked me to speak to you," said Vinay.

"Yes. I got the word. Tell me what can I do for you?" asked Dengrwn.

Vinay smiled faintly. "A war of perception. And I need death to achieve it."

Dengrwn stirred his tea slowly. "And I suppose you came all this way because you've run out of mercenaries with good aim?"

"No," Vinay said, placing a brown envelope on the table. "I came to you because this death needs to be quiet. Political. Symbolic. And deniable."

Dengrwn didn't touch the envelope. "Name?"

"Chandra. Acting head of State Intelligence. Most probably you can catch him in Hyderabad."

That got Dengrwn's attention. He leaned back, whistling softly. "Big fish. Very big. Dangerous waters."

"Shikhandi told me that you were tired of being underfunded. This... could fund your resurrection."

Dengrwn raised an eyebrow. "You are not wrong. My men are gone. Dispersed, arrested, co-opted by ministers who used to curse my name. Bodoland is now a file on someone's dusty desk. But I haven't forgotten how to light fires."

"So light one," Vinay said, voice calm but pointed. "We are not asking for a war. Just one strike. Clean. Surgical."

Dengrwn finally reached for the envelope. He opened it, glanced at the contents--Cash.. Lots of it."

"I have no men in Hyderabad. No footprint. That city eats strangers."

"Shikhandi told me not to ask you how you will pull this. I am sure you will have a plan" said Vinay.

Dengrwn chuckled. "Hmm. I am thinking of a Marxist solution to a bureaucratic problem."

"What do you have in mind?" asked Vinay.

Dengwrn lit a cigarette and exhaled a long plume of smoke. "I know a man. Comrade Mahadev. Operates in the Telangana forest belt. Doesn't ask too many questions if the money flows."

"Good," Vinay said. "Then consider this a business transaction with a shared ideology."

Dengrwn smirked. "You don't have an ideology. You have spreadsheets."

"And you don't have men. You have memory. Let's not pretend either of us are heroes."

The two sat in silence, smoke curling between them. Outside, the street dogs began their nightly howling.

Then Dengrwn nodded once. “Fine. I will broker the kill. Give me a month. You will hear it in the news”.

And just like that the deal was made. One more member of the Mission Insiders is going to be eliminated.

10. PROOF OF CONCEPT

6 December 1992 – Ayodhya

"Babri Masjid came crashing down."

There were people everywhere. The mob had gone out of control. The government–and its entire law enforcement apparatus–had collectively failed.

"It's a success," said Shikhandi, calmly watching the news. "They managed to ignite the passions. How many of our Terminators were involved?"

Dr Reinshmidt glanced down at his notes. "Approximately forty. But we still need confirmation. They were embedded within a crowd of over three thousand. From the surface, the behaviour matched expectations. But I need blood samples to confirm."

Shikhandi turned to Vinay. "Have your men been deployed?"

"They're already there–running a mobile blood donation camp," said Vinay.

Shikhandi raised an eyebrow. "And how do you make the Terminators volunteer?"

Dr Gottlieb pulled the cigar from his mouth, his smile slow and unsettling. "These men believe they're heroes. It's easy to appeal to their better side. All we have to say is that their blood will save fellow warriors in a sacred cause."

Vinay, usually impenetrable, shifted uneasily in his seat. The manipulative glee in Gottlieb's voice unnerved even him.

"Fine," said Shikhandi. "Let's reconvene once the samples arrive."

Two days later.

They assembled again in the conference room.

"Is the blood analysis complete?" asked Shikhandi.

"It is," said Dr Reinshmidt. He removed his glasses, rubbing his temples. Something had clearly disturbed him. "We found something strange. A chemical I thought had disappeared from the human blood chain."

"What is it?" Shikhandi asked.

"A neurotoxin," said Reinshmidt. "A natural one–produced under very rare conditions. We've labelled it Adripoison."

"Adripoison?" Shikhandi's eyes gleamed. "Is it responsible for the violent behaviour?"

"Highly likely," said Reinshmidt. "It activates the reptilian brain. Reduces control. It strips away empathy and complex emotion—leaving only survival instincts and rage."

"Psychological, then?" asked Shikhandi, glancing at Gottlieb.

Gottlieb nodded. "If a man suppresses violent urges his entire life, Adripoison pulls the brakes off. Suddenly he acts on thoughts he once contained."

"So the person becomes capable of unspeakable acts?"

"That was the hypothesis," Gottlieb replied. "We expected some of our Terminators to be malignant psychopaths. But since we sourced microbiological material from ancient Egyptian mummies, we had no way of knowing their exact psychological profiles. We've been studying post-birth behaviour ever since."

"And Stephen?" asked Vinay. "The way he murdered Father Francis. Is that what you expected?"

"Exactly," said Gottlieb. "But that level of violence is rare. Even among our engineered specimens, we haven't seen anything quite like that. Until Ayodhya. This time, the nature of the mob violence—by police, politicians, and citizens—points to an active Adripoison signature."

Reinshmidt nodded. "And yet... it comes with complications."

"Such as?" asked Shikhandi.

"The effects are permanent," said Gottlieb. "The neural changes don't wear off. People act in ways they never imagined. And then... comes the guilt."

"Explain," said Shikhandi, now sitting forward.

Gottlieb's tone became clinical.

"There are three observed outcomes in subjects with sustained Adripoison exposure:

They internalise the guilt. It breaks them. They start believing they were always monsters.

They repeat the violent behaviour, believing it's their nature.

They descend into psychosis. Suicide. Or dissociative dementia. The brain, trying to erase the trauma, simply wipes the memory."

He continued, voice darker now. "Normally, people avoid evil through willpower. Conscience. Fear. But Adripoison hijacks that. Afterwards, the brain either justifies the act... or tries to destroy the memory of it."

Shikhandi leaned back slowly, exhaling. "Unbelievable. There's historical evidence for this compound?"

"There is," said Gottlieb.

Vinay turned to him. "How do you know about Adripoison?"

"My grandfather was a Nazi commander," said Dr Reinshmidt, staring into the distance. "He was executed at the Nuremberg Trials. But my grandmother... she told us stories."

"What kind of stories?" asked Vinay.

"She once told me about a general who served under Joan of Arc. Behind her victories stood this man–secretive, brilliant, and monstrous. After retiring, it was discovered he'd been torturing and killing children. They say he was experimenting–using concoctions, chemicals, alchemy. The villagers burned him alive like a witch."

"That's awful," Vinay muttered. Yet, even as he spoke, adrenaline surged through him at the sheer horror of it. Why does this disturb me and fascinate me at the same time? he wondered, unsettled by his own reaction. "Adripoison began during Joan of Arc's time?"

"Oh no," Reinshmidt continued. "Adripoison didn't begin with Joan of Arc's era. It goes much further back. Nature itself is cruel. Tigers eat their own cubs. So do lions. Ancient human tribes performed child sacrifices. Even Abraham tried to sacrifice his son, according to the scriptures. Some cultures consumed the brains of dead enemies–believing it would give them power."

Shikhandi leaned forward. "I didn't know any of this. It... connects a lot of dots."

"They danced in Adripoison rage," said Reinshmidt. "Temporarily insane, consumed by something primal. But as societies grew larger, more civilised, they began to reject the old rites–torturing children, aborting foetuses to extract Adripoison. The practices were nearly wiped out."

"Then how did that general behind Joan of Arc gain access to Adripoison?" asked Shikhandi.

"There was a bishop in the 6th century," said Dr Gottlieb, stepping in. "He discovered the knowledge on a remote island while preaching. He brought it back to Europe. But the after-effects were so horrific that the Church labelled it witchcraft. Anyone caught practising it was burned at the stake."

"Oh," said Shikhandi, piecing it together. "Is that why early Christians tortured witches? To stamp out Adripoison users?"

"Precisely," Gottlieb nodded. "But they never disclosed the true reason. Imagine the chaos if the masses knew you could make someone insanely violent using just a chemical compound. Every sociopath, narcissist, dictator, and lunatic with a God complex would try to find it."

Both Shikhandi and Vinay shifted uneasily. Gottlieb's words felt like a mirror–reflecting their own deepest motivations.

"So the witch hunts," Shikhandi said, "were partly because society couldn't stomach the cruelty behind Adripoison practices. But the real reason stayed hidden."

"Correct," said Gottlieb. "The Church forbids abortion even today for similar reasons–though no one speaks of it. During mediaeval times, some witches hunted aborted foetuses specifically for extracting Adripoison."

"There were families in France and Italy," added Reinshmidt. "My grandmother told me they perfected the craft. They became enormously wealthy, using the knowledge in secret. They used Adripoison to destroy rivals. To manipulate revolutions. She even said it was involved in the French Revolution."

"The French Revolution?" Vinay asked, surprised. "That was centuries ago."

"Exactly. The mind-controlling properties of Adripoison have been known for millennia. But the formulas were guarded by select families. It's forbidden knowledge."

Shikhandi's eyes narrowed. "How did the Nazis discover it?"

"They found traces of it during the Holocaust," said Reinshmidt. "An old family was imprisoned. Among them was a priest from a chapel in Yugoslavia. The recipe for Adripoison had been passed through his family for generations. But the priest had renounced the violence. He became a monk."

"And the Nazis found him?" asked Vinay.

"My grandfather was part of the team sent to capture him. That's how he learned of it. The priest... killed himself before they could extract the knowledge. He burned the manuscript too. But the fire only destroyed part of it. They managed to save a sheet–one that listed ingredients for a type of Adripoison that could turn crowds into frenzied mobs. But the actual formula was half-burnt."

"What did they do?" Vinay asked, unable to hide his curiosity.

"Himmler ordered doctors to experiment on prisoners–to rediscover the full formula. They tortured thousands. Many died in agony. Eventually, they found one that worked."

"And then?" Vinay leaned in.

"The Nazis sent the formula to Japan. The Japanese refined it. They tested different variants on Allied prisoners. Then they administered it to their own soldiers."

"And the results?" Vinay asked, already knowing the answer.

"The soldiers became terrifyingly violent," said Reinschmidt. "Unstoppable. And eventually... suicidal."

"Oh," Vinay breathed. "That explains the Kamikaze pilots..."

"Yes... And after the Allied forces captured Nazi scientists, the secret of manufacturing Adripoison reached other European powers," said Dr Reinschmidt.

"You know," added Dr Gottlieb, "there were certain mafia-military groups–soldiers without allegiance–who operated outside the official command structures. They joined the war for loot, not loyalty. And some of them got their hands on Adripoison. You'll be shocked by what they did with it."

"What did they do?" asked Vinay.

"They gave the drug to Mahatma Gandhi," Gottlieb said flatly. "And it made him... erratic. Many of his followers were confused. Some abandoned him."

"Those wicked bastards..." Shikhandi grinned. He wasn't horrified–he was amused. "Why target Gandhi?"

"They had two objectives," Gottlieb explained. "One, they wanted to test how effective Adripoison was. Gandhi, a man who preached non-violence–what better test subject to see if a chemical could push even him towards rage? Two, they wanted to destabilise him politically."

Dr Reinshmidt nodded. "Someone at the top wanted to divide India. To create a garrison state–a military-controlled buffer against the rising threat of the USSR. Destabilising Gandhi would help shift the narrative. Make him look weak. Mad. Eccentric."

"A garrison state... you mean a country run by military power?" asked Shikhandi.

Vinay leaned forward. "You're saying... Pakistan?"

"Correct," said Gottlieb. "Pakistan wasn't created to serve the genuine interests of Muslims. That's just the mask. The real motive was geopolitical. A military-controlled entity that could be used to manipulate South Asia."

Vinay chuckled. "Haathi ke daant dikhane ke aur, khane ke aur. Like an elephant–one set of tusks to show, another to use."

"Exactly," said Gottlieb. "That's why Pakistan, despite being born alongside India, has spent most of its existence under military rule."

Vinay shrugged. "Military regimes are easier to deal with. Dictators are useful. You can sell wicked plans to them–democracies require too much convincing."

"So," asked Shikhandi, "did Adripoison turn Gandhi violent?"

"No," said Gottlieb, "but it broke him in other ways. The poison stirred his repressed desires. He became... erotically unstable. Depressed. Paranoid. This happened in the 1940s."

"They saw potential in that," said Dr Reinshmidt. "Even though he didn't turn violent, they realised they could still use the drug to tarnish his image. They recorded his erratic behaviour. His inability to control his thoughts. Then they fed that narrative to his followers. They didn't know he was drugged–they thought he'd lost his way. And many abandoned him."

"But Gandhi wasn't stupid," Gottlieb added. "He knew something was wrong. British allies–who still respected his vision–quietly warned him about the Adripoison. Told him rogue military operatives, still aligned with Nazi ideologies, might be poisoning him. But they begged him to keep it secret. If he spoke out, his friends within the Raj would be implicated."

"He suffered because of that silence," said Reinshmidt.

"Those wicked bastards..." Shikhandi muttered again, but this time it was laced with pleasure, not pity.

"Later, they ran a full-scale trial in Calcutta," Gottlieb continued. "They laced water supplies with microdoses. The result was mass frenzy. Hindus and Muslims turned on each other like animals. The streets were soaked in blood. That became the Great Calcutta Killings."

Vinay's face darkened. "So they triggered Partition?"

"They helped accelerate it," said Gottlieb. "The violence made Partition seem inevitable. The poison worked. Ayodhya, just last week... it's the same model."

He paused, letting the silence weigh in.

"The formula for mob control–how to ignite collective rage–was perfected by the Nazis. But I don't believe they were the first. It was used during the French Revolution. It just disappeared for a while... until the Nazis revived it."

Vinay's voice was now reverent. "So... Adripoison is the secret behind some of the most catastrophic events in modern history?"

"It's darker than you think," said Dr Gottlieb, his voice dropping. "It involves the torture of children, adolescents, young women... even the forced abortion of foetuses."

He paused.

"In this century alone, we've seen scandal after scandal involving child abuse in Christian churches–not because of faith, but because Church priests were being targeted. The real goal? Perfecting mind control through these horrific experiments."

"Why Church priests?" asked Vinay, genuinely puzzled.

"They were replicating a prototype," said Gottlieb. "An earlier success they achieved when experimenting on someone with immense spiritual power. They called it the MK trial."

"MK?" Vinay frowned.

"Mohandas Karamchand," Gottlieb clarified. "Gandhi. They used Adripoison on him. He was revered, disciplined, and deeply spiritual. The test was simple–break him, and you can break anyone. And they succeeded. Not by making him violent–but by making him vulnerable. Erratic. Even erotic."

Vinay flinched at the word.

"They fed those moments to his followers. Subtly. Quietly. Doubt is a virus–it spreads faster than any bullet. Once his followers started questioning him, Partition became inevitable."

"And the same was done to the Church?" Shikhandi asked, eyes narrowing.

"Yes," said Gottlieb. "The same model. Take a symbol of spiritual power–poison it from within. Shatter public trust. Collapse the institution."

"But why haven't we heard of any of this?" Shikhandi asked.

"Because you're in the private sector," said Dr Reinshmidt, stepping in. "Adripoison is one of the world's best-kept secrets. Only a handful of state-level actors even know it exists. And even fewer understand it. The real puppeteers–those who operate inside governments–have used it for decades."

He leaned closer.

"Ever wonder why schools keep getting targeted in mass shootings? Why it's always children? The most emotionally vulnerable? It's not random. It's proof of concept. The experiments are ongoing."

Shikhandi exhaled sharply. "So that explains those school shootings... They're not just acts of madness."

"They're engineered," Reinshmidt said. "Engineered to watch how trauma activates patterns in the brain. Adripoison is not like any drug you've seen. It's not purely synthetic. It's triggered. The human body produces it–but only under conditions of extreme trauma. That's what makes it so hard to control."

"Can we recreate it in our lab?" asked Shikhandi, his voice hushed with greed.

"Not exactly," said Reinshmidt. "It's possible–but convoluted. There's a scientist in Germany. He's been working on synthesising it. Quietly. Illegally. His entire team are closet Nazis–true believers."

"Perfect," Shikhandi said, eyes glittering. "Let's hire them."

"We can't bring them here," said Reinshmidt. "They're under surveillance. German regulators suspect something. If they're exposed, the lab will be shut down overnight. We can't move them. They must operate from their own facility. And they'll be... expensive."

"Money isn't a problem," said Shikhandi. "If we control Adripoison, we'll make more money than entire pharmaceutical giants. You both go to Germany. Secure them. I'll have Finance clear a black budget immediately. Make this a top priority."

Reinshmidt nodded. "We'll fly to Berlin. If we pay them well, they might even prepare a small test batch for us."

"Excellent," said Shikhandi, standing up. "Secure the Adripoison. Test it on one of our Terminators. Meanwhile, I'll alert our contact in the Middle East and propose a proof of concept."

He smiled darkly.

"The profit margins could be extraordinary."

"I've got a better idea," said Vinay. "Why don't we try it on Sarma?"

The suggestion landed like a punch–laced with amusement and old resentment.

Shikhandi raised an eyebrow. “I like that. Let’s use Dubey to deliver it.”

But then his expression shifted, turning contemplative. “Wait... Dubey predicted that Sarma would earn at least a hundred million dollars by 2005–and become one of the world’s richest men by 2020.”

Vinay blinked. “Dubey said that? Then it’s bound to happen. So, we steal it. We steal Sarma’s destiny.”

“How?” Shikhandi asked.

“I’ve got a plan,” Vinay replied. “No matter how much we try to trip him up, Sarma keeps moving towards his fate. So let him. But only we understand his true potential. We’ll gaslight him. Erect a wall around him, make sure no one else sees what he’s really capable of.”

“Oh–like when we used his own relatives to drug him, so that even those who cared about him started to doubt him?” Shikhandi asked.

“Similar idea, but this time we go further. He’s grown up now. If he’s going to become a billionaire, he’ll need to put his talents to work. We know he’s a tech genius. Let him build. Let him write code. And just before he goes public–we strike. Steal his work. Meanwhile, we spread the idea that he’s incompetent, mentally unwell.”

Vinay’s voice lowered.

“And if we can slip in a microdose of Adripoison? That would be the final blow. He might descend into sexual obsession–just like MK, or those church priests. He won’t become violent, but lust will consume him. We trigger a scandal. Use the moment to utterly ruin him."

Shikhandi grinned. "Brilliant. We'll leave him poor while we take everything. Let's see if Dubey's golden prophecy survives that."

Shikhandi picked up the intercom and instructed his secretary, "Call Dubey. Ask him to come in."

With that, the atmosphere in the room shifted. Business resumed.

Shikhandi turned to Vinay. "Shall we talk business?"

"Of course."

"You're brilliant with your sales pitch. Tell me–how do we market our Killer Terminator services? We need to monetise this. Let's discuss the terms."

The two men delved into a long and intense conversation, weighing strategies to pitch and deploy their Terminator programme to high-value clients. After a while, Vinay leaned back and said, "It's a deal."

"I'm glad we've reached an agreement," Shikhandi said, smiling. "A win-win. We'll make a fortune. So, what's next?"

"I've got just the man. Let's send Sulfikar to Lebanon to pitch the proof of concept."

"Sulfikar–excellent choice. But where is he now?" Shikhandi asked.

"He's in Hyderabad. One of his tasks is to track Sarma. He's also keeping tabs on our operations in the Middle East."

"Does Sulfikar know he's one of our Terminators? One of the original million?"

"No... I doubt it. He's driven by money. I pay him handsomely," said Vinay. Then, raising an eyebrow, he added, "Did you say the initial one million? Are there more now?"

"After the original German experiment, we've replicated the model. These days, we've deployed anywhere between ten thousand to a million Terminators in each country."

"How many countries?"

"144," Shikhandi replied flatly. "Send Sulfikar to Lebanon. Keep me updated."

Just then, Dubey entered the meeting room.

"Dubey," Vinay said casually, "take Vanaja with you. Introduce her to Sarma—as your wife."

Dubey frowned. "But... Vanaja isn't my wife."

"We know," Shikhandi interjected smoothly. "She's your mistress, isn't she?"

Dubey's face flushed with embarrassment. "How do you know that?"

Vinay chuckled. "You really think we'd let someone into our world without knowing everything about them?"

Dubey fell silent. He was married—but yes, he had others. Vanaja was the closest thing to love he'd allowed himself. Beautiful. Obedient. Or so he believed.

“Don’t be so tense,” Shikhandi said, his tone disarmingly smooth. “What you consider shameful is perfectly routine here. We’re all carved from the same divine sin.”

He paused, then smiled wickedly. “By the way–Vanaja sleeps around when you’re not watching. She doesn’t trust you. Mistress or not, she’s hedging her bets.”

Dubey froze. Fury surged in his chest. “After all I’ve done for her... the money, the care... pulling her out of the gutter... And that ungrateful–"

“Don’t even think about hurting her,” Shikhandi said coolly, as if reading his mind. “She’s far too valuable to us. Think of her as a toy. Use her for pleasure–never for attachment. Some women aren’t worth a single drop of emotion.”

He leaned back in his chair, eyes glittering. “Vanaja is a seductress. Present her to Sarma as your wife. Let’s see how he responds to her... charms.”

"What news do we have from Ayodhya?" Lucian’s voice came through the two-way radio.

"Father, it’s a success," Batsinger replied. "You were right. The terminators turned within twelve hours after we delivered the BATglue. We conducted a sampling–these machines now carry a sub-program in their neural networks. We can take control of them whenever we wish."

Lucian’s voice crackled back. "Excellent. We can now turn our competitors’ genetically modified zombies into our BAPS.

Time to offer proof of concept to the paymasters. This will bring a windfall–on both ends."

Aiwag furrowed his brow. "Both ends?"

The Accountant interjected, his tone measured. "Our competitors have grand plans for their terminators. If they unleash chaos, we offer our services to restore order. Simple enough, since we now hold the switch that can turn their machines on or off at will. If they ignite the world, we profit from putting out the fire. If they extinguish the fire, we ignite a new one–either way, we win."

He paused, a knowing smirk curling at the edge of his lips. "But knowing how the world's elite operate, no one will be interested in peace. They will all be in the business of lighting fires. Which means, gentlemen, we'll be making money by putting them out."

Lucian's voice remained calm. "Aiwag... Have you switched the blood samples?"

"We did, Father. But why did you want us to mix them with Adripoison?"

Lucian exhaled, as if explaining a simple truth. "Because Adripoison's existence is well-documented. Governments, mafias–they all know about it. If they find traces of Adripoison in their terminators' blood, they will assume that's what caused the behavioral shift. A convenient red herring."

Aiwag hesitated. "But... it's obtained by harming innocents," he said, his voice unsteady.

Lucian's tone sharpened. "Precisely. Our competitors operate like a private mafia. The question is–will they take the bait? Will they resort to harming innocents to source Adripoison, like certain government figures do? Or will they back off?"

The Accountant leaned in. "If they do cross that line, we have recruitment opportunities. Some people never wake up until they're betrayed by the very ones they trust most."

Batsinger cleared his throat. "Father, I have two other pieces of news."

"Go on."

"Shikandi developed a signature drug that bears his name," said Aiwag. "It confuses the gender identity of children."

"What does he want to do with it?"

"It seems they want to use it against the children of the parents who work for Government deep state. He wants to introduce grief into the parents' mind to destabilize them." Aiwag said.

"It is because he saw the pain his parents went through when he outed himself. He liked that pain. It gave him power over them. So, he is now weaponizing it" Aiwag said.

"But our BAT can easily confuse children. All that we need is to copy paste a gender activity of a boy's brain into a girl's and vice versa. We don't need any drug to do that," Batsinger said.

Lucian immediately cut him. "We do not do such things. Leave out that disgusting idea." Lucian said "and what is the other news?"

"DeSantos and Mamadou have both traveled to Bali. They're at Shikhandi's lab."

Lucian's response was immediate. "Who reported this?"

"Our source inside the lab."

Lucian nodded. "Then it's reliable information. Any idea what DeSantos is after?"

Batsinger's fists clenched. His eyes darkened. "He wants a drug that destroys a fetus in the womb–one that causes severe disabilities at birth."

A stunned silence followed.

The Accountant was the first to speak. "Those bastards... What wicked plans are they cooking now? Why would they want anyone to give birth to an unhealthy child?"

Batsinger's voice was tight with barely restrained fury. "DeSantos works for the drug mafia. Their targets are immigrants–Mexicans, Third World workers–maids, nurses, household staff."

Lucian's voice cut through. "Diabolical minds... They want to create dependency."

Batsinger nodded. "Correct, Father. Our source overheard DeSantos explaining it to Shikhandi. The plan is simple: poison the unborn child. The moment the baby is born with disabilities, the family's life is upended. They will need full-time care–nurses, housemaids, support staff. That's where the cartel steps in. They will place their own people inside those families. Once inside, they will have access to the personal lives of the rising elite. CEOs, future political leaders–people climbing the power ladder. Their goal is to infiltrate and control from within."

Lucian let out a long, calculated breath. "Hmm..."

Aiwag frowned. "But why drug the mother? Why not just bribe the hospital staff? A corrupt doctor could easily botch the delivery and cause a deformity."

The Accountant shook his head. "That would be reckless. A surgical error could trigger an investigation–a lawsuit. Insurance companies would get involved. No, no... they need something discreet. A lab-engineered solution. That's why they went to Shikhandi."

Lucian's voice came back, resolute. "Keep a close watch on this drug. Have our source compile a list of parents who will receive it. We might be able to piggyback on the cartel's operation."

"Understood, Father," Batsinger replied.

Lucian shifted gears. "And Mamadou? Why is he at Shikhandi's lab?"

Batsinger's lips curled slightly. "His boss, the great dictator, is complaining about aging. He wants to stay young."

Lucian exhaled sharply. "So, he's there for the Yaayati Serum?"

A wry chuckle came from the Accountant. "Fools chasing eternity."

The Yaayati Serum–named after a king from the Mahabharata who refused to grow old, taking his son's youth to prolong his own life. Shikhandi's lab had developed a similar formula, a drug capable of slowing aging and extending youth unnaturally.

"Yes, Father," Batsinger confirmed. "Mamadou is there to buy the serum for his dictator."

The Accountant sighed, shaking his head. "Stupid people with stupid desires. Human life moves like the seasons–lush in spring, bare in winter. There is grace in accepting the passage of time. Trees shed their leaves without protest, yet men... they scheme to outwit nature. Why tamper with God's design?"

Lucian was unfazed. "Keep an eye on the dictator. Also– where are we in replicating the Yaayati Serum?"

Batsinger's expression turned serious. "We're developing something better. A superior version, one that works with BAT-induced wellness thoughts rather than chemicals. However, the project stalled when Fred fell into a coma."

"And now?"

"We're back on it. I'm working with our lab scientists to perfect the formula."

Lucian's voice was pleased. "Excellent. I will inform the Board. There are billionaires out there, desperate to become modern-day Yaayatis. They will pay anything for it."

The room filled with knowing smiles.

"Anything else before we close our meeting?" asked Lucian.

"Father. I have something regarding the proposed Proof of Concept," said Aiwag. "Our source from Shikhandi's lab told us that they are about to send someone to Lebanon to sell their proof-of-concept. They want to sell Terminator services. They want to drug their terminators with Adriposion."

"Who are they sending?"

"Someone called Sulfikar," said Aiwag.

"Sulfikar? Is he not one on their terminators list?" asked Lucian.

"Yes Father, I cross verified his entry from the Terminators list." saying that Aiwag pushed a piece of paper towards the Accountant. Accountant looked at the paper and said "Unbelievable".

"What is unbelievable? What happened?" asked Lucian over the two- way radio.

"The random number associated with Sulfikar in the Terminators list" said the Accountant.

Aiwag pulled the paper towards him and looked at it. It was written Random number: 1318666 Name: Sulfikar. "What about this number? I did not understand" said Aiwag, a bit confused.

Batsinger took the paper from Aiwag's hand. And said out loud "Book of Revelation 13:18 The new testament."

"This calls for wisdom: let the one who has understanding calculate the number of the beast, for it is the number of a man, and his number is 666." said Accountant.

"So 1318666 is the number of the beast?" asked Lucian. "How coincidental... He is on their terminators list but he is also under our BAPS list. He must be a beast. Where is he now?"

"In Hyderabad," said Aiwag. "But because we pulled all our Human resources out of India we only have satellites tracking."

"If Shikhandi is sending his person to sell their proof-of-concept then let us shadow them. Let them sell. We will offer support services. If things go bad, we have our hands clean," suggested Lucian.

Those words gave great relief to Aiwag. He does not want to directly confront Israel or the USA. It is like standing in front of a hornet's nest and throwing a stone at them. They will be merciless in their response. "Great ideas, Father. We will shadow Sulfikar and report to you," said Aiwag.

"We will chip in and sell our services when necessary to Shikhandi. We already have our hands full in planning Balkans and African conflicts. I believe we get our hands-on good money with these two conflicts at hand. Is my assumption correct, Accountant?" asked Lucian.

"Correct, Father. We can keep the Middle East as option three. It is a good idea for Shikhandi to develop his sales pitch. We can easily piggyback on their work." said Account.

"Perfect. Anything else?" asked Lucian. Nobody replied.

The two-way radio crackled, signalling that Lucian had ended the conversation.

11. KAALA SARPA

Mid-December 1992, Hyderabad, India.

Time...

In Sanskrit, it's called Kāla. A force so immense, so unforgiving, that when it turns against you, it strikes with the venom of a cobra. Hindus believe that even the mighty celestial beings—the SUN and the MOON—are not immune. During solar and lunar eclipses, great serpents, Raahu and Ketu, are said to devour them. But the power of the Sun and the Moon is such that no dark force can contain them for long. The serpents are forced to spit them out, defeated by divine radiance.

Just as the cosmos gets swallowed and released in cycles, so too do humans fall prey to the great serpent of Time. We are but marionettes, dancing on invisible strings in the hands of fate.

Escape? Illusion. According to Jyotisha–the ancient Hindu science of astrology–every single human being must face the bite of Kaal Sarpa, the venomous snake of Time. It's not a question of if, but when.

But there's a purpose to everything–every strike, every sting. Even the most terrifying of creatures, like the Black Mamba or the King Cobra, are not without reason. No creation of God is without value. The truth is, we simply do not understand their design. Suppose, for a moment, that all things are manifestations of Conscious Intergalactic Entities. Then the Black Mamba is no mere snake–it is an incarnated burst of hatred-energy, a KIE in serpentine form. The King Cobra doesn't kill indiscriminately–it strikes only the one it is destined to take down. When Time chooses to bite, there is no antidote. No sanctuary. No saviour.

The air is crisp. There's a certain romance in the cold, especially when it's met with a steaming hot cup of Irani Chai–the pride of Hyderabad. For Sarma, that cup is more than tea. It's one of the few luxuries he allows himself, given the meagre cash he has in hand. Chandra had offered financial help, but Sarma had politely refused. He doesn't take well to charity. Life taught him early: those who give freely often take something far more precious in return–dignity. He doesn't bear grudges. But he's developed a protective shield–suspicion. Especially when the word "free" is involved.

He sits quietly in a near-empty Irani café, sipping slowly. It's early morning–the world is just beginning to wake up.

"Namaste..."

A voice breaks the stillness. Sarma looks up. A medium-built man stands before him, thick hair, a Hitler-style moustache, dressed in a kurta and pyjama. He radiates the aura of an astrologer.

"Namaste," Sarma responds, cautiously warm.

"I'm Kuladarshi Dubey," the man introduces himself.

"May I?" he gestures toward the empty chair across from Sarma.

"Please do," Sarma nods.

"I go by Dubey," he adds, settling in.

"You're new here, aren't you?" Sarma asks, studying him.

"What gave me away?"

"In this part of the world, people don't ask before taking a seat. They just claim it like territory. You asked. That was your mistake." Sarma chuckled.

Dubey smiled, "I'm an astrologer."

"I figured," Sarma said, eyeing the man's attire.

"My outfit gave me away?"

"Absolutely."

"What do you practise? Palmistry? Astrology?" Sarma asked, raising an eyebrow.

"All," Dubey replied, leaning forward. "Let me see your palms."

Sarma extended his hands, curious to know what Dubey would say about his fate.

"You have the letter W on your right palm," Dubey observed, tracing a shape with his finger. "See here? It's quite distinct."

"I do see it," Sarma said, peering at his hand. "What does it mean?"

"It means you're a Watcher," Dubey said, his tone suddenly reverent. "One who observes God's creation, guarding it in silence. Nothing escapes your gaze."

Sarma chuckled and tilted his palm slightly. "Or maybe it's an M."

Dubey's eyes lit up. "In that case, you're a Messiah. You've come to guide the lost–someone who shows the way when all seems dark."

Then, he added, "Put both your palms together, like you're praying in an Islamic way."

Sarma brought his hands together in prayer.

Dubey leaned closer. "Look here," he said, pointing. "These lines curve into a perfect crescent. A half-moon."

Sarma studied them, bemused.

"This moon," Dubey continued, "symbolises your power in prayer. You carry a special antenna in your hands."

"A special antenna?" Sarma echoed.

"Yes. Whatever you pray for–God hears it."

Sarma fell quiet. A pang shot through his heart at the mention of answered prayers. If only that were true... He thought of Kamala. Of wishes whispered in the dark. So many of them unanswered.

He sighed. As a priest, he knew the divine clock didn't follow human time. Still... I keep praying. Waiting. I just hope He doesn't answer too late.

Dubey noticed Sarma's sudden silence. "What is it?" he asked. "You don't believe me?"

Sarma blinked, returning to the moment. Then smiled gently. "No, nothing like that."

"I was researching old palm leaves. There, I found something interesting written about the W or M sign in the right palm of a man" Sarma said.

Dubey leaned forward curiously, "What was written in the palm leaves?"

"It was written that when you look at the right palm it appears like M to yourself. It is not M. But a divine bird Garuda--an Eagle in flight." Sarma said.

"I did not know that. But it is so interesting" Dubey replied. "Garuda is the vehicle of God Narayana. The protector and sustainer of life."

"It is known as Vihanga Yogam. The body in my right hand is formed like an eye. It means, you are right, nothing escapes the person's gaze" Sarma said.

"Then I have to be careful when I am in your presence," Dubey teased.

The conversation flowed. They dove into Jyotisha, planetary positions, karmic debt. Dubey was surprised–Sarma wasn't just well-read; he had depth. Sarma, meanwhile, found himself surprisingly at ease.

"Do you come here often?" Dubey asked casually.

"I study at a nearby computer institute. This is the closest place to get decent tea."

After ten minutes, Sarma stood up to leave. They exchanged nods. Sarma walked off toward the institute.

As soon as he was gone, Dubey stepped outside and headed to a nearby public phone booth. He dialled a number.

"Hello Gupta, I made contact with Sarma," he said, lowering his voice.

"Hold on," came the reply. "Shikhandi is in Indore. He wants to speak to you."

A few clicks. The line shifted.

"Dubey!" Shikhandi's voice crackled through. "So you made contact?"

"I did. I'm honestly impressed by Sarma's knowledge–especially in spiritual sciences."

"Don't get sentimental," Shikhandi snapped. "You're not there to admire him. You're my employee. Kill your conscience."

The words hit hard. Dubey felt the sting of humiliation but swallowed it.

"I remember," he said, his voice quieter than he expected.

"Where are you staying?"

"At Nawab's farmhouse. Vinay arranged it."

"Good. That farmhouse may change hands soon. Nawab owes us money. We are going to ask the Nawab to give it to someone as a payment. But you can continue staying. We will tell your new owner that you will continue to stay." Shikhandi said.

"Alright"

"We're sending you the Adripoison ampoules. A contact from Berlin—someone embedded in a Hyderabad-based pharmaceutical firm—is flying in. He lands this evening. Head there tomorrow and collect the package. Gupta will give you the exact address."

Dubey hesitated. "It won't kill Sarma, right? I'm not looking to rot in jail."

"Relax. It's non-lethal. But it will alter his behaviour. He'll become erratic. That's exactly what we want. You know the plan—Vanaja will handle the next step."

Dr. Gottlieb wanted a real-world test: to see how a pacifist priest reacts under the influence of a behavioural-altering substance. Vanaja's job was to get close enough to Sarma to observe and report.

"Alright," Dubey said. "I'll collect the drug."

"If you need anything, Gupta is your contact. Don't mess this up." With that, Shikhandi hung up.

Dubey stood for a moment, phone dangling. His thoughts churned.

Back at the institute, Sarma walked quietly, mind abuzz. Dubey intrigued him—not just as a person but as a resource.

What if I write a program in C to generate astrological charts? he wondered. The idea struck like lightning. Maybe this meeting wasn't just random. Maybe it was Kāla's bite—sharp, sudden, and strangely synchronised.

He smiled. He needed to talk to Dubey again.

The next day onwards Sarma and Dubey landed up in many more discussions. Sarma started writing the C program, while Dubey is entertaining Sarma's company but secretly plotting on how to deliver the Adripoison to Sarma.

One day, Dubey leaned forward during their usual chai conversation and asked casually,

"Sarma, are you a practicing priest?"

The question hung in the air.

Sarma hesitated. He seldom told people he was a priest—seldom. And he had his reasons.

In Hindu dharma, there are three types of priests—each with a distinct role and tradition.

First, there's the Āśrita Purohita. These priests are attached to specific families. They handle all the family's religious ceremonies, guiding them through rituals, life events, and spiritual duties. Their loyalty is exclusive—they serve only those families and no one else.

Then there's the Grāma Purohita, the temple priests. They don't visit homes or perform domestic rituals. Their duties are bound to the temple premises. Their livelihood is taken care of by the temple trust or community donations.

But then... there is a rare, almost forgotten kind: the Rāja Purohita.

Unlike the others, a Rāja Purohita is not tied to a salary, a temple, or a patron family. In the old days, kings would identify great scholars, sages with deep spiritual insight and learning, and bestow upon them wealth, land, and titles. These Purohitas were expected to serve any citizen—rich or poor—who came seeking help. And they were to do so without expectation of reward.

Sarma was a Rāja Purohita—but without a kingdom to support him. He had no lands, no ancestral wealth, no royal treasury to fall back on. Just his learning, his convictions, and a vow to serve.

And that vow had a cost.

Sometimes, poor families approached him for help—for rituals, for last rites, for ceremonies. Sarma couldn't turn them away. His dharma wouldn't allow it. But the expenses had to come from his own pocket: travel, materials, offerings. There were times when performing a ritual meant skipping a meal or borrowing money just to buy the bare essentials for the puja.

That's why he kept his priesthood private. Not out of shame, but out of necessity. If people knew, they might call upon him—not out of respect, but out of convenience. And offer him a token, a pittance, not realising the weight of what he was doing, or what it cost him.

So when Dubey asked, Sarma simply smiled and replied,

"I study spiritual sciences. I help when I can."

"My wife Vanaja has a Kāla Sarpa Doṣa. Can you come to my home and perform the ritual?" Dubey asked.

Kāla Sarpa Doṣa is a planetary alignment in Hindu astrology where all seven major planets fall between Rahu and Ketu. It is believed to trigger karmic blockages, delays, and emotional turmoil. Special rituals are performed to appease these shadow planets and alleviate the spiritual and material hardships they cause.

Sarma hesitated. He never liked accepting priestly requests, especially when they clashed with his routine.

"I'll pay you well for your services," Dubey continued. "We live on the outskirts of Hyderabad, in a farmhouse." Dubey shared the address.

"But it's too far," Sarma replied honestly. "I have my computer classes in the morning and a job in the evening. I hardly get any time."

"I understand," said Dubey. "But it's mid-December. Everyone gets a few holidays this time of year. How about this weekend? You can stay the night with us."

Sarma couldn't argue. Dubey had a point.

"I'll make the necessary arrangements," Dubey added before taking his leave.

Sarma sighed. He had no choice now.

That weekend, as agreed, Sarma arrived at the farmhouse. Dubey welcomed him warmly.

"This is a nice place you're staying at," Sarma complimented.

"Oh, it's a rental. We're from North India, so we rented this from a Nawab of Hyderabad. He owns the farmhouse. We've taken a portion of the outhouse on lease," Dubey explained.

There are many landlords in this region who follow the Islamic faith, so the fact that Dubey was staying at a property owned by a Muslim didn't come as a surprise to Sarma.

"Please come in..." Dubey said, ushering Sarma inside.

There stood a lady–draped in a pure white saree with golden edges, a bright red tilak on her forehead, and a delicate garland of mogra flowers tucked into her long, dark hair. She wore traditional ornaments and had covered part of her hair with the edge of her saree, in the classic style of a devoted, traditional Hindu wife. A sweet, intoxicating perfume wafted from her presence and lingered in the air, reaching Sarma's nostrils and making him feel momentarily light-headed.

Vanaja had clearly taken great care in her appearance. It was obvious she had spent at least an hour making herself look graceful and presentable.

Sarma, however, didn't dwell on her beauty. One thing he always observed as a priest was strict adherence to the ancestral codes of conduct. There were rules–definite dos and don'ts–especially when it came to women.

"Sarma, please meet my wife, Vanaja," said Dubey.

But what Dubey didn't realise was that when Sarma enters his priestly mode, he shifts into another dimension of perception. His senses become finely attuned–not just to the physical world, but to the divine, to truth, and to subtle vibrations. In that state, it becomes incredibly difficult for anyone to hide deception from him.

As Dubey introduced Vanaja as his wife, Sarma noticed something–an almost imperceptible change in Dubey's tone. There was a faint hesitation, a slight modulation in his voice. Dubey rubbed his nose and his eyes twitched rapidly.

In ancient India, telling a lie was considered a serious transgression–punishable by the symbolic (and sometimes literal) cutting off of one's nose. That's precisely what happened to the demoness Surpanakha. She had lusted after Rama and approached him, begging him to marry her. Rama, loyal to his wife Sita, refused and redirected her to his brother Lakshman. But Lakshman saw through her deception. He knew Rama was her first choice, and that her approach to him was driven by lust, not love. Her lie, her transgression, was punished: Lakshman sliced off her nose, a symbolic disfigurement for dishonesty.

Since those ancient times, human conscience–timeless, eternal, and beyond the bounds of linear perception–has clung to a primal association. Even today, those who lie often, perhaps unknowingly, touch or rub their noses. It is a vestigial cue, buried deep in the collective memory of humankind, a relic from a distant past.

Dubey had done just that. As he introduced Vanaja, his fingers brushed against his nose–subtly, almost imperceptibly.

That was enough for Sarma. He knew Dubey was lying.

'But why?' Sarma wondered. 'Why would this man lie to me? Is she not his wife? Perhaps she's a mistress... or a second wife...'

Every human being is unique. Who Vanaja was to Dubey—wife, lover, companion—was entirely his business. After all, Hinduism has, at various times, allowed for polygamy. Whatever arrangement they shared, it wasn't Sarma's place to question it. He was here to perform his priestly duties, not to pass judgment.

Sarma nodded politely and greeted Vanaja. "Hello."

"Please come in. I'll show you the puja place," Vanaja said.

Sarma set up the altar required for the puja and havan. As was his custom, he preferred to explain the meaning of the ritual to those present.

"For us Hindus, every being is potentially divine," Sarma began. "The Vedas say: 'Mother is God, Father is God, Teacher is God, and Guest is God.' Do you know why that is?"

Dubey, momentarily forgetting the dark purpose of his visit, found himself genuinely curious. "Why?"

"The Sanskrit word deva is usually translated as 'God,' but its deeper meaning is often missed. Have you heard of Yaskacharya?" Sarma asked.

"No," Dubey admitted.

"The Vedas come with their own dictionary to prevent misinterpretation of their terms. This is called Nirukta. It's one of the six limbs—shadanga—of Vedic knowledge."

"I see... The Jyotisha I practice, which is astrology, that's one of the six limbs, isn't it?" Dubey asked.

"Not entirely correct—but that's a longer debate," Sarma replied gently. "The Jyotisha we practice today in India draws more from Buddhist traditions than from the original Vedic framework. But yes, technically speaking, Jyotisha is one of the six limbs."

"So, who is Yaskacharya?" Dubey asked.

"He was one of the great sages, who lived thousands of years ago. He compiled the Nirukta."

"So I suppose he said something about deva?"

"Exactly," Sarma nodded. "According to the Nirukta, deva means one who gives, one who governs, and one who guides. A mother gives her body and risks her life to give birth–that's why she is considered a goddess. A father provides and protects, steering us away from danger and ignorance–that's why he is divine. A teacher imparts knowledge and shows us the way–that's why we say the teacher is God."

"Adoration, or puja, in Hindu dharma is incredibly intuitive," Sarma continued. "Say you want to invite your teacher home. What would you do?"

Vanaja, now fully engaged, responded, "We call him to our home."

"Exactly," Sarma said. "But even before that–you must know who your teacher is."

"Correct..." she nodded.

"Knowing is the first step in a Hindu puja. We call it dhyanam–contemplation, visualization. Once you know, you invite them. That's avaahanam. Second step in Puja. Then you offer a seat–aasanam. Third step. You speak kindly to them, praise them–that's the recitation of the 108 names. You offer food–nivedyam. In total, there are sixteen steps. These are the same courtesies we extend to any guest. In our view, the entire universe is divine."

Dubey and Vanaja exchanged glances. A flicker of guilt passed between them.

We invited this priest to trap him. But his knowledge... it surpasses all our expectations.

'They say that if you want to harm someone, you must create a story, a reason to hate them,' Dubey's mind churned. 'You need someone to supply you with that hate story so you don't feel guilty about the evil things you do to someone. In the story of Jesus Christ, the Roman general knew that the Rabbi Jesus was innocent, but he had to go along with the narrative and crucify him.' Desperately, Dubey tried to conjure up a reason, a story to justify the evil he was about to inflict upon Sarma, the trusting priest.

Dubey's thoughts spiralled. I need a story like that–something, anything–to justify what I'm about to do to this priest. A reason to numb my conscience.

He walked into the kitchen and returned with a steaming cup of tea–Sarma's favourite. It was already laced with Adripoison, a rare neurotoxin specially procured from Berlin.

He was about to offer it, saying, "Please drink this before you begin the puja..."

But then, Sarma resumed speaking–his words layered with depth, reverence, and profound simplicity. Dubey froze.

Something shifted.

He turned silently and walked back into the kitchen. With trembling hands, he poured the poisoned tea down the sink.

After that, Dubey returned and sat silently beside Vanaja. Sarma continued with the puja, now completely absorbed in the ritual. He opened a book–the sacred manual that detailed every step–and began to read aloud from it.

Ever since his memory was damaged by the poisoning incident in Bangalore, Sarma had lost confidence in his ability to recall mantras and verses accurately. Puja was no casual affair. A single misstep, a mispronounced syllable, could render the whole ritual meaningless. This was serious–sacred work. On the advice of one of his spiritual mentors, he had begun using the book to guide his recitations.

By the time the ritual concluded, the sun had already set. Birds were flying back to their nests, filling the dusky sky with their calls. Sarma, exhausted, thought of the day ahead. He had to wake early, wash his clothes, clean his room, and then catch a bus from one end of the city to the farmhouse, tucked away on its rural outskirts. The puja had been a success–but the day had drained him.

They had dinner.

After the dinner, "I'm quite tired now," Sarma said. "Could you please show me where I can rest?"

They guided him to the guest bedroom. He lay down on the bed and fell asleep almost instantly.

Meanwhile, Dubey's phone rang. It was Vinay.

"Did you deliver the Adripoison?" Vinay asked bluntly.

"Yes," Dubey lied.

What Dubey didn't know was that Vinay had already anticipated this. He knew Dubey, a Brahmin, might feel sympathy for another Brahmin—especially one as devout and gentle as Sarma. So Vinay had taken precautions: he had instructed the household servant to observe everything.

And the servant had seen it all.

He watched Dubey lace the tea with the poison… and then, after a long pause, pour it down the sink.

"You fool," Vinay hissed. "Do you even know what you've done? That poison cost us a fortune. You owe us a hundred thousand dollars now. And if you don't pay, we'll take your family. You'll suffer pain you can't even imagine."

Dubey stood there, frozen. His world began to collapse around him.

What have I done? he thought. *I made a pact with the devil for money… and now I can't walk away. I thought I could lie my way out of it. I didn't want to drug the priest. But I underestimated the evil I agreed to serve. Vinay has eyes and ears everywhere.*

Tears welled up in his eyes.

Vinay's voice remained cold and merciless. "What's the use of crying now?"

"What do you want me to do?" Dubey asked, his voice breaking.

"I knew you'd lose your nerve. That's why I had the househelp mix the poison into the *kheer*—the milk-sweet you served for dinner. Sarma ate it."

Dubey went pale. His mind blanked.

Vinay continued, "And don't think you can get away. That vial you wasted? It was custom-synthesized. You owe us. One hundred thousand dollars. You poured it down the drain."

"I—I can't pay that. I don't have that kind of money."

"Then we'll take your family," Vinay said, his voice chilling. "Piece by piece."

Dubey trembled. The cruelty in Vinay's words was not an act—it was real, pure evil.

"I'm sorry," he sobbed. "Please... give me another chance. I'll do anything. Just... one more chance."

There was silence on the other end. Then Vinay spoke, calm and terrifying.

"Fine. Here's what you'll do..."

He laid out the next steps. Dubey listened, numb with fear.

There was no way out now. He had entered the devil's den, and the door had locked behind him.

It was the middle of the night. Sarma lay in bed, half-asleep, half-aware—adrift in a dream, yet lucid within it. Something primal stirred inside him. Kamala lay beside him, her beautiful form entirely bare.

"Oh, I miss you..." he whispered, wrapping his arms around her.

"I missed you too," she murmured.

He melted into her embrace. Her skin–soft, warm, real–ignited a deep, aching longing. She pulled him closer.

"Come into me," she whispered.

He was about to give in, lost in the dream's intensity... but then, something stirred within him–something older, deeper than desire. Years of training in esoteric Hindu practice rose from the depths of his awareness.

An ancient reflex surged–like a mantra rising from his marrow. The tale from the Mundaka Upanishad broke through the haze.

Two birds.

One eats. One watches.

That silent watcher–it was still within him.

And it was screaming.

The teaching came alive: the tale of two birds on a tree. One on the lower branch eats the fruit–sweet and bitter, pleasure and pain. The other watches in silence. The eater is the experiencer; the watcher, the Paramātman–the eternal witness.

Sarma awoke into that witness state.

From that elevated awareness, he saw his own body–entwined with Kamala's form–but something was wrong. The ache of missing her had turned into an erotic hallucination. This wasn't just a dream.

Kamala was real. Tangible. Flesh beside him.

But she was thousands of miles away.

This is not her...

Then it hit him.

Witchcraft.

He was under the influence of a powerful illusion–seductive, dangerous, designed to bypass reason. But that sacred witnessing pulled him back from the edge. He began oscillating between the two birds–his higher self and lower self, sākṣī and experiencer–until clarity pierced the fog.

It was not Kamala.

It was Kaamini.

The erotic spirit. A shapeshifting seductress. Draped in lust and deception.

She had taken Kamala's form to ensnare him.

He tried to open his eyes, but his head was spinning–still under the lingering effects of Adripoison. Kaamini, now attempting to possess Vanaja's body, suddenly shrieked–like something struck by divine fire.

Earlier that morning, Sarma had tied a sacred thread–bṛhatsāma rakṣā–around Vanaja's wrist during ritual. The sanctified thread now burned Kaamini's ethereal form.

She recoiled into a shadowed corner, her eyes flaming with rage.

Sarma jolted upright, the spell broken. He shoved Vanaja away and quickly wrapped himself in cloth.

"What happened?" Vanaja asked, breathless. "I thought you were enjoying it."

Still reeling, Sarma stared at her. "You're Dubey's wife... how could you?"

"Does it matter?"

"It matters to me," he said, voice heavy. "I don't betray trust. As a priest, that's a vow I uphold."

Vanaja's voice turned sharp. "What if you weren't a priest? Would you still push me away? Don't you find me desirable?"

"I do," he admitted. "You are profoundly attractive. But I will not lay a hand on another man's wife or lover. To do so would violate a sacred bond. If someone betrayed me like that, I'd be shattered. I refuse to cause that kind of pain."

He steadied himself. "What you've done–what you tried to pull me into–it ends now."

She clung to him again, desperate, pleading–but Sarma pushed her away and sat up.

From the shadows, Kaamini's voice slithered out–venomous, mocking.

"You tied that sacred thread to her wrist. Otherwise, I would have devoured you. You escaped tonight, priest... but not for long. I will return."

With that, she vanished.

Something shifted in Vanaja. As if waking from a trance, she rose abruptly, wrapped her saree around her body, and slipped silently out of the room.

Sarma sat on the bed, shaken.

What just happened? What did I almost allow? How could I falter so close to breaking my vows?

He reminded himself: Hindu priests are not forbidden from sexual union. But there are rules.

A follower of dharma must never engage with a married woman, nor one in a committed relationship. Exceptions are made only if the woman is truly separated, and even then, only after two full moon cycles have passed.

This had not been that. This was a deception. A trap.

He stood up, dressed swiftly, packed his few belongings, and stepped out into the night.

It was past midnight. No buses, no autos. The road ahead stretched ten miles through the wilderness. But Sarma feared no darkness. He feared only human treachery.

And so, he walked. Alone, into the night.

In the adjacent room, Vanaja stepped in quietly. Dubey stood there, trembling, a camera in his hand. Sweat ran down his face.

"He didn't touch you," Dubey whispered, voice quaking. "He... he woke up."

"You never showed me the kind of respect that priest showed," Vanaja said coldly. "You were willing to sell me for money. But he respected you—more than you ever did."

Her voice cracked slightly. Her mind was struggling to process everything. Something inside her had changed.

"Delete that footage," she said sharply. "If the federal police ever get their hands on it, we're finished. Sex trafficking. Rape charges."

"I–I can't delete it. I have to send it to the people funding us. Otherwise, they'll destroy me."

"But why rape?" Dubey asked, confused.

"Because he wasn't looking at the camera. He didn't know it was there. He wasn't aware. He pushed me away. That's all the footage shows. And to any honest prosecutor, that's rape. It's assault on camera. They'll see the truth. We'll go to jail."

Dubey swallowed hard. The weight of what they'd done was beginning to crush him.

Vanaja, no stranger to seduction, had lured many powerful men into traps before. But this time... this man... something about him had shaken her to her core.

She made up her mind.

She needed to know more about Sarma.

Not to trap him.

But to understand how a man like that still existed in this world.

Beirut, Lebanon - Early January, 1993:

The Boeing 707 descended through the amber-streaked sky, its engines roaring as it touched down on the tarmac of Beirut International Airport. The sun hung low on the horizon, casting long shadows across the war-scarred city. It was 5 pm, and dusk was creeping in, the scent of the Mediterranean breeze mingling with the lingering aroma of aviation fuel.

As the aircraft taxied to a halt, Sulfikar unbuckled his seatbelt and rose from his seat. The flight from Kuwait had been nearly empty, making for an eerily quiet journey. With barely a handful of passengers, the immigration process was swift-- a few stamps, a few cursory glances, and he was through. Stepping into the arrivals hall, the dim yellow lighting flickered overhead. A few weary travelers shuffled past, dragging their bags, while airport staff moved with practiced indifference. Then, amidst the sparse crowd, Sulfikar spotted a man holding a handwritten sign:

“Sulfikar - International Olive Traders.”

The letters were scrawled hastily on a piece of cardboard, the ink slightly smudged. The man holding it adjusted his coat, squared his shoulders, and strode toward the waiting stranger.

Sulfikar walked up to him. "Salaam Alekum."

"Alekum wa assalam wa barakatu," the man replied, his voice measured. He raised the sign slightly. "You are Sulfikar?" His eyes flickered with an unspoken need for confirmation.

"I am Sulfikar."

The man lowered the sign. "I am Suleman. Sheikh Nasir sent me. Please, follow me."

Suleman gave Sulfikar a once-over. "No luggage?" he asked.

"I am here only for two days," Sulfikar said.

Suleman nodded, as if that was expected. "Come."

They stepped out of the airport. The parking lot was coated in a fine layer of dust–signs of long, dry summers and desert winds. The moment Sulfikar stepped beyond the air-conditioned confines of the terminal, a wave of heat wrapped around him, thick and oppressive. He shrugged off his jacket, folding it over his arm.

Suleman led him to a Mercedes-Benz, an older model, its once-luxurious frame now riddled with scratches and dents. The front bumper bore the scars of careless driving, and the back was slightly crumpled, as though it had kissed one too many obstacles.

Suleman pulled the creaking door open, motioning for Sulfikar to get in.

Sulfikar slid into the seat, the worn leather sighing under his weight.

The car rumbled to life, and Suleman pulled out of the parking lot. The airport lay on the city's outskirts, with the road ahead snaking towards the heart of Beirut. But just as the city's lights came into view, Suleman made a turn—away from the city.

A weathered road sign loomed ahead:

"Bekaa Valley - 40 Miles"

Sulfikar glanced at Suleman but said nothing.

The journey was taking him somewhere far from the city, and he had a feeling—this was where things would begin.

The battered Mercedes-Benz rattled over the uneven road, its headlights slicing through the gathering dusk. Suleman drove in silence, his fingers wrapped tightly around the wheel. The further they went, the fewer signs of civilization remained.

Beirut's distant glow faded behind them, swallowed by the dark silhouette of the Lebanese mountains.

The road was long, stretching through the valley like a serpent, flanked by rocky hills and scattered vineyards. Even now and then, Sulfikar spotted abandoned buildings--some riddled with bullet holes, others reduced to crumbling shells.

They passed a checkpoint, a makeshift barrier manned by armed men in civilian clothes. One of them, a bearded man gripping an AK-47, stepped forward and rapped on Suleman's window.

Suleman rolled it down. Arabic words exchanged--low, clipped, businesslike.

The man's eyes flicked toward Sulfikar, lingering just long enough to register his presence. Then he stepped back, gesturing for them to pass.

Suleman drove on.

About an hour later, a rusty road sign emerged from the darkness:

"Syrian Border - 10 Miles"

"Hermel - 5 Miles"

Sulfikar knew the name. Hermel--a remote town, a known Hezbollah stronghold. The further they drove, the heavier the air felt. This wasn't just some distant war zone--this was a place where fighters trained, where supply routes were guarded, where politics and warfare blurred into something far more dangerous.

The car veered off the main road onto a narrow dirt track, weaving through the barren landscape. It was darker now, with no streetlights, just the faint glow of a distant village nest;ed in the hills.

Suleman finally spoke.

"We are close."

Sulfikar shifted in his seat, following the weight of the night press around them. He wasn't here for pleasantries--he was here for business. And in places like this, business was often a matter of life and death.

The Mercedes-Benz slowed as it approached the dimly lit compound, nestled in the shadow of the hills. A group of armed men stood near the entrance, their rifles slung casually over their shoulders. One of them raised a hand, signaling the car to stop.

Sulfikar exhaled slowly. It was time.

The door opened, and Suleman stepped out. He exchanged a few words with the man who had halted them, his voice low and measured. After a brief discussion, he returned and opened the door for Sulfikar, giving him a subtle nod.

"Sheikh Nasir will see you in the morning. We've arranged a guest room for you. I'll take you there now. But first, I need your passport," Suleman said.

"My passport?" Sulfikar asked, frowning slightly.

"Security precaution," Suleman replied. "We do not allow visitors to keep their passports with them. InshaAllah, you will get it back when you leave."

Sulfikar hesitated for a moment but then handed over his passport. Without another word, Suleman led the way, and Sulfikar followed.

A dusty path wound behind the building, leading them toward an old stone well. As they approached, Sulfikar noticed a set of stairs descending into the well's dark depths. His steps slowed slightly.

Suleman glanced back. "Air raids. We never know when the Israelis will bomb us. We live in underground bunkers," he explained.

The air was thick with the scent of gunpowder and damp earth. The faint glow of an electric lamp flickered along the narrow corridor at the bottom of the well. The entrance to a man-made tunnel yawned before them, its walls rough and unpolished. Sulfikar hesitated.

"Come," Suleman urged, stepping forward.

With no other option, Sulfikar followed. The tunnel stretched ahead in eerie silence, the only sound the soft echo of their footsteps against the stone floor. After ten minutes of walking, they reached a narrow corridor lined with doors. It was clear that others–fighters, guests, or both–were living behind them.

Suleman stopped at one of the doors and pushed it open. "This is your room," he said, stepping aside.

The room was small and dimly lit. A single cot stood against the wall. A metal tripod held a clay water pot, a steel glass resting on its lid.

Sulfikar stepped inside, the weight of his journey settling onto his shoulders. Tomorrow, he would meet Sheikh Nasir. But tonight, he would rest in the depths of the earth.

Early in the morning. A faint call for the early morning prayer Fajr is heard. Sulfikar woke up. He had a disturbed sleep. He hurriedly completed his ablutions and went to the adjacent hall. It is a room that can host 30 people. There are not many in there. But everyone is praying. Next to them lying on the ground are AK-47 rifles. Grenade launchers. It looks like they are ready for combat but for now praying. The atmosphere appeared surreal because Sulfikar never witnessed that kind of intensity. A heavy contrast between prayers which are supposed to give you peace anchored with the rifles which can destroy that peace at any moment. Sulfikar can sense unknown eyes watching him observing carefully his prayer style and his demeanour. Only one familiar face he could see -- Suleman. He is leading the prayers.

After the Fajr prayers, Suleman approached Sulfikar with a nod.

"The Sheikh is waiting for us... Come, let's go."

"Now? This early in the morning?" Sulfikar asked, frowning.

"We start our day early here. The afternoons are for rest," Suleman replied matter-of-factly.

Without another word, he turned and led the way. They walked through a series of corridors, crossing several heavy doors before arriving at one that looked different. Suleman knocked twice, paused, then knocked three times in quick succession.

The pattern was precise–not just a signal, but a code.

A faint metallic clunk echoed from the other side, and the door creaked open. As Sulfikar stepped inside, he realized it wasn't just an ordinary door. It was steel-reinforced, thick and formidable–the kind used in bank vaults to secure millions.

The room inside was a fortified bunker, its walls two feet thick, designed to withstand blasts. A three-seater sofa and two single-seater chairs faced a low wooden table in the center. On it, a large world map was spread out, marked with pins in four cities: Tokyo, London, Bombay, and New York—four of the most expensive and densely populated metropolises in the world.

At the head of the table sat a man, his long white beard flowing over his chest, his turban wrapped tightly around his head. His eyes, sharp and calculating, were fixed on the map. He barely moved as they entered.

"Salaam Alaikum, Ya Sheikh Yasir. I have brought Sulfikar," Suleman announced.

The man finally lifted his head. His gaze was piercing, cold and unreadable, his face a mask of hardened authority.

"Wa Alaikum Assalam," he responded, his voice steady, businesslike. But his expression remained detached, unreadable.

His eyes scanned Sulfikar up and down, scrutinizing him with the kind of calculated intensity that could strip a man down to his soul.

Sulfikar, though accustomed to high-stakes negotiations and power plays, felt a chill crawl up his spine. He forced himself to hold the gaze, resisting the instinct to shift uncomfortably.

"So, you are Sulfikar," Sheikh Yasir finally said, his tone devoid of warmth.

"Salaam Alaikum," Sulfikar greeted, keeping his voice even.

The Sheikh gestured toward a single-seater sofa to his left.

"Come, be seated."

Sulfikar noticed another man already seated to the Sheikh's right—his posture composed, his presence deliberate. He was dressed in a flowing white gown, a white silk cloth draped loosely over his head without any harness. It was an unmistakable attire—the traditional dress of the Muttawwaḥs, the religious scholars and enforcers of Shariah law in Sunni Islam.

Sheikh Yasir motioned toward him.

"This is Abdullah," he said. "He represents the interests of our Sunni brothers."

Sulfikar gave a slight nod. So, this was a Muttawwaḥ. His presence confirmed what Sulfikar had suspected—this wasn't just a meeting; this was an alliance.

Islam's sectarian divide between Sunnis and Shias had shaped geopolitics for centuries. Yet, when faced with a collective threat, their factions often found pragmatic alliances.

And for Sulfikar, this was good news.

If he could sell the solution to the Sunnis as well, his market had just doubled.

Their conversation shifted into Arabic, a language Sulfikar knew well.

"So, what news do you bring us?" Sheikh Yasir asked, his voice calm yet expectant.

"You know what happened in Ayodhya," Sulfikar said, watching their reactions closely.

Sheikh Yasir remained silent, his expression unreadable.

It was Abdullah who spoke first. His voice was stern, unwavering. "We are upset with what was done in Ayodhya."

Sheikh Yasir's fingers tapped lightly on the table, his gaze fixed on Sulfikar.

"It is time they learned a lesson," he said, his voice low but laced with menace. "Not just Ayodhya, but the rest of the world." He leaned back slightly. "So, what is your proposal?"

Sulfikar straightened. "Consider our services as human resources. We provide motivation for your soldiers."

Yasir's eyes narrowed slightly. "Motivation?" His voice held a note of scepticism. "What kind of motivation?"

Sulfikar met his gaze evenly. "The kind that can turn a man into a suicide bomber. The kind that makes him willing to do anything you command."

A heavy silence filled the room.

Sheikh Yasir and Abdullah exchanged a look. No words were spoken, but something passed between them—a shared understanding, or perhaps, a silent calculation of risks and rewards.

Finally, Abdullah broke the silence. "We saw suicide bombers in the Sri Lankan war. We tried to motivate our people, but we rarely succeeded." He folded his arms. "You claim you can provide this 'motivation'. How is your approach any different?"

Sulfikar smiled slightly.

"I represent the interests of a business group," he began, his tone controlled, measured.

He launched into his presentation, carefully balancing secrecy with persuasion. He revealed just enough to make Sheikh

Yasir and Abdullah believe in his proposal, yet kept his business secrets tightly guarded.

For the next hour, the room was filled with intense discussion–questions, counterarguments, silent calculations. Sulfikar watched their reactions, adjusted his pitch, and pushed them just enough to bring them to the brink of agreement.

At last, Sheikh Yasir leaned forward.

"Are you sure this works?"

Sulfikar’s reply was immediate, unwavering. "We are confident."

Abdullah stroked his beard. "And the cost? Each event, depending on its severity, will have a price?"

Sulfikar nodded. "Correct. This is business. We offer our services. In return, you achieve your political objectives."

Sheikh Yasir and Abdullah exchanged a glance.

Then, after a long pause, Yasir spoke. “Give us two days. You will remain our guest. We’ll meet again and give you our answer.”

Two days later, they reconvened.

Sheikh Yasir leaned forward, his fingers resting on a world map spread across the table. His voice was calm, deliberate.

“Here is our proposal,” he began. “We will not disclose our plans to you. We make our own plans. We assemble our own teams. But, as you suggested, we will over-prepare. For every operative we require, we will gather four. If we need two, we’ll assemble eight.”

Sulfikar nodded. "Exactly. And once you have those eight names, you send them to us. We'll conduct a 'motivational class'—and afterwards, we'll tell you which two to select."

Abdullah, seated beside Yasir, leaned in. "Some of our operations are planned for distant lands. In those cases, we'll need to assemble local teams. How would that work?"

Sulfikar met his gaze. "You already have connections with local organisations, don't you?"

"Of course," Abdullah replied.

"Then outsource the execution to us," Sulfikar said smoothly. "Give us the names of your local contacts. We'll identify the best candidates, prepare them, and carry out the operation on your behalf."

A slow, knowing silence settled over the room.

Then Sheikh Yasir tapped the map with his finger.

"Alright. Let's start with two cities," Yasir said, his finger landing on a marked location. "We were planning an attack in New York."

Abdullah's eyes darkened. "After Ayodhya, we agreed—Bombay must burn as well. But before that, we need to teach the police a lesson. They failed to protect our shrine."

"What are you thinking?" asked Sulfikar.

"Assassinate a high-ranking police officer," Abdullah said flatly. "We don't care who. Just someone near the top. But the act must never trace back to us. Sometimes we don't want attention—we want deniability. This will prove whether your people can demonstrate that."

Sheikh Yasir leaned forward, locking eyes with Sulfikar. "This will be a test of your operational capability. Kill the officer. That act will trigger the next phase. Within a month of his death, we strike New York. And a month after that, Bombay. That will mark the beginning of our Holy War."

Sulfikar nodded. "We can handle it."

He reached into his pocket and pulled out a small calculator. His fingers tapped rapidly, crunching numbers–projecting the profits that mass bloodshed would bring.

When blind faith mixes with greed, it brews the devil's concoction–a formula for destruction with no antidote.

That day, deep in an underground bunker in Lebanon, a pact was sealed.

The fires they lit would smoulder for decades.

12. KALKI

New Delhi, India - Early January, 1993

Inside a classified intelligence operations room, the low hum of secure-line chatter and the rustle of paper filled the air.

Brigadier Bipin sat overseeing Mission Insiders. There was a knock on the door.

"Enter," he said.

Chandra stepped in.

"Chandra, we met just last week. Anything urgent?"

Mission Insiders had been a slow grind—too slow. Each month, the top team would assemble, dissecting what little progress they'd made. They still had no clue where the mind-control suitcases had vanished. Sarma, their central focus, remained absorbed in his education in Hyderabad. Aghora had disappeared back into the Himalayas, retreating to his shadowed existence.

Nothing had moved.

So why was Chandra here now?

"You know we've been tracking those around Sarma in Hyderabad," Chandra said.

Bipin leaned back, fingers drumming on the wooden armrest. He already knew the background. His mind flashed back to their very first briefing on Mission Insiders—Dr Sood's voice still echoed:

"There are enemies who've tried to harm Sarma since childhood," Dr Sood had said, his voice edged with conviction. "Because Dr Rao's guru, Sastry, identified Sarma as the reincarnation of Mohan."

"So?" Chandra had asked.

"Find out everyone—whether in government or private sector—who tried to sabotage Sarma. Some submitted false reports. Others administered drugs to destabilise him as a child. We even have evidence suggesting some of his girlfriends were manipulated. They lied to him. One was in contact with those responsible."

"I don't understand," Chandra had said. "Why does Sarma tolerate such abusive relationships? Why not walk away?"

"We are to blame," Sood had said. "Sarma was trapped between two opposing evils. One comes from within our own ranks—insiders pretending to be allies while serving their own interests. They infiltrated his personal life. He was young, traumatised, and searching for companionship. He was easy to exploit. Some of those women drugged him and misreported his behaviour. Rather than supporting him, they became agents of the very machinery we, as citizens, finance."

"And the second evil?"

"The one behind the mind-bending suitcases. Possibly a third, still unknown."

"So you're suggesting we monitor everyone with links to Sarma?" Chandra had asked.

"Precisely. He's seen the suitcase–we believe he can identify it again. Someone will eventually approach him. That's inevitable."

Bipin blinked–returning to the present.

"Yes, I remember. Dr Sood asked you to keep eyes on Sarma's circle," Bipin said. "Anything unusual?"

Chandra nodded. "A man named Sulfikar has caught our attention. But our civilian trackers have lost him. We need MoD's help."

"Tell me more."

"He runs several businesses," Chandra said. "One's a recruitment agency supplying labour to the Middle East. More recently, he's opened an olive trading company."

"Why does that interest us?" Bipin asked evenly.

"He just landed in Beirut. And now–he's vanished."

That got Bipin's full attention.

"Can we track him with our defence satellites?"

Chandra hesitated, then nodded. "I know repositioning a satellite is expensive. But the MoD operates some of the most advanced imaging systems in the world. And I don't believe Sulfikar's in Lebanon to sell olives."

"Do we have a visual?" Bipin asked.

Chandra slid a grainy photograph across the desk. A dented, older-model Mercedes-Benz with Middle Eastern plates.

"That's the car he's travelling in."

Bipin gave it a quick glance, then pressed his intercom.

"Get me satellite imagery on this vehicle's movements in Lebanon. Immediate priority."

One hour later...

A lieutenant stepped into Bipin's chamber, file in hand. He saluted crisply and laid high-resolution satellite images on the desk.

"The car is currently stationed in Hermel, sir."

Bipin studied the satellite images, tracing the route the car had taken through the winding streets of Hermel.

"Certainly, he's not there to sell olives," he muttered.

Chandra picked up the phone without hesitation and dialled Dr Sood.

"We've found him," he said, voice steady. "He's in Hermel."

"When is he returning?" Dr Sood asked.

"According to the flight ticket, he's landing in Hyderabad the day after tomorrow," Chandra replied. "What do you want to do about Sulfikar? Shall we detain him for questioning? I'll be in Hyderabad for the next week—I can organise it."

Dr Sood paused for a moment.

"No. Let's not do anything just yet. Simply wait and observe. We have too much at stake. Questioning him—or even hinting that we're aware of him—won't benefit us at this point."

Chandra nodded, though Dr Sood couldn't see it. "Understood."

Once the call ended, Dr Sood moved swiftly. He relayed the intelligence directly to Dr Rao—the man who made the final decisions.

Rao was buried in paperwork, barely glancing up at first. But the moment he heard the words "Sarma," "Hermel," and "Sulfikar," he sat upright.

"We need to alert the Israelis. We can't risk the welfare of our allies."

Dr Sood hesitated. "They might already know."

"They might," Rao replied, tapping his pen against the desk. "But they need to know that we know. That will impress them."

Sood raised an eyebrow. "You think we need to impress them?"

"Sometimes, overt gestures strengthen alliances," Rao said calmly. "Staying silent isn't always the smart move. Besides—do you know why we must inform the Israelis?"

"Why?"

"Do we have anyone on the ground in Hermel?" Rao asked.

"No... we don't."

"Exactly. But I'm sure the Israelis do. If we signal our interest in Sulfikar, we can request access to any intel they've gathered."

Sood leaned forward. "What exactly do we tell them?"

Dr Rao took a breath, choosing his words carefully.

"Tell them the truth: we know what we know. We also know what we don't know. And, importantly, we're aware that there are things we don't even realise we don't know."

Sood blinked. "Unknown unknowns."

"Precisely," Rao said. "Take the mind-controlling device. Until recently, it was beyond the reach of even our speculation. If we build trust with the Israelis—share what we do know—then perhaps..."

He paused, steepling his fingers.

"...they'll help us uncover what we don't know."

The room fell into a contemplative silence.

"Also..." Rao looked up again. "Inform Saudi Intelligence as well. Tell them we're tracking Sulfikar."

Sood's expression tensed. "Should we tell the Saudis about the existence of the mind-control devices?"

"No. Not yet," Rao said firmly. "Until we have concrete proof, it stays between us. We tell none of them. We don't know which country is behind the technology. Everyone is a suspect. We can't risk our national security."

He paused.

"If we speak without evidence, we'll be ridiculed. And if a hostile power really is behind it... they'll do anything to silence us. It's not in our interest to let anyone know that we know. Not yet."

"Understood," Sood said quietly. Then, after a beat, he asked, "What about the USA? Should we inform them as well?"

Rao shook his head. "The Soviets are still smarting from the collapse of the USSR. If we turn to the Americans now, the Russians will feel we've abandoned them. That would weaken our non-aligned stance."

He smirked slightly. "Besides, if we tell the Israelis, it's as good as telling the Americans."

Sood couldn't help but chuckle at that. The deep ties between Mossad and the CIA were no secret.

He picked up the secure line and began dialling the Israeli and Saudi embassies.

Location: IBSB Regional Office, Delhi

Chandra was buried in a case file when a knock broke his concentration.

Detective Inspector Shree stepped in.

"Sir, may I come in?"

"Yes, come in, Shree," Chandra replied, looking up. "What's the matter?"

"It's Vyas sir, from Hyderabad. He's on the secure line."

Ever since they discovered their regular phone lines were being tapped by unknown adversaries, Chandra had imposed sweeping changes to communication protocols. Sensitive matters were no longer discussed on standard calls. High-level conversations were either held in person or through the Special Secure (SS) Hotline Terminal—a dedicated, encrypted channel.

Chandra stood, exited his office, and entered the adjacent chamber housing the SS Terminal. He activated the encrypted line.

"Hello Vyas. Jai Hind," Chandra greeted.

"Hey Chandra, Jai Hind," came the reply.

"What's going on?"

"I wanted to talk about one of your boys—Sarma."

Chandra's eyebrows arched. "What about Sarma?"

"There's a lot of chatter. A full-blown smear campaign, actually. Some people claiming to be his old friends and relatives are spreading rumours. Mainly about him getting close to a girl from Pakistan."

Chandra paused. "I'm aware."

"You are?" Vyas sounded genuinely surprised. "Then why haven't you given him cover? Or at least a ring?"

In their world, giving cover meant making it known—especially within intelligence circles—that someone was an insider, protected, and not to be touched. A ring symbolised that the person was effectively ring-fenced from scrutiny.

"It's deliberate," Chandra said, his tone firm now. "This is a highly sensitive operation. It touches on national security concerns across multiple countries. Sarma is working with us on an international investigation. We're avoiding internal alerts or usual protocols–because right now, we can't tell who's compromised. The threat is real, and it's deep."

Vyas was silent for a beat.

"Blimey... I didn't realise it was that serious. So, you don't want my team to offer him protection?"

"That's right. Sarma can handle himself for now. No interference."

Chandra paused, then added, "Besides, you know how devastated he was after losing Kamala."

"Right..."

"He's beginning to smile again. And this girl–whatever her background–seems to lift his spirits. Why rob him of that? A little light in his life doesn't make him a traitor. Dating someone from Pakistan isn't a crime."

"What about those so-called friends and relatives stirring the pot?"

"That's his past," Chandra said, dismissively. "Most of it stems from jealousy. I once read something interesting–there are three important things in life: what you think the world thinks about you, what the world actually thinks about you... and the third is the most important."

"What's the third?"

"Who you really are," Chandra said. "I might think people see me as a sharp and feared officer. In reality, they might see me as something else entirely. But no one really says what they truly think. Society trains us to wear masks. In genuine relationships, the less we hide, the better."

"So what matters most... is who you really are," Vyas repeated, thoughtfully. "And who are you, Chandra?" he teased.

Chandra chuckled. "I won't tell you. That's a secret I keep to myself. But knowing who I am—that's what gives me the confidence to work without pretence."

"And who's Sarma then?"

"The people he grew up with—they have a version of him stuck in their memories. But Sarma outgrew that. They didn't keep up. So what they think, or what he thinks they think—it doesn't matter. What matters is who Sarma really is."

"And who is he?"

"He's intelligent, sharp, and, most importantly, a good human being. He's got discernment—rare these days. I had plans for him. If not for his heartbreak with Kamala, I would've pushed him into the police force, maybe even mentored him into a top position."

"But it's not too late, right?"

"He's resisting. Wants a private-sector life. Maybe we can still convince him. But one thing I admire most—his integrity. You can trust him completely. He won't break it."

"Good to know," Vyas said. "I'll still try to give him as much discreet cover as possible, without drawing attention."

Chandra paused, thinking. Sarma needed support. And bringing Vyas into the loop could be an asset.

"Vyas," he said finally, "can you fly down to Delhi? I'd like to bring you up to speed on the full mission. We could use your help."

Sulfikar had spent more time than he initially thought in the underground bunker in Lebanon. After the meeting concluded, all three men emerged from the bunker. Sheikh Nasir shook hands with Abdullah and Sulfikar, kissed them both on the cheeks in farewell, and quickly vanished back inside.

Suleman was waiting near the car. They got in.

"Are you coming with me to the airport?" Sulfikar asked.

"I have a flight to catch–Kuala Lumpur," replied Abdullah. "Malaysia will be our new hub. We're expanding our network across Indonesia and the surrounding countries."

The rest of the journey passed mostly in silence. After a few hours, they arrived at Beirut International Airport. Sulfikar boarded a transit flight to Kuwait, from where he would eventually reach his final destination: Hyderabad.

Abdullah took a different route. He boarded a flight to Dubai, and from there, to Kuala Lumpur.

Sulfikar sat in the transit lounge of Kuwait, waiting for his connecting flight to Hyderabad. Boarding was still some time away.

He leaned back in his seat, closed his eyes, and tried to relax.

A rustle beside him broke the stillness. Someone had taken the adjacent seat.

The man wiped sweat from his forehead, glanced at Sulfikar, and said with a tired smile, "It's scorching outside. Then you step in here–it's like the Himalayas. The air conditioning is heavenly."

Sulfikar gave a polite nod. Small talk wasn't his strength–and he wasn't in the mood for it.

"Salam. I'm Sultan," the man continued, extending a hand. "I work for Pakistan's Ministry of External Affairs."

There was a trace of pride in his voice–like he expected instant recognition or respect.

Sulfikar's posture stiffened slightly. That line triggered his internal radar. He shook the offered hand. "Hello."

"Where are you from?" Sultan asked casually.

"Hyderabad."

"Hyderabad in Pakistan or India?" Sultan raised his eyebrows. "You know, both our countries have a city by that name."

"India," Sulfikar replied.

"Ah, beautiful city! Great educational institutions there. InshAllah, we'll soon have ours on par with global standards too," Sultan said, his tone hopeful.

Sulfikar didn't respond.

"What do you do?" Sultan asked, pressing on.

"I trade olives."

"Olives? Interesting." Sultan smiled. "May I have your business card?"

Sulfikar handed it over without hesitation. Networking in airport lounges was common, especially in international hubs like this.

Sultan studied the card briefly. "One of our directors, Imran Sahab—his son Mustafa and daughter Noor are both studying in Hyderabad."

That made Sulfikar pause. Name-dropping family details—especially ones that sounded vaguely sensitive—wasn't standard behaviour in casual chats with strangers.

Naive or dangerously overconfident, Sulfikar thought. How does someone like this end up in the Ministry? Must be either well-connected—or very well-funded.

"Good to know," he said flatly. "I hope they're enjoying their time there."

"If we ever need help, I hope we can stay in touch," Sultan added with a grin.

"Sure," Sulfikar replied with a diplomatic smile.

Sultan glanced at his watch. "Oops—my flight's boarding. Nice meeting you. Please remember me."

With that, he walked off, leaving Sulfikar alone again—thoughtful, and mildly amused.

He glanced at his wristwatch. Timing was critical.

Vinay's network operated through a narrow orbital window—an encrypted communication cluster that piggybacked on a rotating trio of low-earth satellites. The most secure one was currently in range, passing over the Bali segment for exactly 63 minutes.

At the far end of the terminal was an old-fashioned telephone booth, tucked discreetly behind a smoked-glass partition.

Sulfikar stepped in, picked up the handset, and dialed a number. It rang four times. He hung up.

Then he waited.

Exactly sixty seconds later, the phone rang.

Vinay.

They had agreed on this protocol weeks ago. Sulfikar would never initiate a conversation—only trigger the handshake. The real call would always come from Vinay, routed through a call-back relay triangulated via three mid-orbit military satellites—old Soviet-era tech, now repurposed by a rogue syndicate in Central Asia. The group leased secure bandwidth to clients in exchange for gold, weapons, or drugs—never money.

The line crackled once, then settled into a sterile silence.

"Bali window is open," Vinay said.

"Not for long," Sulfikar replied.

"Sulfikar?"

"Yes, boss."

"Myself and Shikhandi we both are in the room," Vinay indicated that Shikhandi is also listening into the conversation. "How did the meeting go?" Shikhandi asked.

"It was a success. They're ready to pay top dollar. Payment will come through oil tankers. We can sell the oil and collect our share."

"Perfect. We don't want any direct cash trails. What are the targets?" Vinay asked.

Sulfikar briefed them on the deal.

"So they want to take out a high-ranking police officer before the business begins?" Vinay asked.

"Yes, boss."

"Well, they're in luck. Something is already set-up. It'll satisfy our client's... expectations." Vinay chuckled. "What time does your flight land?"

"By midnight tonight." Sulfikar said. "Boss, tell me who is going to be bumped off. Who is this officer?"

"You know him..." Vinay said. "Chandra"

"Chandra?" Sulfikar felt shivers in his spine. "But he is too high ranking. We will be in serious trouble."

"Nothing that we can't handle. Are you still watching Sarma?"

"I've been monitoring him. But he's a dull subject. Spends mornings learning advanced computing. Afternoons till late night, he works as a systems analyst. No social life. I don't get a chance to spike his drink or anything. It's a waste of my time."

"Don't worry about that. We're sending someone else to handle him."

"Anything else I should know about Sarma?"

"Yes. He's developed a close friendship with a Pakistani girl. Her name is Noor. She has a brother Mustafa. I've seen them together around Golconda Fort and the Old City. Also spotted them multiple times gossiping sitting at an Irani chai shop."

"How'd that happen?"

"No idea. But they seem to bond over music, art, philosophy–or so I gather."

That triggered a spark in Sulfikar's memory.

"Boss, something just clicked. I had a strange conversation earlier..."

He recounted the lounge encounter with Sultan.

Vinay listened, then asked, "What's interesting about that?"

"The girl Sarma is close to is named Noor. And she has a brother named Mustafa. Ring any bells?"

A pause.

"Did Sarma figure out anything related to the murders in Karjat? I asked you to find out what he would tell the police?" Vinay asked.

"I have no luck with that. Sarma occasionally meets Chandra. But I am not sure what they discuss." Sulfikar said. "But I was sitting right behind Sarma and Noor while they were having tea at Irani chai. I heard Sarma tell her about his previous employment at Sleep research lab and the death of his friend Priya. That is all."

Vinay looked at Shikhandi who was listening to the conversation over the speaker.

"They're high-value targets. Since you're tracking Sarma, track them too." Shikhandi said.

"Understood. Anything else?"

"That's all, boss. When will I get my payment?"

"It's done. A local lawyer in Hyderabad will complete a gift deed for a farmhouse and five-acre vineyard in your name. Give it a year, then sell it." Vinay said.

"Thanks, boss. I appreciate you paying me a farmhouse with a five acre vineyard." Sulfikar said.

"Use it as a base for all our operations. It will be safe and discreet" Vinay said.

"Understood, Boss, Signing off."

The call ended.

What Sulfikar didn't know: Sultan had planted a discreet listening bug on his carry-on bag. He couldn't hear Vinay's voice—but Sulfikar's half of the conversation was enough.

As Sulfikar exited the booth, Sultan reappeared.

"Salam. Here we meet again," he said, smiling. "My flight got delayed, so I came back to kill some time."

Sulfikar forced a nod and walked away, uninterested.

Sultan brushed past him casually—and in the same movement, removed the listening device from the bag.

Sultan didn't work for Pakistan's Ministry of External Affairs.

He was part of Lucian's ground crew—and reported directly to Aiwag.

He stepped into the booth Sulfikar had just left, and dialed a number.

Malaysia, nestled between the Gulf of Thailand and the Andaman Sea, is separated from Sumatra by the narrow Malacca Strait. In Port Klang—just 25 miles southwest of Kuala Lumpur—a luxurious yacht lay docked. Half of its mid-deck had been transformed into a high-tech operations cabin, its walls glowing with an array of monitors and encrypted terminals.

Aiwag picked up a secure satellite phone.

"Aiwag here."

"Sultan speaking."

"Did he take the bait?"

"He did—hook, line, and sinker. They'll now be watching Noor and her brother closely," said Sultan.

"Excellent. Father will be very pleased."

"How is Sulfikar getting paid for his services?" Aiwag asked.

"A Farmhouse with a five acre vineyard" Sultan said. "But there's something else—something more interesting."

"What is it?"

"Apparently, some guy named Sarma has grown close to Noor. They've been seen together quite a lot—visiting places, hanging out. He also mentioned about Sleep research lab and Priya"

“Sarma? Is he a Hindu priest?” Aiwag asked, suddenly alert.

“I’m not sure. I think he works at some computer lab,” said Sultan.

“Alright,” Aiwag replied, then ended the call without another word. Sultan disappeared into the crowd.

Aiwag sat still for a moment, the name looping in his mind. Sarma... why does that sound familiar?

While he was in his thoughts. The phone rang.

“Bikku here.”

“Tell me”

“I am ready with my men at the airport. Waiting for the arrival of Abdullah.” said Bikku.

“Make sure you aim right. Don't kill him” said Aiwag.

“Sure,” replied Bikku.

Alwag thought for a second. And said “Bikku”

“Yes, Aiwag?”

“When you were investigating the COMxBAT malfunction in South India, you looked for any Jesuit priests in that region, right?”

“Yes. But we didn’t find any.”

“But you said you found a priest from another religion?”

“Yes. There was someone named Sarma. He was close to Nalini. He was a teacher but also a Hindu priest.”

“When did you find this out?”

"I went back to that area to tie all loose ends. I came to know there was a priest close to Nalini. But he disappeared from there. Apparently, the workplace where he was working fired him. You pulled us all out of India. I did not probe any further...," Bikku said.

Aiwag's eyes narrowed. "And Nalini...?"

"She was neutralized, as instructed. Why?"

"Never mind," Aiwag muttered, and cut the line.

He leaned back, thoughts racing. Sarma... the name again. From Kodur, wasn't he?

One of the COMxBAT units controlling a BAPS named Nalini had gone down. At the time, a priest named Sarma had been friends with her. Then during Operation Schrödinger's Cat in Karjat, another COMxBAT unit failed–coincidentally, a priest from Andhra Pradesh named Sarma had briefly worked in that lab. And now he was in Hyderabad–being tracked by Sulfikar, who works for Shikhandi, their competitor.

Could it be the same Sarma?

Aiwag went to his records room and accessed a file. It has the title "Schrödinger's Cat". He opened the file. Inside there is a name next to Schrödinger's Cat: Dr Priya Kotwal

A surge of excitement rushed through Aiwag. Ever since Fred tampered with the BAT code to protect "a priest," they had been hunting for that priest's identity. Father was obsessed. A year and a half had passed, and they'd hit dead ends. Fred still lay in a coma. But this–this could be the breakthrough.

Heart racing, Aiwag strode down the hallway toward Lucian's private chamber.

He knocked once, then entered.

"Father, I believe I've found the priest Fred tried to protect," Aiwag announced.

Lucian turned slowly from the window. "That is very good news. Who is it?"

Aiwag recounted everything–the lounge encounter, Sultan's report, the COMxBAT anomalies, the old connection to Nalini, Schrödinger's Cat and the recurring presence of a single name: Sarma.

After travelling for 12 hours, Abdullah landed at Kuala Lumpur International Airport. He collected his luggage and stepped outside. A private car driver was waiting with a placard.

"Salam Alaikum," greeted the driver. He knew Abdullah well–he was the regular chauffeur assigned to him during every visit to Kuala Lumpur.

"Wa Alaikum Salam," Abdullah responded warmly.

The driver took over the luggage trolley and led the way to the parked car. Abdullah followed.

Just as the driver opened the door, Abdullah moved to get in. He stepped in with his left leg, momentarily shifting all his weight onto his right. Suddenly, there was a sharp crack–a "fussak" sound–and he screamed in pain.

"Allahu Akbar!" he cried out, collapsing into the back seat.

"What happened, sir?" the driver asked, alarmed.

"I think I broke my leg," Abdullah groaned, his face twisted in agony. "Drive to a hospital–fast."

The driver wasted no time. He radioed ahead to the nearest private hospital's A&E while speeding through the city.

A team of nurses was already waiting at the hospital entrance. Abdullah was swiftly wheeled in. A doctor met him in the ward.

"Hello, I'm Dr. Katy," she introduced herself. "What happened?"

"I think I've fractured my leg. The pain is intense," Abdullah replied, his eyes half-closed from the shock.

"Any other pain? Anywhere else in your body?"

"I'm not sure. I feel something in my upper arm, maybe."

"In that case, we'll do a full-body scan. But first, let's manage your pain."

Dr. Katy administered an injection and began basic checks. The nurses completed the necessary formalities and transferred Abdullah onto a stretcher.

Soon, he was wheeled into the MRI room.

"This is a state-of-the-art machine," Katy assured him. "Brand-new installation. If there's any problem in your body, we'll find it."

Abdullah closed his eyes as the machine hummed to life. The tunnel engulfed him with a mechanical whir.

Meanwhile...

Inside the Yacht, in the Operations room, Batsinger stood watching one of the monitors closely.

"Is the MEDxBAT connected?" Lucian asked, seated nearby. Accountant and Aiwag were also in the room, their attention fixed on the screen.

MEDxBAT—short for Medical Event Data cross-linked with Brain Activity Transformer—was originally developed by Fred to extract brain dumps from humans near death. Batsinger had since enhanced it. Now, it could harvest data even from hospital patients under MRI or while in ICU or in some other conditions.

"Yes, Father," Batsinger confirmed. "Abdullah is inside the MEDxBAT tunnel. We patched it into the hospital's new MRI system."

Text began appearing on the monitor—one line after another. Some were simple Arabic words: "Airport," "Taxi," and others.

"Are you in pain?" Dr. Katy asked, her voice coming through the hospital feed.

"Just a little," Abdullah replied.

The monitor then displayed: "Katy, beautiful doctor."

Batsinger chuckled. "Father, it seems the attending doctor made quite the impression on Abdullah."

Lucian raised an eyebrow. "Is her name Katy?"

"Yes. That's what his mind says," Batsinger confirmed, pointing to the line.

The AI began organizing Abdullah's subconscious thoughts. As the minutes passed, a pattern emerged. MEDxBAT started outputting coherent data—everything Abdullah had recently experienced, including the meeting in the underground bunker.

"They're planning to assassinate a high-ranking police officer in India," Batsinger explained. "Then they aim to target New York... followed by Bombay." He handed a printed mind map to Lucian. The AI, trained in advanced NLP, had translated Abdullah's thoughts into a human-readable structure—a branching tree of intent and context.

"How are they getting paid?," Accountant asked.

Lucian read it carefully, then passed it to the Accountant.

"Okay. They are paying in Oil," said the Accountant after reading the mind map. "I will make necessary arrangements for us to steal it during price negotiations while they are in the process of sale."

"I heard Sulfikar is getting paid a farm house and five acres of vineyard?" Aiwag said.

"I suggest we send a COMxBAT attached to that farmhouse. I am sure any plans they carry out we would know" Batsinger said.

"But we don't have any ground crew or BAT operatives in India right now," Aiwag pointed out.

"We don't need BATs for the police assassination," Lucian replied calmly. "Shikhandi will handle it. Officially, we're not involved—just observers. We're piggybacking, waiting for the right time to offer our services."

"And what about Bombay and New York?" Aiwag pressed.

"If we don't have boots on the ground, we can't steer those events," Batsinger warned.

Lucian was silent for a moment. Then: "We already have our team in the USA, but send Bikku and his crew back into India. Temporarily. Send someone to attach a COMxBAT to Sulfikar's farmhouse. I want eyes and ears on the ground."

"Father, if our intention isn't to steer outcomes post-attack, why send the COMxBATs at all?" Batsinger asked.

Lucian didn't answer immediately. His focus was still on the mind map.

"We need to. Remember Option 3—our plan to profit from Middle Eastern chaos," said the Accountant. "Let Shikhandi's people think they're in charge. Meanwhile, we ride the wave."

Batsinger nodded slowly. "I remember."

"This is an opportunity," Accountant added. "People will flee India in fear. We'll piggyback on that exodus. We'll gain intel on Pakistan and Afghanistan. I'm betting those regions are future war zones."

Lucian gave a small nod, still reading.

"I'll make arrangements to send Bikku and his team," Batsinger confirmed.

"And I'll give you the list of targets—homes where we'll plant the COMxBATs," said Accountant.

Just then, an alarm sounded—a signal that the yacht was about to set sail.

With a low hum, it detached from the dock and began its quiet journey into international waters.

Sulfikar sat in the corner of the Irani café, cradling a steaming cup of tea. The ceiling fan above spun lazily, doing little to dispel the thick air of unease. Ever since Vinay had said that Chandra was going to be "eliminated", Sulfikar had felt a growing knot in his stomach. Something about the whole thing didn't sit right.

"Nothing will go wrong," Vinay had assured him. "It won't come back to us."

But Sulfikar wasn't convinced. Things had a habit of going wrong–quickly, and often violently. He needed a way out. A clean escape route. If it all went south, he had to be holding something he could use to vanish without a trace.

"I'm doing this for Jihad. The holy war," he muttered under his breath, trying to justify the plan to murder a law enforcement officer. But the words rang hollow. Instead of feeling resolute, he felt exposed–unsafe.

He checked the time. Sarma was late. They were supposed to meet here–neutral ground, busy but discreet. After a few more minutes, Sarma finally walked in.

"Hey Sulfikar."

"Hey Sarma. How are you? Thanks for coming," Sulfikar replied, forcing a smile.

He turned towards the counter. "Chotu! Two teas, please!"

Chotu, the young server, nodded and headed to the back.

Originally from Uttar Pradesh, Chotu wasn't just another waiter.

Once Dubey discovered that Sarma favoured the tea at a particular Irani café, he had wasted no time. He pulled strings, made calls, and placed someone there–someone who could be trusted. That someone was Chotu.

He had been handpicked.

Chotu had an ailing mother back home. Rent was overdue. Medical bills were mounting. That's when Dubey had swooped in like a guardian angel. He arranged a rent-free room for Chotu in a chawl on the city's outskirts and ensured a regular supply of medicines–courtesy of Shikhandi's contacts in an international pharmaceutical firm.

All Dubey asked in return was simple.

Get a job at the Irani café.

Wait.

Watch.

That was it.

But after the initial failure to poison Sarma with Adripoison, Vinay grew impatient. He ordered Dubey to persist. "Just keep dosing him," Vinay said. "Tiny amounts. Over time, it'll break down even the strongest minds."

Dr. Gottlieb–one of their shadowy scientific advisors–had assured them of this: that the human will, no matter how disciplined, could be cracked through sustained biochemical tampering. Repeated microdoses would erode cognitive resistance, dissolve psychological boundaries, and eventually turn even the most devout into a puppet.

A few days ago, Dubey had passed Chotu a small packet.

Inside were several clear ampoules–2ml vials of a transparent, odourless liquid. Chotu didn't know what they were made of, only that they had been flown in from Germany... from labs with a history that whispered of dark experiments and buried war crimes.

The box had a single label stamped on it.

Adripoison.

The name meant nothing to Chotu.

But the fear in Dubey's eyes when he handed them over?

That told him everything he needed to know.

Dubey's instructions were straightforward: whenever Sarma ordered tea, pour a single drop from one of the ampoules into his cup. At first, Chotu panicked. It had to be poison. But after seeing Sarma return again and again–alive, cheerful, sipping tea as usual–his fear began to fade. Dubey had changed his life. He would do anything for him.

That day, as usual, Chotu stepped into the back, retrieved an ampoule, and snapped it open with practised hands. He glanced around to ensure no one was watching, then discreetly let a single drop fall into one of the cups.

When he returned, tray in hand, he noticed the café owner eyeing him from the corner. Something in that gaze made his palms sweat. His hands trembled. In his nervousness, he got it wrong.

He switched the cups.

The one meant for Sarma—the one laced with Adripoison—landed in front of Sulfikar.

Chotu had no idea what he'd just done.

Because Sulfikar wasn't merely a radical operative. He was something else entirely—lab-engineered. A terminator. A weapon in human skin.

And Adripoison? It wasn't made to kill him. It was made to disrupt him.

Soon, something inside Sulfikar would begin to shift—quietly, dangerously.

"So why you called?" Sarma asked while sipping the Chai.

"I called to tell you that there is a job opportunity in Saudi Arabia. They pay you very well. Tax-free." Sulfikar said. He took a sip from the cup. Put the cup on the table and pulled a paper from the attache he is carrying with him. He handed over the printout for Sarma to read. It is a job advertisement about a Systems Analyst job in Saudi Arabia. Sarma read the paper.

The payment sounded too good to be true. He must first discuss with Chandra before taking up the offer.

"I will think of it," Sarma said.

"Do not think for too long. Let me know by tomorrow." Sulfikar said. After discussing it for another ten minutes.

While they were there Noor arrived at the café with her friend followed by her brother Mustafa. She saw Sarma and waved her hand. He said, "Hello".

Noor came close to the table. "Hi Sarma, how are you?" said Noor. It is great to see you here. I told you my friend Asma is coming from Pakistan?"

"I suppose this is your friend Asma?" Sarma replied smilingly.

"Yes, I am Asma. Noor told me so much about you. Finally, I get to see you," Asma smiled introducing herself.

Sulfikar felt awkward. He does not like the way Noor and Asma freely approach and chat with Sarma. Something in him stirred. A type of anger. He is already angry at Sarma. He is angry at everything. Adripoison started working inside him.

"Meet Sulfikar. He's a job search agent," Sarma said, gesturing to the man beside him. "He's advising me about a position in the Middle East."

Noor offered a polite smile. "Salaam."

"Hello," Sulfikar replied curtly, his eyes brushing past her with a flicker of disinterest. Cold. Calculated. Almost territorial.

Then, without ceremony, he stood up. "I have to go. Think about the proposal I gave you," he said to Sarma, his voice clipped, as if punctuating a deal already done. And just like that, he left.

Asma immediately slid into the chair Sulfikar had vacated, claiming it like it belonged to her. Noor settled into the seat next to her, and Mustafa plopped down beside Sarma.

"What proposal?" Noor asked, her tone light but her curiosity sharp. She had grown bolder around Sarma lately—comfortable enough to speak her mind, to poke and prod a little.

Sarma silently handed her a folded printout.

She unfolded it and scanned the document. Her eyes lit up.

"Masha Allah," she breathed. "Only the truly blessed get a chance to live so close to the House of Allah. You know Jeddah is just a stone's throw from the Holy Kaaba."

Sarma gave a faint smile, his eyes distant, thoughtful–but he didn't respond.

Noor glanced at him, reading between the lines. "I'm sure Kamala would love it there too..." she said gently. Sarma had confided in her about everything–his love, his loss. Noor had listened, quietly absorbing the weight of his story without judgment.

"Inshah Allah," she continued, her voice softening even more, "if you two end up moving there, I'll come visit. I'll stay with you–just imagine! I could go to the Kaaba every single day."

There was a flicker of warmth in her eyes, a mixture of joy for him and a wistful longing of her own.

Sarma looked at her–not just with appreciation, but with that rare kind of gratitude reserved for those who truly see you... and still choose to stay.

They chatted for another half hour, laughter and quiet understanding flowing easily between them.

"I want to show Asma around the old city," Noor said, turning to him with a hopeful smile. "Why don't you join us?"

Sarma shook his head gently. "I've got some other things to take care of. You two enjoy it."

He stood to leave.

"We're planning to visit Golconda Fort tomorrow," Noor added, her voice light but expectant. "Will you come?"

Sarma paused for a moment. "Golconda... hmm. I'll try. Let's see. Bye for now."

And with that, he walked away–leaving behind the faint echo of a maybe.

"Apaa, you two go ahead and enjoy the tour. I need to study and catch up a bit. See you later," Mustafa said, slinging his backpack over one shoulder before walking off.

"Come on," Noor said, turning to Asma with a bright smile. "I'll show you the old city. Hyderabad has a fascinating history–it's like walking through a storybook."

They stepped out of the Irani café and headed down the bustling lane. Neither of them noticed the black van parked discreetly about fifty meters away. Its windows were heavily tinted, masking the figures inside.

Behind the glass, a group of men sat watching intently.

"They've exited the café. Shall we proceed?" asked the man in the passenger seat, eyes fixed on Noor and Asma.

"Proceed," came the cold reply from the back.

It was Sulfikar.

He had made up his mind. The Adriposion running through his system had fogged his judgment–normally calculating and precise, today his mind was erratic, his actions impulsive. The drug was making him volatile.

"Where should we bring them?" the driver asked.

"To my farmhouse," Sulfikar said, his tone flat.

The van rolled forward, keeping a discreet distance as Noor and Asma wandered into the quieter parts of the old city—narrow lanes where the crowd thinned and the noise of the bazaar faded.

The moment they reached a more secluded stretch, the van suddenly surged forward and skidded to a stop. Before the women could react, the side doors slid open. Two men jumped out.

Everything happened in seconds.

Rough hands grabbed Noor and Asma. They screamed, but the alley swallowed their voices. White cloths drenched in chloroform were pressed tightly against their faces. They struggled briefly—then went limp.

Unconscious.

Their limp bodies were hauled into a van that vanished into the labyrinth of backstreets. No one saw a thing.

By the time they regained consciousness, they found themselves locked in a cold, dim room. The air was thick with damp and dread. Every inch of the place reeked of mould, mildew, and paranoia.

The farmhouse now belonged to Sulfikar—a gift from Vinay, payment for a favour no one dared ask about. After taking ownership, Sulfikar ordered major renovations. Construction was ongoing.

As per Lucian's instructions, a new COMxBAT unit had been embedded into the site—hidden beneath the façade of construction gear. But this was no ordinary surveillance tool. It wasn't just recording. It was listening, sensing, analyzing. It had already flagged two anomalous heat signatures. Biometric data—elevated heart rates, stress markers, erratic breathing—was now streaming straight to AIWAG's command center.

"I think Sulfikar's farmhouse just got two new guests," said Batsinger, eyes locked on the COMxBAT feed.

"Who?" asked Aiwag.

Batsinger picked up the satellite phone and dialed.

"Nayeem here," came the calm reply. His voice didn't betray it, but Nayeem was on edge. He was the one who had installed the COMxBAT unit—masquerading as a construction technician, just another cog in the machine. No one questioned him. That was the plan.

"You near the farmhouse?" Aiwag asked.

"Almost there," Nayeem replied.

"There are two new occupants—but not in the main house. They're in the outhouse. It's divided into two sections. One still houses a couple—a man and his wife who've been there since before the property changed hands. But now, we're picking up activity in the other section—the one that's been vacant until now."

"Understood," said Nayeem. "I'll get eyes on them."

He made his way towards the outhouse. The guards barely looked up. Everyone on-site knew him. He was the quiet worker, always busy, never intrusive.

But two new men stood by the outhouse door. Their stance was different–alert, on edge.

"Hey, who are you?" one of them barked.

"Renovation guy," Nayeem replied casually. "I left a toolkit inside–I need to grab it."

"Come back tomorrow. Not today," the other said, firm.

Nayeem nodded silently and stepped away. Around the back, out of sight, he pulled out a thin listening device and pressed it against the wall.

A moment later, voices.

"Asma, are you okay?" It was Noor's voice–weak, dazed, as if swimming through the fog of chloroform.

"I think so. Where are we?"

"I don't know..."

Nayeem froze.

Noor.

His sister.

And Asma. Sajjad's sister.

Nayeem froze. His blood turned to ice. His heart slammed against his ribs like a battering ram.

What the hell were they doing here?

Panic clawed at his throat, threatening to rise, but he crushed it down. He couldn't afford to lose control. Not now. Not with everything on the line.

One wrong move, and the COMxBAT system would register the anomaly. If that happened—if his cover was blown—Father Lucian wouldn't hesitate. He'd descend like a storm. Everyone connected to Nayeem—his father, his mother, his sister, his siblings, his friends, even the innocents—would be wiped out. No warnings. No explanations. Just annihilation.

He forced himself to think. Fast. Discreetly.

Slipping to the rear of the building, he found a grimy, cracked window. He peered through. A faint yellow light buzzed inside, casting long shadows across the concrete floor. The room was bare, industrial, almost clinical. He saw them—Noor and Asma—both seated against the wall.

Their ankles were shackled to steel rings bolted into the floor. Their hands, mercifully, were free. A small table sat beside them with a few fruits and a jug of water. Just behind them, a narrow door—likely a bathroom. The chains were long enough for them to drag themselves there, if needed.

"Who are these people? Why did they take us?" Noor whispered, her voice trembling.

"I don't know," Asma said, her tone tight with fear.

They looked exhausted. Hollow. But unharmed.

"Alhamdulillah... they didn't hurt us. But how long will that last?" Noor said, breaking down into sobs. "May Allah protect us."

Asma leaned in, wrapped her arms around Noor, and the two women clung to each other, crying quietly. The sound, even muffled through the glass, twisted like a knife in Nayeem's chest.

He wanted to call out. To tell them he was there. That they'd be okay. But he couldn't. Any noise–any move–could trigger a response from the COMxBAT. The system was always listening, always scanning. If it detected him, it would respond. And that response would be lethal.

He clenched his fists.

Think. There has to be a way.

His earpiece crackled to life. A voice, sharp and cold:

"Who's in the house?"

It was Aiwag.

Nayeem swallowed hard. He steadied his breath.

This wasn't just a mission anymore. This was personal. And any mistake now would cost lives.

"Just the housemaids," Nayeem lied, his voice even. But his mind was racing, calculating a way out for Noor and Asma.

He stepped away and quickly dialed a number.

"Mustafa," he said, trying to keep his voice steady. "It's me–Nayeem."

"Nayeem bhai! Where are you calling from?" Mustafa's voice lit up, unaware of the storm swirling on the other end.

"I'm in Old City. Some work," Nayeem replied.

"That's great! Come to Banjara Hills if you can. Noor Aapa's here. Asma too–she came from Pakistan a couple of days ago."

Nayeem hesitated. A heartbeat passed.

"I know," he said quietly.

"You... know?"

"I just met them," he said, forcing the words out. "They're with me now. They won't be home tonight. But they're safe. That's all you need to know."

"Okay," Mustafa said, a little confused. "Bring them home for breakfast then. I'll wait."

"Alright," said Nayeem. He hung up, pocketed the phone, and turned back to the farmhouse–his face blank, but his heart already mapping the rescue.

Nayeem had never known dread like this–not once in his life.

He kept vigil near the outhouse where Noor and Asma were held captive. He wouldn't let harm come to them–not while he still drew breath.

It was 8 p.m., nightfall. Just then, the gentle echoes of the Isha call to prayer drifted through the darkness, the fifth and final obligatory prayer of the day. It was performed only after twilight had completely surrendered to night.

Quietly rising, Nayeem performed his ablutions, then spread his prayer mat on the cold, unforgiving ground. With a focused intensity born of desperation, he moved through each prayer posture, seeking divine clarity and strength.

As he concluded, a verse from the Qur'an surged powerfully into his mind, resonating like a whispered revelation:

"How should ye not fight for the cause of Allah and of the feeble among men and of the women and the children who are crying: Our Lord! Bring us forth from out this town of which the people are oppressors! Oh, give us from Thy presence some protecting friend! Oh, give us from Thy presence some defender!" – Qur'an 4:75, Pickthall

A shiver raced down his spine.

"Ya Allah... show me the way," he murmured urgently. "Send me a protector, a friend–I must rescue my sisters."

Hands raised in silent supplication, an idea struck him with sudden, unmistakable clarity:

The priest.

Yes, of course. Bikku had told him that Fred, the creator of BAT, had secretly altered its code. The priest's biosignature no longer registered in the system. It shields him from any harm.

That meant the priest could enter and exit without getting harmed by the blasts of COMxBAT.

He might hold the key. But this required careful planning. Urgently, Nayeem called Sajjad on the satellite phone.

“Sajjad, are you still aboard our boat?” Nayeem asked quietly.

"I'm about to leave for Bombay," Sajjad replied.

“Have you secured the COMxBAT units for delivery?”

“Not yet. I am going back to the main Yacht, why?”

"Listen carefully–in the COMxBAT's storage area, there's a file named Kalki. Fetch it. Carry it with you. Call me back immediately after you reach our boat."

"Understood."

Thirty tense minutes passed before Sajjad's call came through again.

“Nayeem, I've found the file titled Kalki. The note inside reads: 'The righteous Brahmin who will rise against mighty kings driven by lust for power–Kalki, the King Slayer.'”

Nayeem felt his pulse quicken. Fred had anticipated the darkness Lucian would unleash--this override was his quite rebellion, his secret legacy, woven into the fabric of his creation as a beacon of hope. Kalki was Fred’s hidden vulnerability within the seemingly invincible BAT that can make anyone a monster, that can cause chaos at unimaginable proportions. Yet he held back this crucial detail; Sajjad didn’t need further confusion. The less he knew, the safer they all were.

Instead, Nayeem swiftly gave Sajjad precise instructions. He withheld any mention of Asma’s immediate danger.

Now, all that remained was to wait patiently until dawn, when his plan could finally unfold.

13. HORNET'S NEST

Hyderabad. Late January 1993.

It was just past 5 a.m. when Chandra awoke. He was getting ready for his usual jog at the nearby stadium when the phone rang.

"I'm Nayeem. You don't know me," said the voice on the other end.

"I'm listening," replied Chandra, already wary. He knew Nayeem's name from Karjat. The trail ran cold. Nayeem vanished into thin air. Now receiving this call but not sure if this is the same Nayeem they were looking for.

"You're searching for a mind-controlling device, aren't you?"

Chandra instantly snapped to full alert. “And I suppose you know where to find it?”

“I do… but I won’t tell you.”

“Then why are you calling?”

“Because your priest–Sarma–knows.”

Chandra’s expression tightened. Only a handful of insiders knew that Sarma had ever seen the device. This was no hoax.

“How do you know he knows?”

“Because the creator of the device had a change of heart after something Sarma did.”

“Who is the creator?”

“I can’t tell you,” Nayeem replied. His voice was heavy with grief and inner conflict. “But I have a reason for calling.”

“My sister and her friend are being held captive by someone named Sulfikar. I want you to send Sarma to rescue them.”

Chandra frowned. “Sarma is a simple priest. If your people are being unlawfully detained, I can send in a proper police unit to carry out the rescue. Just give me their details.”

“No. Do not do that,” Nayeem said quickly.

“Only Sarma can go.”

“Why?”

“Because the creator of the device built a special safeguard–a programme. It’s programmed not to harm Sarma. And our supreme boss has also issued standing orders that Sarma is not to be touched. Anyone else who interferes will alert the entire system. We won't just retaliate–our organisation will eliminate the threat entirely. The device will track and destroy anyone who disrupts the setup. Only Sarma has immunity. That's why he must be the one."

Chandra exhaled slowly. "That's... interesting. And if I agree to send Sarma, what do we get in return? You must offer something."

"I'm not high enough in the organisation to make real promises," Nayeem admitted. "But I can give Sarma two notebooks."

"What sort of notebooks?"

"One is called Savage Birds, the other Fire Breathers."

"Colourful titles. But how are they of any use to us?"

"Savage Birds contains the names of potential mind-controlled hijackers."

"And Fire Breathers?"

"That one lists the preachers who can radicalise and activate the hijackers."

"You mentioned hijackers. What mission are they preparing for?"

"I don't know. Nothing might be planned yet. But in the future, if there's a hijacking, you'll know who was involved–because the names are all in that book."

Chandra went quiet.

"So... Do we have a deal?" Nayeem pressed.

“Send me the books,” Chandra said at last. “I’ll consider the rescue.”

“No. Sarma must rescue them first. Only after my sister and her friend are safe will I hand the books to him directly.”

“I’ll think about it.”

“You’ve got twenty minutes. Please hurry. We don’t have time.”

Chandra stepped outside and dialled a number.

“Hello, Advanced Systems Computer Institute,” said the receptionist.

“Can I speak to your lab assistant, **Sarma**?” asked Chandra.

A few minutes later, Sarma came on the line.

“Sarma, do you know anyone named Nayeem?” Chandra asked.

“No, sir. I don’t.”

“What about Sulfikar?”

“Sulfikar? Yes, sir. He’s a job consultant. He’s been trying to help me get a placement abroad.”

Interesting, Chandra thought.

“Can we meet?”

“Of course, sir. But I’m tied up in the lab for another three hours.”

“This is an urgent matter. Skip the lab work for today. Meet me at Begumpet Police Station as soon as you can.”

"Okay sir, give me an hour. I am in the middle of the lab. I will hand over this to someone and come." Sarma said.

Chandra hung up, lost in thought. *This could be real progress. A gift from the universe–unexpected and perfectly timed.*

He considered calling **Dr Sood** or **Brigadier Bipin**–but decided he'd speak to Sarma first, then loop them in.

The phone rang again. Nayeem.

"So? What have you decided?"

"It's a deal. But Sarma is busy now. He will meet me after an hour. Send me the details."

"No. I'll send the information directly to Sarma. You or your officers must stay out of it. Just inform Sarma that he has to do this on your behalf. That's all."

"Alright," Chandra replied. "I'll tell Sarma he has to carry out the rescue." He continued.

"Know this–if you had asked me for anything else, I wouldn't have entertained it. But because it's about rescuing two innocent girls, I've agreed. As police officers, we're sworn to protect lives. So rest assured, your sister and her friend will be safe. But send *everything* through Sarma."

Chandra ended the call. He called Vyas and spoke to him for a few minutes.

He has an hour before Sarma arrives. He can use that hour to jog. The sky was beginning to warm with the first signs of dawn. Dressed in his navy-blue tracksuit, Chandra ran a steady pace along the inner lane of the empty stadium. As always, he'd refused any security.

"Routine makes you predictable," someone had warned him.

"Only if someone's watching," he'd replied with a laugh.

He didn't know someone was.

High above, from the top tier of the stadium stands, two men lay prone behind a rusted service gate. They carried an imported rifle fitted with a silencer and thermal scope–Maoists, smuggled into the city, housed in a safe flat arranged by Dengrwn's contacts.

"Confirm identity," whispered the shooter.

"Target confirmed. Blue tracksuit. Wristband. No security detail."

Chandra slowed to stretch near the west gate, wiping his brow. His breath rose in faint clouds in the cool morning air. He turned to resume his jog.

Two muffled cracks echoed, faint as distant hammering.

The first bullet struck his lower back–shattering his spine.

The second tore through his neck, exiting with a fine spray.

Chandra collapsed in a heap on the track, twitching once–then lying still.

And just like that, another member of the ultra-secret operation known as The Insiders fell to the bullets of those who intended to bring grave harm not just to India–but to the stability of nations far beyond its borders.

Sometimes, even fate remains silent in the face of such questions.

Sulfikar woke with a jolt. The microdose of Adripoison had finally dissolved from his system. As the fog lifted, reality came crashing in.

What had he done?

He had abducted two women. Two civilians. The blowback would be catastrophic if word got out.

Shaken, he stepped out of the house and made his way to the outhouse. There, sitting calmly on his prayer mat, was the construction worker—Nayeem. Sulfikar barely registered him. His eyes moved past to the two guards stationed at the entrance.

"What are you doing here?" Sulfikar asked, his voice low.

"You told us to guard the women," one replied, confused.

"Well, I changed my mind. Go home. I'll handle it from here."

The guards exchanged a glance, then left. Sulfikar waited until they were gone. He couldn't risk anyone else seeing the women. Their captivity was insurance—his leverage if things went south after Chandra's assassination. Once that was done, he'd figure out what to do. One step at a time.

He crossed to the other side of the outhouse and knocked gently.

Vanaja opened the door. She looked sleepy but curious.

"Hey Vanaja. I need a favour," he said, trying to sound casual. "There are two women in the other room. Can you look after them for me?"

Vanaja—his mistress now—tilted her head. “Who are they?”

“They’re... important. I’ve imprisoned them. But from now on, it’s your job to care for them. Quietly.”

“What should I tell Dubey?” she asked, frowning.

“Don’t. Say. Anything. Just tend to them when Dubey’s not around.”

“For how long?”

“For as long as I say,” Sulfikar replied, already turning away.

Vanaja hesitated, then walked over to the other section of the outhouse. She unlocked the door and stepped inside.

Two women sat on the floor, chained by their ankles. A jug of water and some fruit were placed nearby.

She froze. Noor?

Vanaja recognised her instantly. Just a few days earlier, at the Irani café, she had seen this woman—Noor—sitting close to Priest Sarma.. They looked... intimate. A pang of jealousy had surged through Vanaja then, sharp and unwelcome. Dubey had later mentioned the girl's name in passing: Noor. Vanaja hadn’t approached them at the time—Dubey had been in a rush—but she hadn’t forgotten that face. There was no doubt now. It was her.

Why is she a prisoner? Vanaja wondered.

As the door creaked open, Noor and Asma lifted their heads.

“Hi... do you need anything?” Vanaja asked gently.

"Who are you? Why did you imprison us?" Noor's voice was hoarse, drained.

"I don't know," Vanaja replied honestly.

"Please," Asma pleaded. "Let us go. We won't tell anyone."

"I'm sorry. I can't. I'm just a caretaker," Vanaja said. "But I'll be back in an hour. If you need anything, just tell me."

She gave them a final look, then stepped out and quietly shut the door behind her.

News of Chandra's assassination spread like wildfire. It was on every channel–breaking news, round the clock. The world was awake, reeling in shock.

Except for two souls.

Sarma, buried deep inside his computer lab, oblivious.

And Nayeem–keeping vigil outside the outhouse, guarding his sisters like a silent sentinel.

He clutched a satellite phone in his trembling hands. He had managed to get Sarma's number from Sajjad, who was still aboard the yacht. Once Aiwag found out that Sarma was the priest Fred had tried to protect–his identity recorded in a ledger–he knew this was the only shot they had.

He had to call Sarma. He has to wait an hour–he needed to brief him after Chandra briefed Sarma.

Suddenly, the satellite phone buzzed. It was Sajjad.

"Did you hear the news?"

"What news?" Nayeem asked, distracted.

"Chandra is dead. Assassinated. We knew it was coming–but not this soon. Aiwag wants us to stay alert."

The words hit Nayeem like a bolt of lightning.

Chandra–dead?

His whole plan was built around Chandra. His hope was that Chandra would instruct Sarma to carry out the rescue. Now, that hope lay in ruins.

Man proposes, but God disposes.

For the first time in his life, Nayeem felt the raw, intimate pain of loving someone deeply–and watching harm inch closer and closer to them. It hurt. It hurt badly.

And yet, in the name of a so-called holy war, he had plotted, planned, and justified hurting other people–people who were someone else's loved ones.

"Ya Allah... You are showing me what it means to feel this pain," he whispered, gazing up at the stars. "Punish me if You must. But not my sisters. Spare them... Please show me a way."

He slumped onto the prayer mat, tears soaking into the fabric. The sense of helplessness was crushing. The death of his sisters felt inevitable. He could call Aiwag and beg–but Father Lucian was ruthless. There would be no mercy.

In that moment of despair, a memory surfaced–his father.

Imran.

It had been years since they last spoke. Their relationship had shattered the day Nayeem announced he was dedicating his life to jihad. Imran had pleaded, argued, cried. But Nayeem had walked away.

Now, everything inside him longed to speak to his father. His hand moved on instinct. He picked up the satellite phone and dialled the number.

In Pakistan, Imran was sitting on the living room sofa. That morning, he'd planned to reread the notes he had brought back from his recent visit to the Holy Land. He reached for the small briefcase he always carried and opened it.

Inside, among folded papers and scribbled reflections, lay a simple sheet with four drawn roses.

A prayer paper.

Noor had given it to him, asking that he read it near the Kaaba.

He picked it up, curious. His eyes landed on the first line:

"I pray that my father and my brother Nayeem reconcile."

Imran sighed deeply, filling his lungs with air. He had honoured Noor's request. But reconciliation... that was in Allah's hands. As long as Nayeem walked the path of violence–hurting innocents in the name of religion–Imran could not accept him.

"That boy never understood what a true holy war is," he thought bitterly.

Just then, Fatima walked in from the kitchen with a tray of tea. She sat beside him, handing him a cup.

"I don't know why, but I've been thinking of Nayeem, Noor, and little Mustafa all day," she said.

"Me too," Imran replied, handing her the prayer paper. "Noor asked Allah to reunite me with Nayeem. But how can I accept a son who believes God wants him to spill innocent blood?"

"Inshā'Allah, he will change," Fatima said softly. "We must keep hope. A mother always does."

At that moment, the phone rang.

Imran rose and answered.

"Baba..."

It was Nayeem. His voice was faint, hollow–like someone who had lost everything.

"Beta... Nayeem... is that really you? How are you? Where are you?" Imran asked, heart swelling with emotion. In that instant, the years of anger and silence dissolved. Only love remained.

"Baba... please pray for us. We're in serious trouble," Nayeem said, then began to sob.

Fatima stood beside Imran, her heart pounding. She could hear the pain in her son's voice.

"Beta, what happened? Allah will help us. Just tell me–what's hurting you, my son?" Imran pleaded.

"I just needed to hear your voice, Baba. That's all. I'm... I'm so sorry. You told me a thousand times. But I didn't listen. I thought I understood what holy war meant. I didn't. It makes no sense to hurt the innocent. But I think... it's too late for me now."

"No, beta. Never say that. Don't despair. Allah's mercy is greater than your mistakes. Tell me where you are—I'll come to you right now. Are you in danger? Tell me the country. I'll contact the embassy—get help."

"I can't, Baba. If you knew... you'd be in danger too," Nayeem wept.

Fatima gently took the phone from Imran's hand.

"Beta... Nayeem... it's Ammi," she said, her voice trembling. "Don't worry. Baba will help. Allah will make a way. Just tell us what kind of trouble you're in."

"I'm sorry, Ammi... Please forgive me..." he said between sobs. But he shared nothing more.

The line went silent.

Nayeem had ended the call.

The silence that followed was deafening.

Imran and Fatima sat there, stunned—hearts heavy with worry, hands tied by distance and secrecy.

Imran slowly stood, retrieved his prayer mat, and laid it out.

"Come," he said softly. "Let us pray for our children—wherever they are, whatever danger they're in. Only Allah can protect them now."

Together, they knelt and began to pray.

Vanaja had been waiting for the right opportunity to get close to Sarma ever since he slipped away from her in the middle of the night. She wasn't angry anymore–now she simply wanted to befriend him. Learn from him. Understand him.

And seeing Noor imprisoned in the outhouse? That was her chance.

If I call Sarma and tell him that his friend is in distress, maybe... maybe I'll get the chance to get closer to him, she thought.

Dubey had gone out early to read someone's astrological chart. The moment the door closed behind him, Vanaja picked up the phone and dialled Sarma's number. She was sure he'd be in the computer lab.

Sarma had just wrapped up the lab session and handed over the remaining classes to a colleague. He needed to leave early–he had an appointment with Chandra. As he approached the reception, he noticed something odd: the receptionist wasn't her usual self. She was clutching a small transistor radio to her ear, eyes wide with alarm. A few students stood nearby, murmuring.

"What's going on?" Sarma asked. "Why aren't you in the lab?"

"Did you hear the news?" the receptionist said, not looking up.

"What news?"

"The IBSB Regional Head–Chandra. He's been assassinated. Radicals, apparently."

Sarma's legs almost gave out. Chandra sir? Dead? He'd just spoken to him an hour ago. They were about to meet. His mind reeled, refusing to process the loss.

Nobody knew the depth of his connection with Chandra—it was a closely guarded secret. And now, that secret would be buried forever. But more than that, Sarma had lost someone who was like an elder brother. His mentor. His protector.

He sank into the nearest sofa, numb and hollow.

Just then, the telephone rang.

The receptionist answered and turned to him. "Sarma, it's for you."

"Hello, Sarma here."

"Sarma-ji, I hope you remember me... It's Vanaja," came the voice.

Sarma froze. A surge of heat rushed to his face. Memories of that night with her—his moment of weakness, the bizarre illusion of Kamala—flooded back. He hated himself for it.

"Why are you calling me?" he asked sharply.

"I want to help," she said, her voice expectant, almost like she was waiting for his gratitude.

"What kind of help?" Sarma wasn't in the mood for games.

"It's about your friend. Noor."

His jaw clenched. "What about her?"

"She and her friend are being held prisoner."

Sarma stood up, stunned. "What are you talking about?"

Vanaja explained everything she had seen.

"Are they still at your farmhouse?" he asked urgently.

"Yes. But listen–I'm taking a huge risk telling you this. You can come and rescue them. I'll help."

"Tell me everything. Are there guards?"

"There were a few, but they've left. Only one construction worker is around. The rest won't be back for another couple of hours."

"I'm on my way. Don't move," he said, then rushed out of the lab.

Sarma had once befriended an auto driver, hoping to learn to drive in case he needed extra income. That auto driver happened to be sitting idle nearby.

"Anna, I need to borrow your auto for a few hours. Please," Sarma pleaded.

The driver, who had borrowed Sarma's help many times, agreed and handed over the keys.

Sarma drove straight to the farmhouse. Vanaja was waiting at the gates.

"They're still in the outhouse. The man who locked them up went out for some errands. Only the construction worker is here now."

Sarma didn't reply. He marched past her and towards the outhouse. Vanaja unlocked the door. Inside, Noor and Asma looked up, chained and exhausted.

On the yacht, COMxBAT flickered to life. Batsinger's screen showed static and glitchy distortions–as if digital dust were falling from the monitor.

"What's happening?" Aiwag asked.

Father Lucian had instructed them to monitor all activity following Chandra's assassination.

"The COMxBAT just connected to Sulfikar's property," Batsinger said.

"So?"

"I think the priest–Frederick's protected asset–just entered the blast zone. Look at that flicker. That's the override code 'Kalki' Fred embedded. It's shielding him from our weapon."

Aiwag stared. "He's actually there?"

Batsinger nodded, still taking notes. "Yes. And the system recognises him. That priest just walked into the lion's den. Does he know that place belong to Sulfikar... A terminator?"

"Sarma!" Noor yelled. "Please help!"

Sarma rushed to her. Vanaja handed him the key. He unlocked the chains.

"We'll talk outside. We don't have much time," he said, pulling Noor by the hand. Asma followed. All three stepped out into the sunlight.

Nayeem, the lone construction worker, saw Sarma and the girls. He quickly retreated behind the building, not wanting Noor to spot him.

His satellite phone rang.

"This is Aiwag. Can you confirm if the priest is on-site?"

"Yes, I see him," Nayeem replied calmly.

"What's he doing?"

"He's here to pick up the maids," Nayeem answered. It was the perfect cover. "Only God could arrange such a flawless disguise."

"Alright," Aiwag said, satisfied.

Sarma loaded Noor and Asma into the back of the auto. He turned to Vanaja.

"Thank you. But it's not safe for you here. Come with us."

"Don't worry. I'm good at creating stories. I'll say they overpowered me and escaped. But remember this—I'll ask for something in return someday."

"I promise," Sarma said, then drove them away.

Noor sat silently, overwhelmed with relief. Her ordeal was finally over.

At Banjara Hills, Sarma dropped them off.

"Noor, you're safe now. Call the police. Report everything. Talk to your parents. I'll come with you to the station as your witness."

"Sarma, please come in."

"Not now. I need to return the auto."

Inside, the phone rang. Mustafa picked it up.

"Noor Aapa, it's for you. Nayeem Bhaiya."

Noor grabbed the receiver. "Bhaiya! Is it really you?"

"Are you safe?" Nayeem asked gently.

She burst into tears. "Yes. Asma too."

"Good. Don't cry. I know everything."

"You know we were abducted?"

"Yes. But the important thing is–you're safe."

"Sarma said we should inform the police."

"No. Don't. It'll create a scandal and put us all in danger. Call Baba in Pakistan. Say your prayers worked. And leave India. Immediately."

"But when will I see you again?"

"Insha'Allah, soon. I'll come to Pakistan. Don't tell anyone about this."

"Okay."

Sarma returned that evening. Noor and Asma were packed and ready.

"Sarma, we're leaving. Nayeem said not to report anything to the police."

"But–"

"We must trust him. We're leaving tonight. I'll stay in touch. Thank you... we'll never forget you."

That evening, they left India–for good.

Four days later, a courier arrived at the lab for Sarma. Inside were two notebooks and a note.

One book read: Savage Birds.

The other: Fire Breathers.

The note read:

"Sarma, you don't know me, but I know you. I promised a dead man I'd deliver this for your help. I also made a vow to my father—and to Allah—that I would mend my ways.

The 'Savage Birds' notebook lists potential hijackers.

'Fire Breathers' lists those capable of inciting mass violence.

Please keep these safe.

I know you'll do the right thing.

I'll be watching. Insha'Allah, our paths will cross again.

–XXX"

Sarma went to Begumpet police station. Vyas was there.

"Sir, I'm sorry about Chandra."

Vyas nodded, grim. "He was a great loss. A ray of hope. He called me just before he died. Told me two girls were in distress. That you'd rescue them. And in return, we'd get vital intel about the minds behind the mind controlling devices."

Sarma handed over the notebooks.

Vyas opened them and looked stunned. "These... these are the notes."

He looked at Sarma. "How did you get these?"

Sarma explained everything.

"Vanaja is in danger," he added. "She helped me."

"We'll protect her," Vyas said, still reading.

After Chandra's assassination, Sulfikar went into hiding. But as Vinay had promised, there was no fallout. The murder was blamed on radicals.

A few days later, Sulfikar returned to the farmhouse and found the outhouse empty.

"What happened?" he asked Vanaja.

"They overpowered me and escaped," she said, weeping convincingly.

Sulfikar felt oddly relieved. He couldn't understand what madness had led him to imprison two innocent women. But now that they were gone–and no police had shown up–he felt at peace.

"This secret stays between us," he told Vanaja.

The phone rang. It was Vinay.

"See? Just as I said. No one knows what happened," Vinay said, proud.

"Congratulations," Sulfikar replied.

"Now... Bombay. You go there. Begin planning the next phase."

"Alright. I'll book my tickets," Sulfikar said and hung up.

--XXX--

---Satyam eva jayate nānṛtaṁ ....

Truth alone triumphs, not falsehood...---

'Mundaka Upanishad'

REFERENCES AND WORD MEANINGS

BAT

Brain Activity Transformer. A device that can alter human behaviour.

COMxBAT

Communicator crossed with Brain Activity Transformer. This works in tandem with BAT.

SANI

A LEO Low Earth Orbit Sattelite that acts as a go between BAT and COMxBAT.

MEDxBAT

Medical Event Data crossed with Brain Activity Transformer. It collects brain data from patients in critical conditions.

ATTATAYI

papam evasrayed asman hatvaitan **attatayinah**

tasman narha vayam hantum dhartarastran sa-bandhavan

sva-janam hi katham hatva sukhinah syama **madhava** - Bhagavad Gita 1.36

In Sanskrit, the term "Attatai" (अत्ततायी or अत्तातायी) refers to a deadly assailant, aggressor, or an armed attacker who poses a serious threat to life and safety.

The word अत्ततायी (Attatāyī) is used in Hindu scriptures, including the Manusmṛti and Dharmaśāstra, to describe individuals who commit heinous crimes such as:

1. Arsonists (setting fire to homes or property)
2. Poisoners (attempting to kill with poison)
3. Assassins (those who attempt to murder someone)
4. Looters or Plunderers (who rob or attack innocent people)
5. Kidnappers (who forcibly abduct someone)
6. Land Grabbers (who unlawfully seize others' property)

According to Manusmṛti (8.350) and other legal texts, killing an Attatāyī in self-defense is not considered a sin because they are already engaging in adharma (unrighteous acts) that endanger lives.

So, in Sanskrit and Hindu legal traditions, "Attatai" (अत्ततायी) refers to a criminal aggressor who commits grave offenses against others.

YOGINI SULABHA

Sulabhā (सुलभा).—A female ascetic (Sannyāsinī). She acquired several powers (Siddhis) by tapas. She had the power of giving up her body and receiving new bodies. Once she went to Mithilā and held a learned discussion with King Janaka. She went to Mithilā as a beggar woman. By her yogic powers she entered the mind of Janaka. She and Janaka were thus in the same body when they carried on the discussion. After remaining in Janaka's body for a day, she left the palace. (Mahābhārata Śānti Parva, Chapter 320).

MIND CONTROLLING REFERENCE FROM MAHABHARATA:

https://www.wisdomlib.org/hinduism/book/the-mahabharata-mohan/d/doc826279.html

O lady of the ascetic order, I have respect and affection for you. However, this affection should not stop me from saying that your behavior does not match the principles of the lifestyle you've adopted. You possess a delicate build and a very attractive appearance. You are young and endowed with self-control—or at least that's doubtful. Using your yogic powers, you've entered and taken control of my body (mind-controlling me) to test whether I am truly liberated or not. This act contradicts the very ascetic life you represent. The triple staff (carried by ascetics) is not suitable for a yogi who still has desires. You yourself do not seem to adhere to the discipline symbolized by your staff. Even those who are truly liberated must guard against falling from their path.

Now listen carefully as I explain how your actions towards me are inappropriate. What reason justified your entry into my kingdom or my palace? Under whose authority did you invade my inner self? You belong to the highest order, a Brahmana woman. I, however, am a Kshatriya. There can be no union between us, so do not cause an improper mixing of the castes. You follow a path leading to spiritual freedom, while I live as a householder. Your action has created yet another problem—an unnatural union between two entirely different lifestyles.

I don't know if you belong to my family lineage (gotra) or not. Similarly, you don't know mine. If it turns out you belong to my lineage, then by entering my body, you've committed another wrong by causing an unnatural relationship. Moreover, if your husband is alive and living far away, you've committed yet another wrong by creating an unlawful union, because you and I cannot lawfully be together. Are you committing these wrongdoings to achieve some specific goal? Or are your actions driven by ignorance or distorted thinking?

If your improper conduct results from your uncontrolled nature, let me assure you that anyone who knows the scriptures can easily see that your actions are entirely wrong. There's yet another fault in your behavior: you're disturbing mental peace. In your eagerness to show off your superiority, you're displaying traits characteristic of a wicked woman. Your desire to prove your victory isn't just about me—you clearly wish to show your superiority over my entire court of learned Brahmanas. By gazing arrogantly at all these wise Brahmanas, you're evidently trying to humiliate them while glorifying yourself at their expense.

Driven by jealousy of my power, you have arrogantly mixed your consciousness with mine, thereby blending nectar and poison. The union between a man and a woman who both desire each other is sweet like nectar. But the union where a woman desires a man who does not reciprocate her feelings is not noble at all; rather, it becomes toxic and harmful like poison.

Stop mind-controlling me immediately. Know clearly that I follow righteousness.

HUM DEKHENGE SONG SOURCE

Hum dekhenge song: Translation source:
http://ghazala.wordpress.com/2008/01/08/hum-dekhenge/)

BAPS

Brain Activity Pacified Slaves. These are individuals who become zombies when BAT with COMxBAT takes temporary control of their brains. BAPS usually have only two outcomes. They destroy everyone in their vicinity, and they destroy themselves in the process.

TERMINATORS

A list of bio-engineered humans maintained by SHIKHANDI. They are no longer humans because they have behavioural patterns hardwired into them.

Printed and bound by CPI Group (UK) Ltd, Croydon, CR0 4YY
14/05/2025
01871999-0001